IMAGES
of America

WOOD-RIDGE

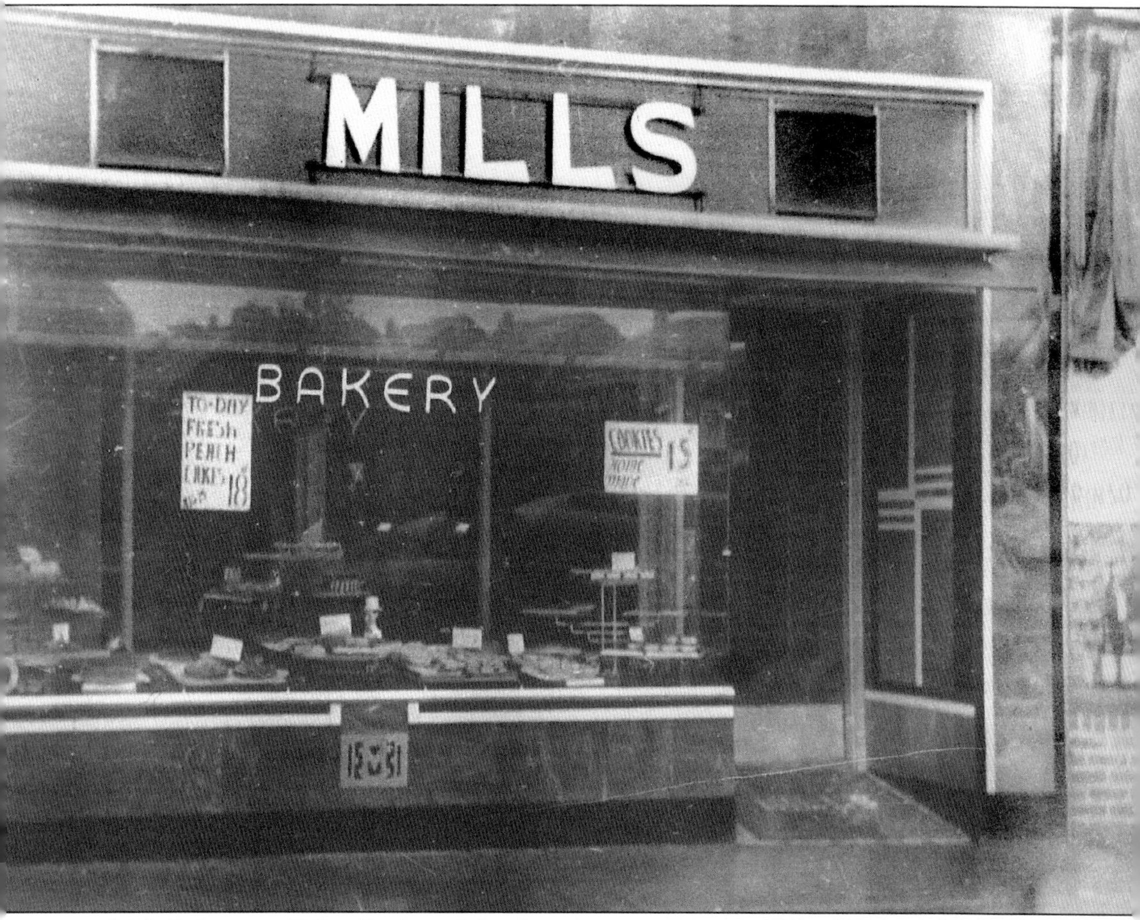

Mills Bakery, on Valley Boulevard, has long been a mainstay of Wood-Ridge. This photograph was taken in the 1930s; note the prices in the window. Still going strong, Mills continues to use some of its original recipes. Former residents are known to stop at Mills when in the area.

On the cover: Students at Wood-Ridge Public School No. 1, Mount Pleasant School, gather in 1910 for a class photograph.

IMAGES of America

WOOD-RIDGE

Patricia Helbig Sloan and Catherine Cassidy
for the Wood-Ridge Historical Society

ARCADIA
PUBLISHING

ISBN 978-0-7385-3556-2

Published by Arcadia Publishing
Charleston SC, Chicago IL, Portsmouth NH, San Francisco CA

Printed in the United States of America

Library of Congress Catalog Card Number: 2004102488

For all general information contact Arcadia Publishing at:
Telephone 843-853-2070
Fax 843-853-0044
E-mail sales@arcadiapublishing.com
For customer service and orders:
Toll-Free 1-888-313-2665

Visit us on the Internet at www.arcadiapublishing.com

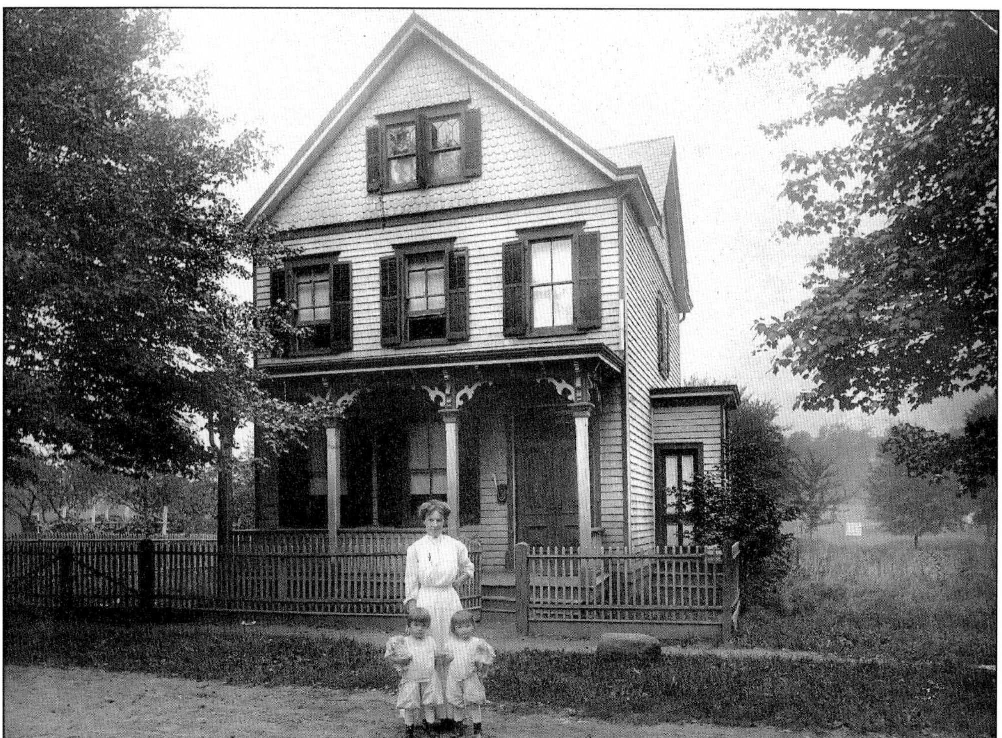

The house at 107 Third Street was the home of the Laurent family. The Laurents were the grandparents of former library director Patricia Hannon and *Wood-Ridge Independent* editor Bob Hannon.

Contents

ACKNOWLEDGMENTS

This book would not have been possible without the work of the History of Wood-Ridge Committee and its research for the "blue book" history of Wood-Ridge, which was published in 1964. Also, we are grateful to the members of the Wood-Ridge Historical Society for their knowledge and support during the process of creating this book.

We would like to thank and acknowledge all the people who helped in the creation of *Wood-Ridge*: the staff at Wood-Ridge Borough Hall, Ruth Stumm, Lou Metzger, Dorothy Dobek, Carolyn Cassidy, William Sloan, Isabelle Helbig, Eileen Helbig Toughill, Kay Duddy Sloan, Helen Rumsby, Carl Dittmann, library director John Trause, Rosemarie Costantino Cristofolo, Marie Cherichella, Peter Traina Sr., Phyllis Gorab, Debi Mueller, Rick Gennarelli, Jackie Sharkey, Bernice Slattery, Jacki Goldklang, the Tuesday morning bingo ladies, Carol and Nick Valdez, Helen von der Osten, Doris Meyer, Martha Preli, Christopher McAlinden, Bernice Linden Moran, Bob Hannon of the *Wood-Ridge Independent*, Ron Williams, Nancy Williams, Kevin Jones, Lee Bracey, and Julia Hofbauer Stapleton. If we inadvertently omitted anyone, we apologize. Everyone's help is greatly appreciated.

This book was written in memory of the early settlers and dedicated to the members of the Wood-Ridge Historical Society, past and present, whose goal is to preserve and promote the history of Wood-Ridge.

The information used for this work is as accurate as possible. When researching old files, information is sometimes conflicting, and we apologize for any inaccuracies that may be found. All photographs, unless otherwise noted, are from the files of the Wood-Ridge Historical Society.

INTRODUCTION

In 1669, lord proprietors Sir George Carteret and Lord John Berkeley awarded a land grant to Capt. John Berry. The territory extended approximately from Hackensack to Newark between the Hackensack, Passaic, and Saddle Rivers. At the time, the Lenni Lenape Indians inhabited the area. The tract was gradually divided into farms, and by the early 1700s, the area that is now Wood-Ridge began to appear in county records. An old Indian trail extending from the northern part of Bergen County to points south was laid out by Berry as a roadway *c.* 1707. Named Polifly Road, it is now known in Wood-Ridge as Hackensack Street.

The land became part of the township of New Barbadoes. In 1825, when Lodi Township was formed, it split off from New Barbadoes. Wood-Ridge and its surrounding areas became a part of Lodi Township. Wood-Ridge was an area used as a hunting ground by the Indians. Artifacts found in the vicinity lead historians to believe that the Indians inhabited land closer to the surrounding rivers.

The eastern section of the land consisted of marshes and swamps, but upland from these were dense woods. Chestnut, hickory, maple, and ash were among the variety of trees found. When the land was cleared, the soil was found to be rich for farming.

By the early 19th century, farms began to appear, with some of the earliest names found in borough records being Schoonmaker, Van Bussum, Brinkerhoff, Anderson, Berry, Engel, Terhune, and Vreeland.

At first the farms were established to sustain the inhabitants and the surplus was either bartered or sold. By the time of the American Revolution, farms had begun to take produce to markets in Newark and New York City, transporting the crops by horse-drawn wagons and by boats in nearby creeks that sailed down the Hackensack and Hudson Rivers.

Besides farming, inn keeping became one of the oldest types of businesses. The first known tavern in Wood-Ridge was the Windisch Hotel, located on old Polifly Road. John Adelung built a hotel in the southeast corner of the town after the railroad came to Wood-Ridge *c.* 1870. His hotel sat across from the depot, along with a few stores and the Lobravico Cigar Factory.

By 1890, shops began to appear up the hill. A bakery was established on the southeast end of Hackensack and Center Streets, followed by a butcher shop, and a small grocery store. Industry began in Wood-Ridge as early as 1880, when the Standard Oil Company of New Jersey built a large pumping station on the west side of town where the Curtiss-Wright Company would later stand. Standard Oil had established a pipeline extending from the oil fields of Pennsylvania to the refineries in New Jersey, providing pumping stations about every 20 miles and ending in

Bayonne. The Wood-Ridge plant was the last on its line.

In 1889, Anton Molinari built a house and factory for the manufacture of surgical instruments on the site where Assumption School now stands. Other industries followed, but Wood-Ridge remained predominantly a residential town, as it still is today. Around this time the people began to consider forming a separate town, and in 1894, the borough of Wood-Ridge was incorporated.

One

A Farming Community

Along with the early farmers and business owners, some of the first property owners named in old records include members of the Frederick Kohbertz family (who owned a large estate on what is now the southern part of Seventh Street), Leopold Windisch, and Frederick Merkel. The Stahl family owned property east of Hackensack Street, and James Van Bussum owned a large farm in the western end, near the vicinity of the Standard Oil Company property. Toward the later 1800s, the Young family is found in records, along with the Bushmans, Franks, Kempfners, Kochs, and Schmidts.

Leopold and Walter Brandenburg owned large tracts of land in the borough, roughly from Wood-Ridge Street between Highland Avenue and Windsor Road to the railroad line near Wallington. Leopold Brandenburg owned the former Brinkerhoff farm, an 18th-century structure built of brownstone with a combined gambrel and mansard roof. The Brinkerhoffs were well known throughout Bergen County. They were among the original landowners in Wood-Ridge. The Leopold Brandenburg home was saved from the wrecking ball and became the Wood-Ridge Memorial Library in 1954. Walter Brandenburg owned land between Marlboro and Innes Roads. Parts of the housing development Sunshine City were built on Walter's property, as well as Leopold's. The Brandenburg family donated numerous artifacts and photographs to the History of Wood-Ridge Committee, now the Wood-Ridge Historical Society.

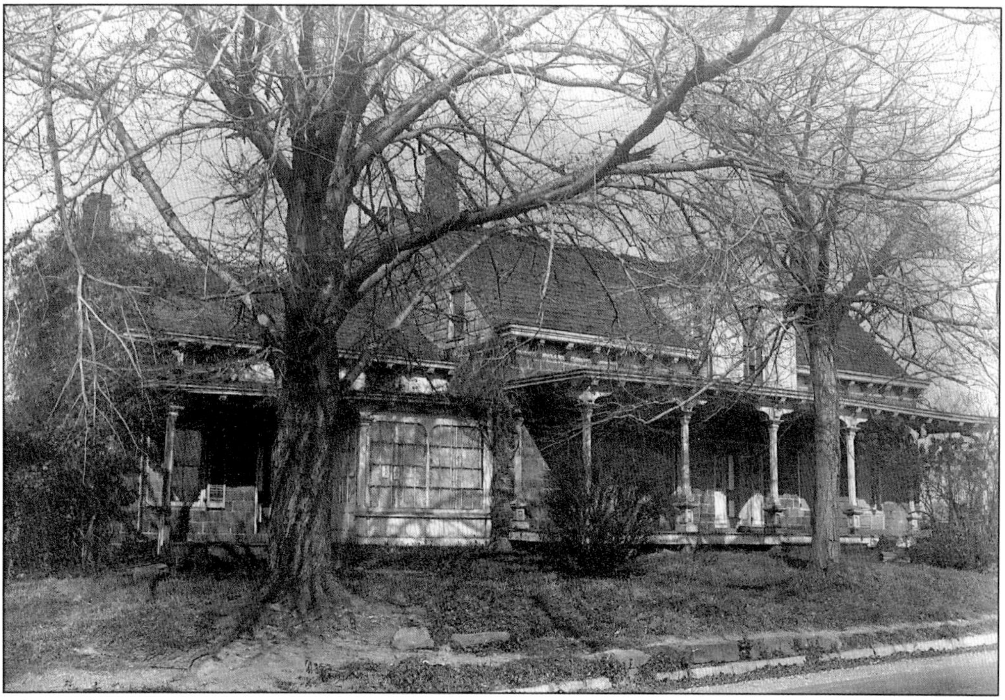

The Walter Brandenburg farmhouse was located on Hackensack Street between Marlboro and Windsor Roads. Numerous businesses and the first section of Sunshine City now stand on the old farm. This photograph is dated January 1911.

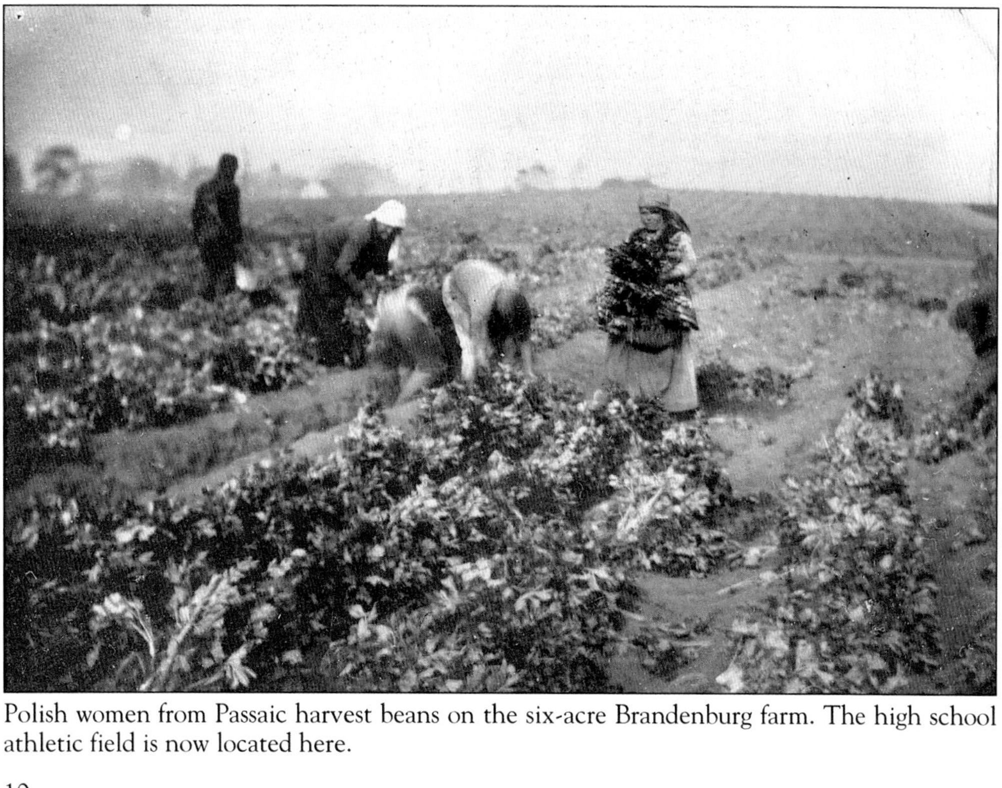

Polish women from Passaic harvest beans on the six-acre Brandenburg farm. The high school athletic field is now located here.

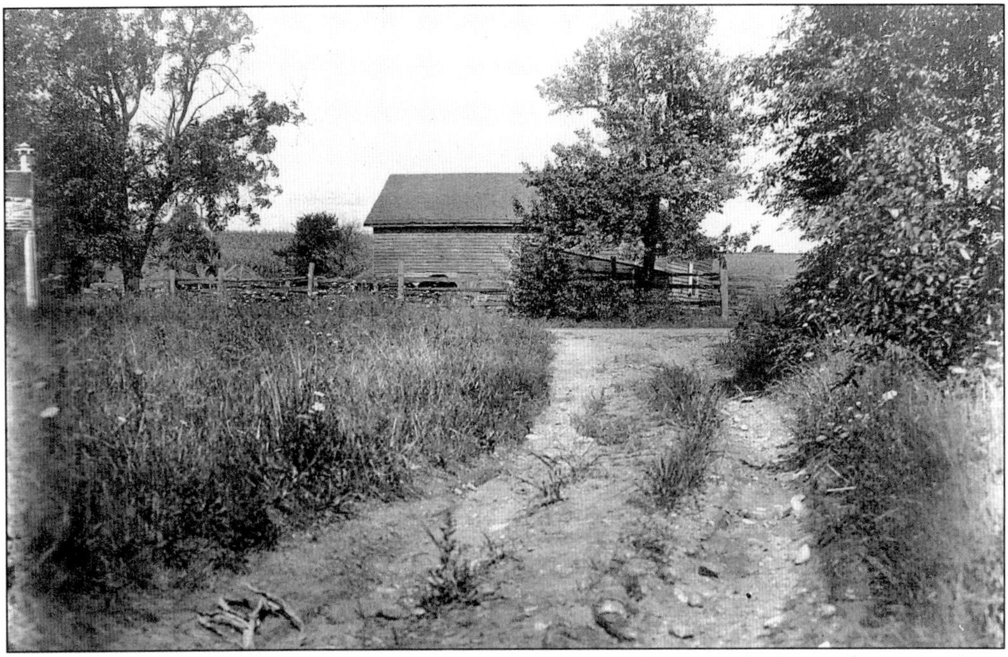

This summertime view shows Windsor Road leading to Walter Brandenburg's farm. Sunshine City was built on the Brandenburg farm in the late 1920s.

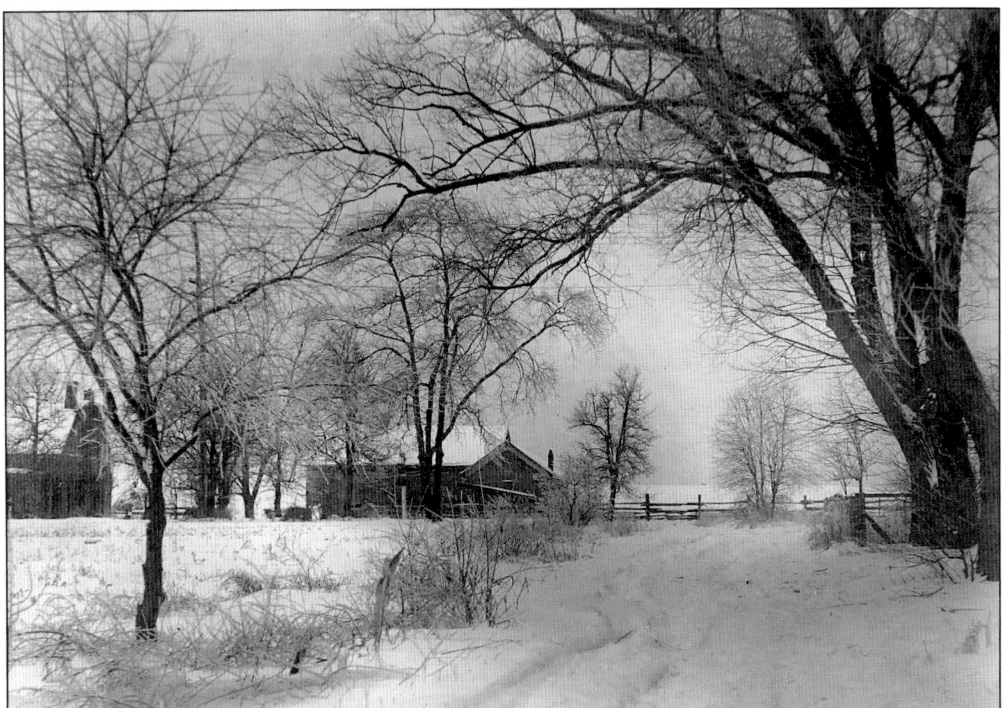

This winter view shows Windsor Road leading to Hackensack Street. Walter Brandenburg's barn is in the center, and his house is on the left.

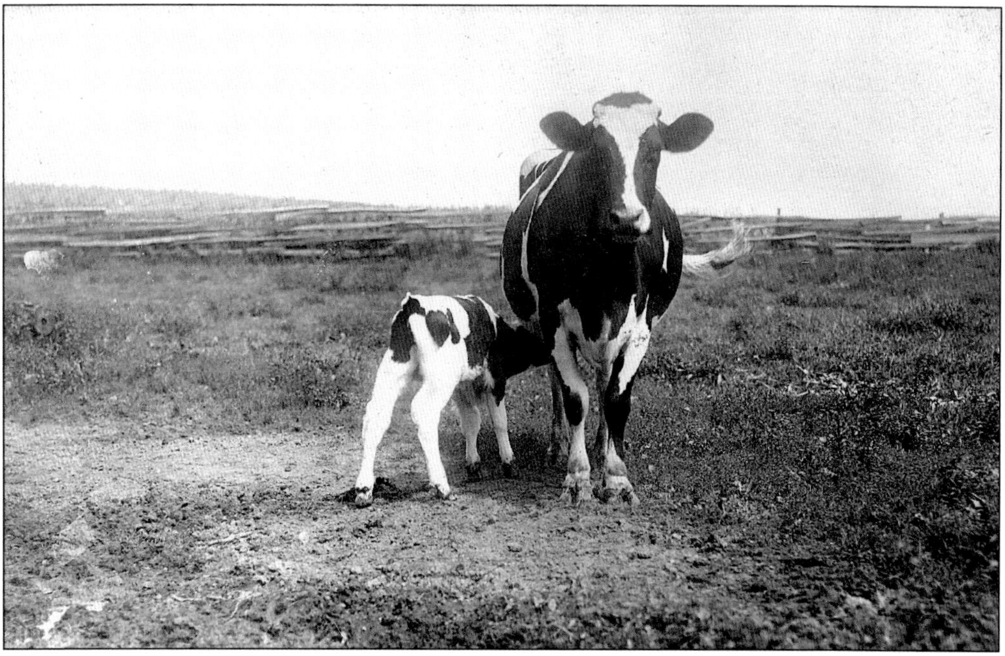

Pictured in 1918 are two inhabitants of what is now Sunshine City. Farms and dairies were an integral part of early Wood-Ridge.

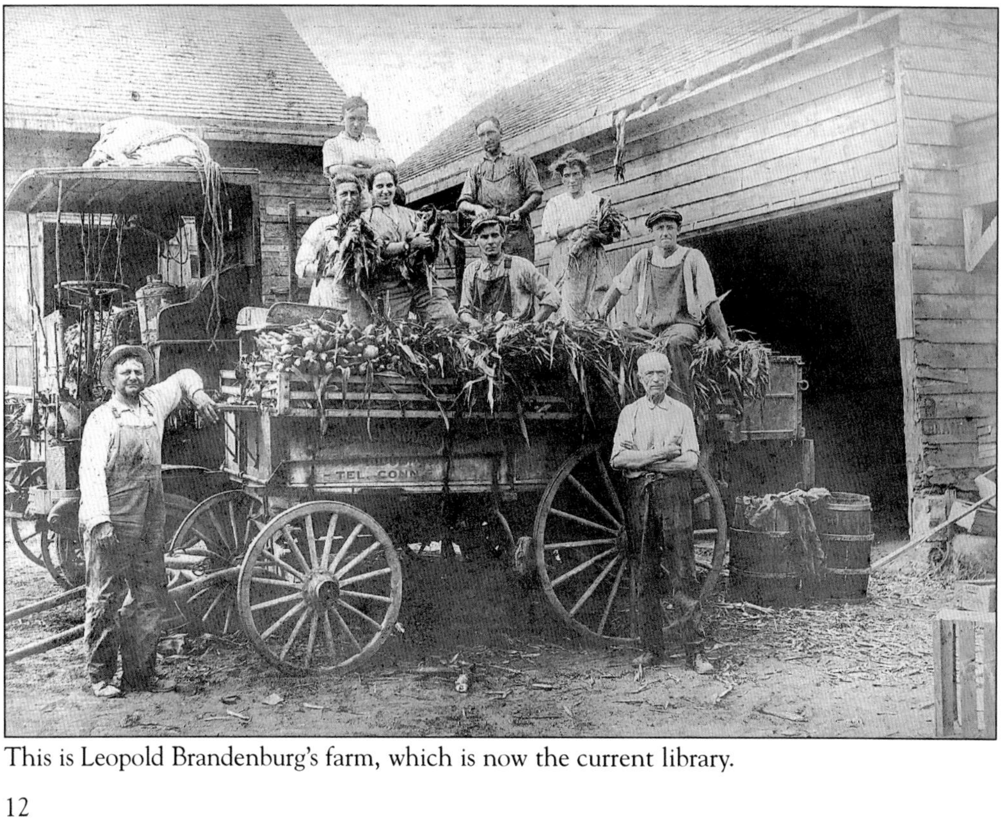

This is Leopold Brandenburg's farm, which is now the current library.

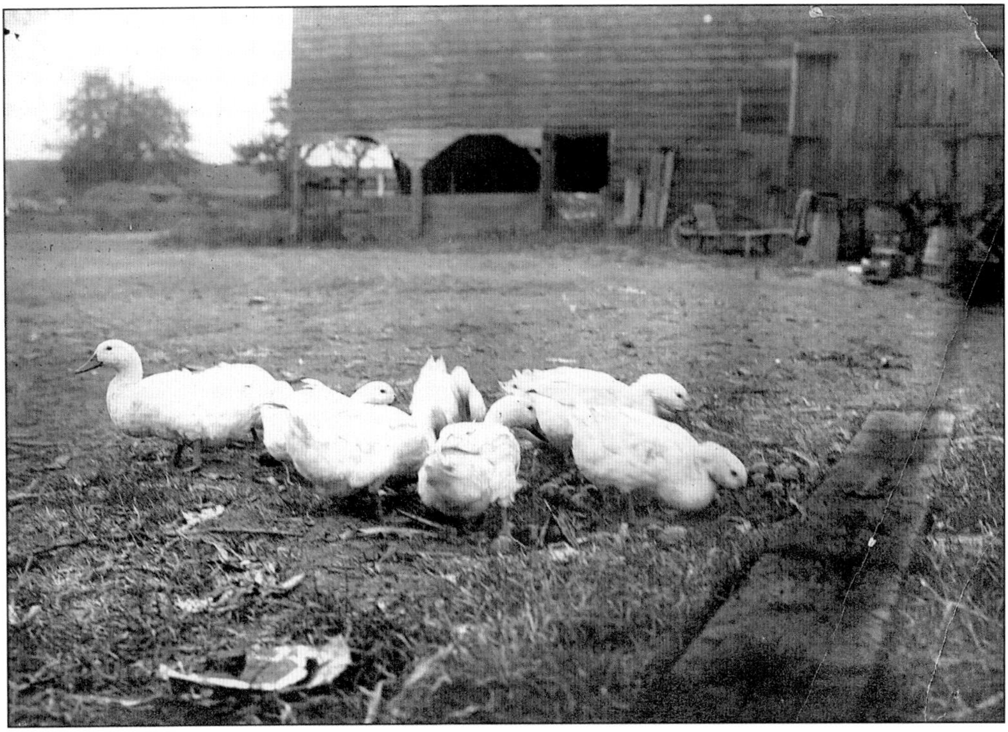

These ducks are on the Brandenburg farm.

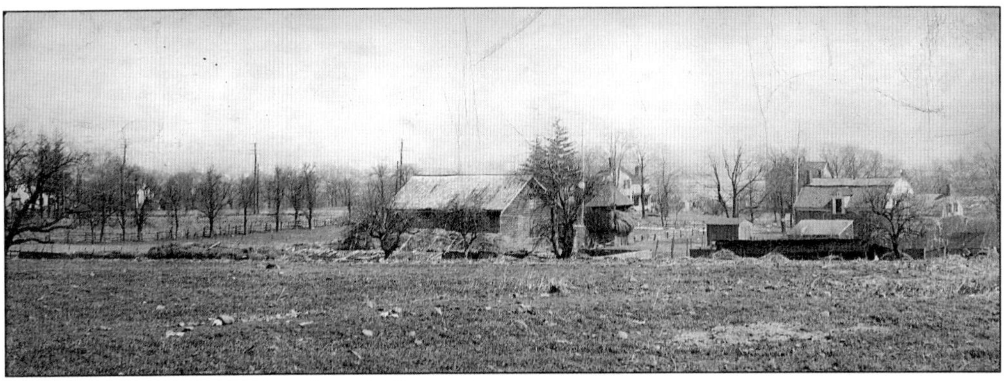

This eastern view was taken from Hillcrest Avenue.

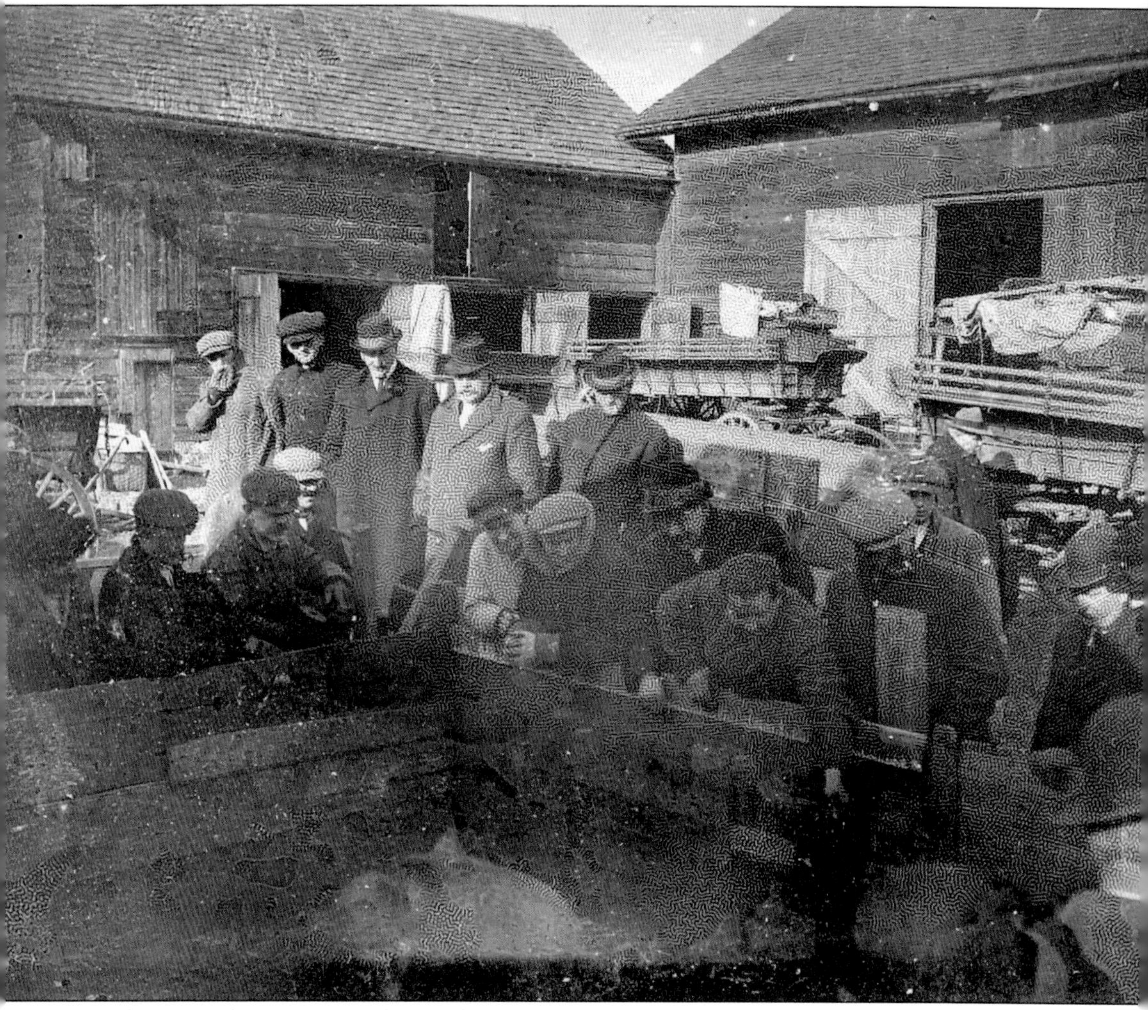

This was the auction sale of the Schoonmaker farm and property. The Sunshine City development was later built on parts of this farm.

Two

Early Homes

By 1861, there were some 10 houses in the area that is now Wood-Ridge. Many of the homes were constructed of brownstone, a style frequently seen in early Bergen County. A large windmill graced the property of the Boland-Meyer homestead, and on Independence Day, red, white, and blue lanterns were hung on it. A white picket fence surrounded the Arnault House (now the Bianchi House). The property included a coach house, a grape arbor, stables, and an outhouse. The house of Anton Molinari (Wood-Ridge's first mayor) was located where Assumption School now stands; it was a 16-room structure topped by a large tower with shutters and Gothic arches. The 1870s saw the construction of the Kohbertz mansion. It contained 20 rooms in all, with hot and cold running water and gas service throughout the house. The house, later a meeting place for the Ku Klux Klan, eventually became a restaurant. It was razed in 1940 after sustaining severe fire damage.

Change was in the air. Between 1885 and 1895, there was an increase in residences and farms, as well as industries and businesses, and the first church was established. By 1894, several areas of Lodi Township had decided to incorporate into smaller, individual boroughs, and it was at this time that some of the residents of what is now Wood-Ridge began to favor such a move. Promoters of incorporation were aware that some residents were opposed; thus, when the boundary lines were established, several residences were cut out. A later borough ordinance included the properties of the people not included in the original boundary lines.

The plan was put to voters, and in December 1894, 96 ballots were cast—56 for and 40 against. The borough of Wood-Ridge was born. At the first election, on January 15, 1895, Anton Molinari was elected mayor, defeating Frederick Imbert, who was the leader of those opposed to incorporation. The ticket in favor was called the citizen's ticket, and the opposition, the workmen's ticket. On Madison Street, the opposition erected a hall known as the Workmen's Association, later occupied by the Masons.

One of the first major improvements sought by the new council was the installation of streetlights. In all, 23 were installed along the paved sections of Hackensack Street and Moonachie and Anderson Avenues. Further lighting, water, gas, and electric lines soon followed.

In the early 1900s, trolley tracks were extended from the Monroe Street terminus in Carlstadt to what is now Valley Boulevard in Wood-Ridge and on to the city of Hackensack. At this time, increased population made it necessary to enlarge School No. 1, and *c.* 1908, a three-story addition was added. In 1911, land was sold to developers Lint, Butscher, and Ross to build homes between Hackensack Street and Twelfth Street.

By 1918, Wood-Ridge still had several farms, but in future years farmlands were divided and sold and more houses began to appear on the landscape. After the population explosion of the 1920s, a new school was required. Six acres were purchased from Leopold Brandenburg, and in 1922, the cornerstone for School No. 2 was laid. This building eventually became Wood-Ridge High School.

The period between the 1920s and 1935 saw much progress in Wood-Ridge. The sewer system was planned and constructed in the 1920s during the administration of Mayor Walter Innes, thanks to the hard work of Councilman Albert Gorab. The *Wood-Ridge Independent*, still published weekly, was founded in 1928 by Fred Caston. The trolley system was discontinued, bus service was provided, and Sunshine City was developed.

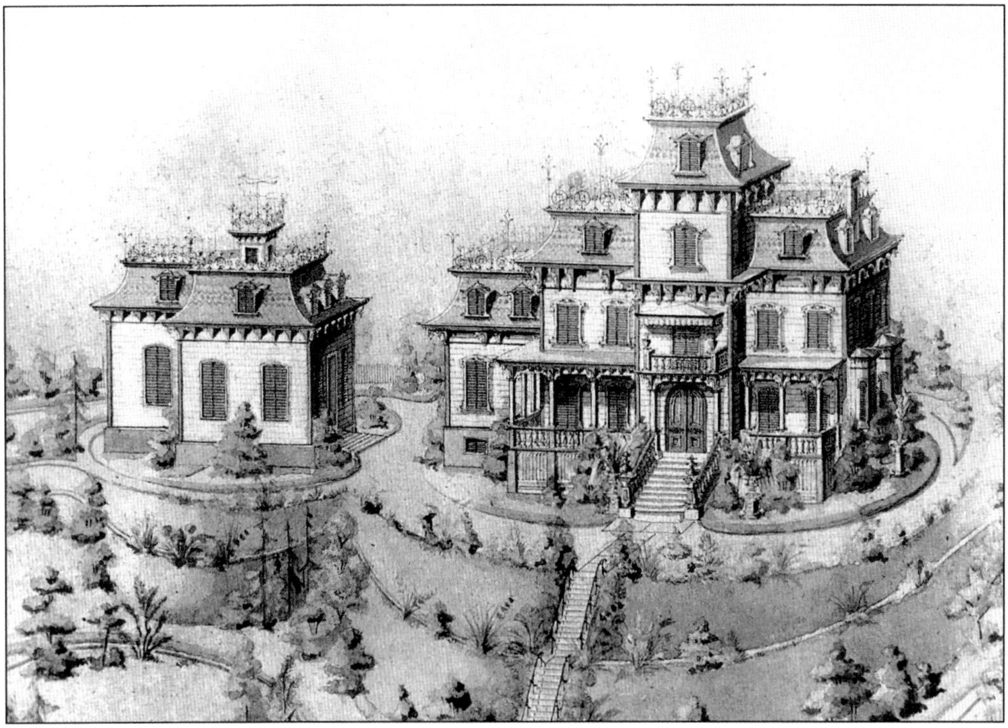

Here is a sketch of the Kohbertz mansion. The home was built on what was known as Pfannkuchen Hill, the highest elevation in town. The mansion was turned into a restaurant in the 1930s and then was torn down in 1940, after being partially destroyed by fire. The only remaining structure is the coach house, to the left. Spadola Brothers salvaged cornices and molding, which now adorn a house in Pine Bush, New York. The location is between Sixth and Seventh Streets and Union and North Avenues.

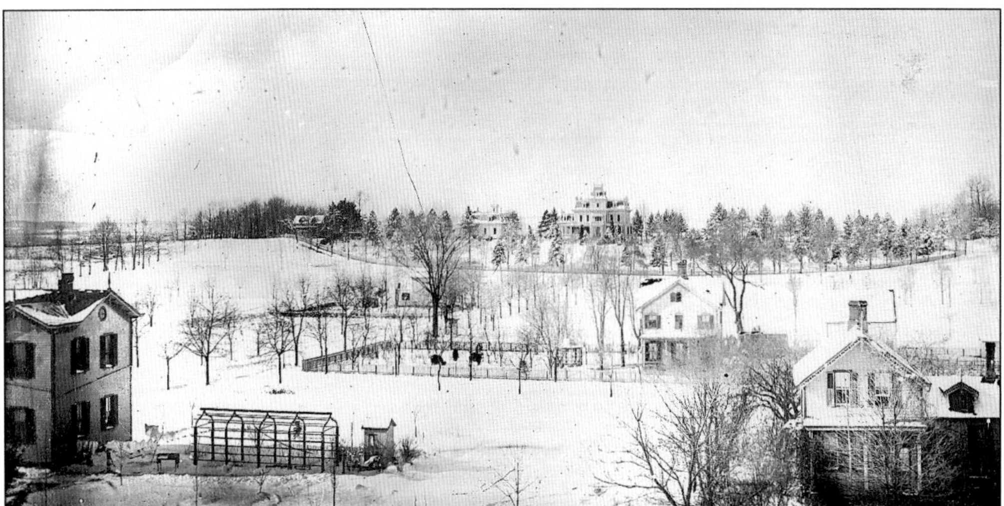

This view of the Kohbertz mansion was taken from a building on Hackensack Street. Because of his ardent promotion of development in Wood-Ridge, Frederick Kohbertz has been considered the founder of the town. Portraits of him and his wife, Anna, hang in Wood-Ridge Borough Hall.

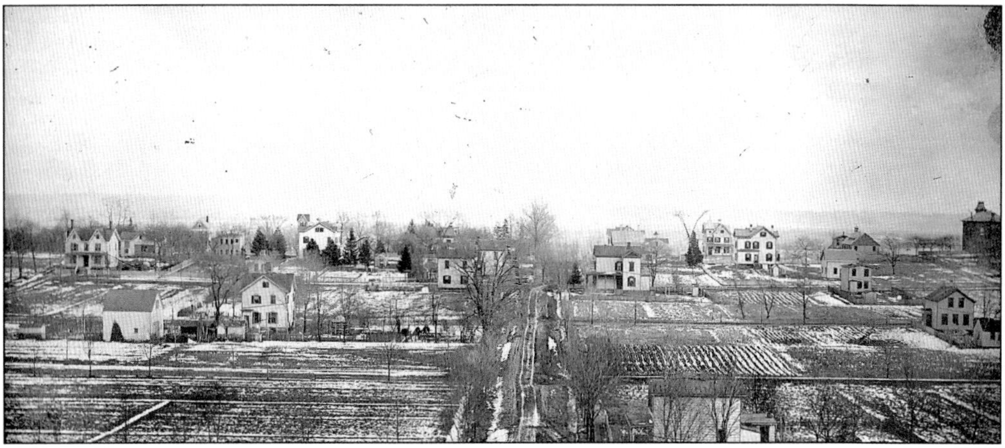

This photograph was taken looking east from the Kohbertz mansion. Note Mount Pleasant School at the top right. At the time, Mount Pleasant School was known as School No. 36 of Lodi Township. It was known as School No. 1 within the borough.

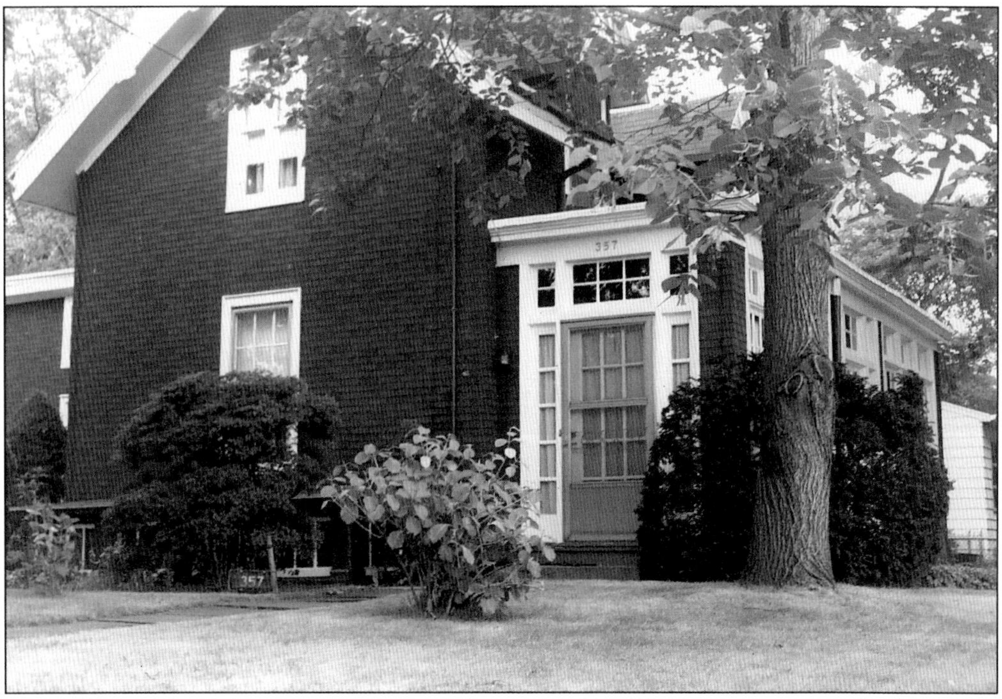

Shown here is the Kohbertz mansion coach house in 1980. The entire estate was built in 1869 at a cost of approximately $75,000. This home was also known as the Pfannkuchen House.

Here is a rear view of the Kohbertz mansion coach house *c.* 1920.

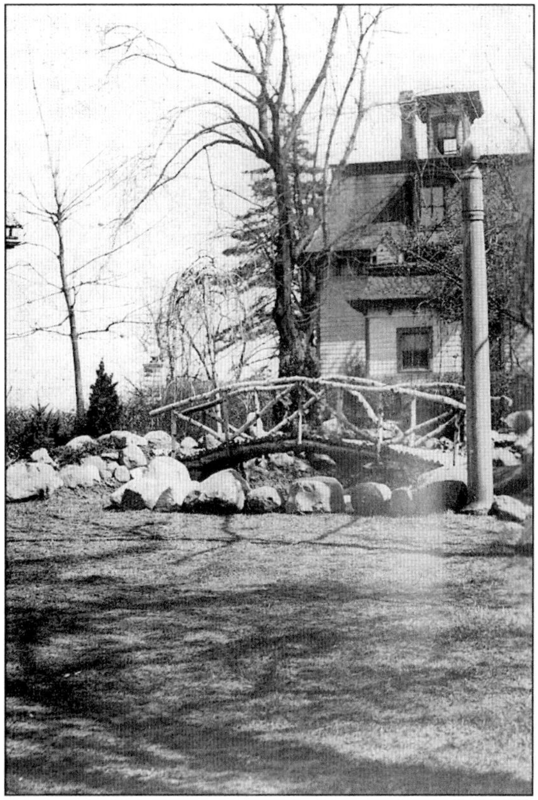

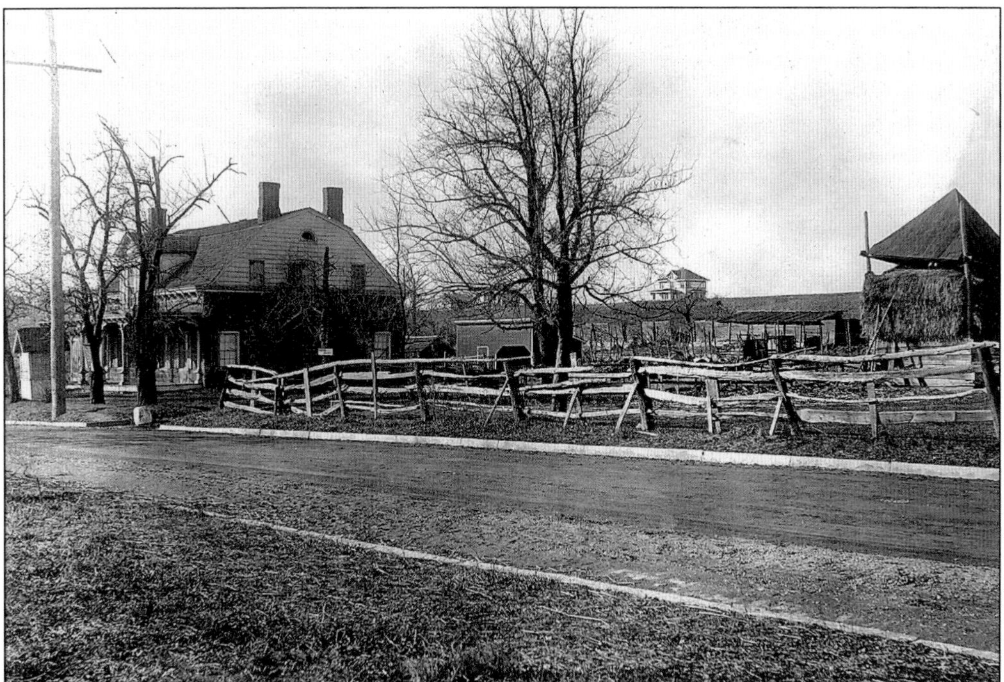

This beautiful brownstone house is located on the Brandenburg Farm on Hackensack Street.

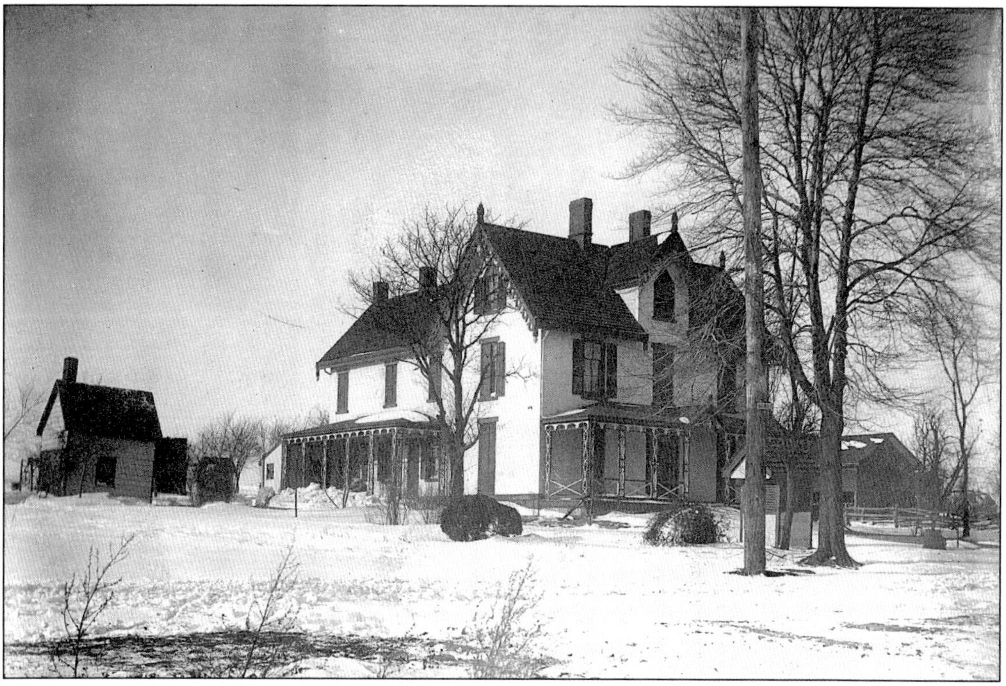

The Isaac Schoonmaker House once stood in the area across the street from the 7-11 Convenience Store. It had four chimneys, with the bricks coming from Little Ferry and the brownstone from the Olnes Mill in Hasbrouck Heights.

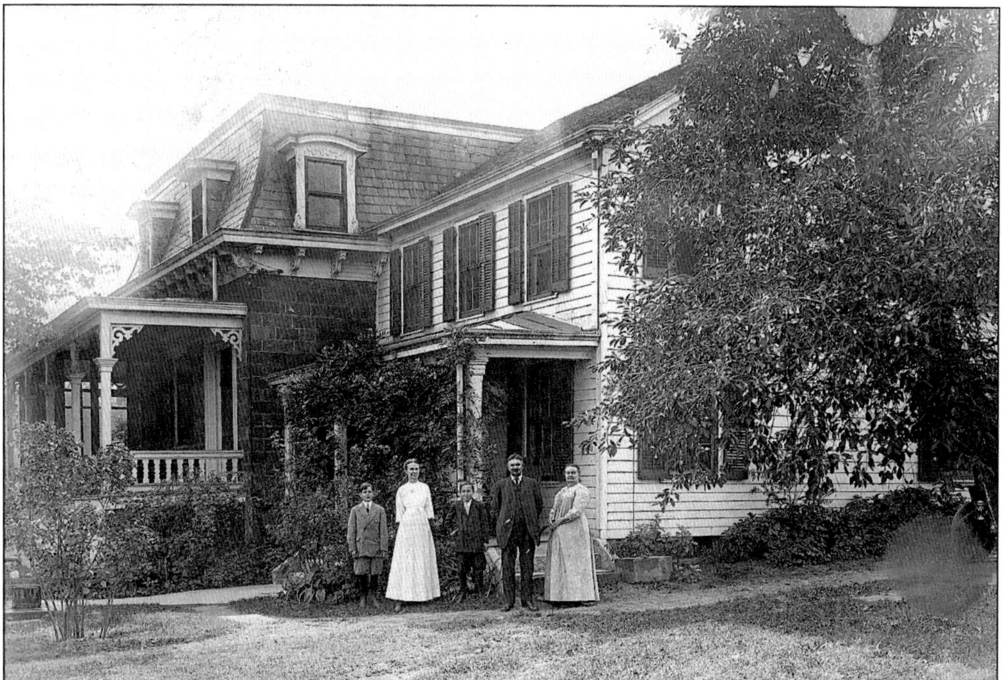

The Brandenburgs pose in front of their home, which was once owned by the Brinkerhoff family. This building is now the Wood-Ridge Memorial Library.

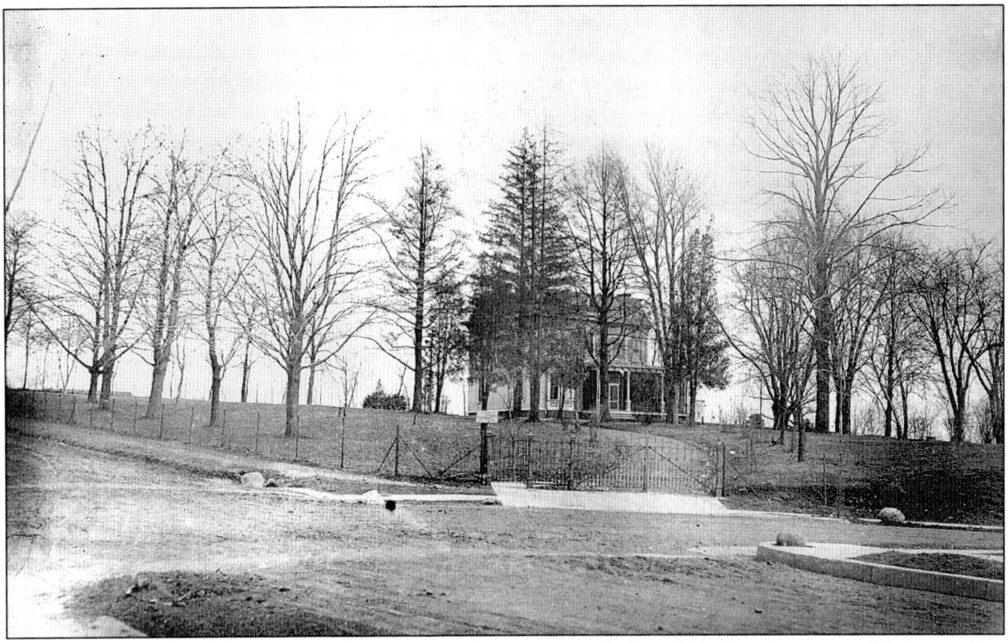

Mayor Charles Ruegger's home stands on the corner of Wood-Ridge Street and Moonachie Avenue. Today, garden apartments are on this site.

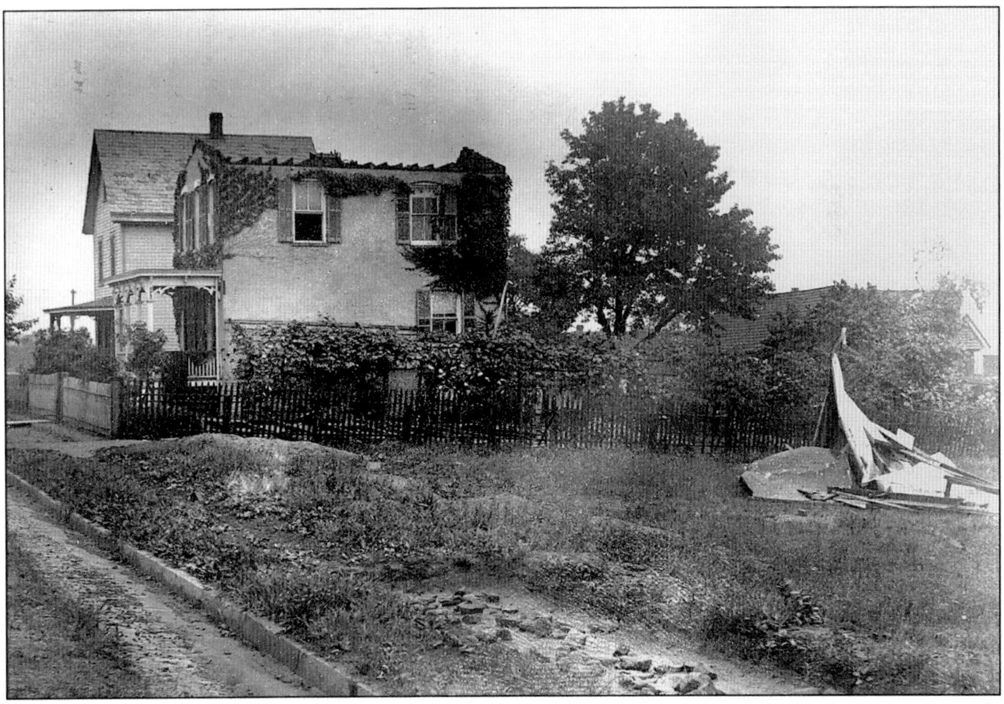

Shown c. 1911 is the home of Joseph Mahlbacher, on Madison Street, after hurricane winds tore off the roof.

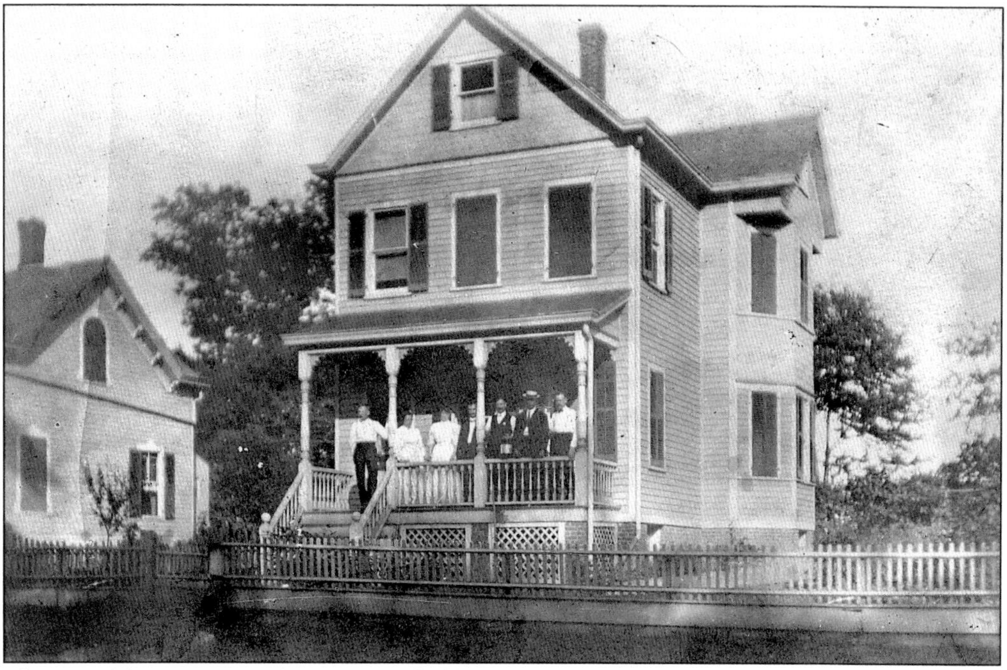

The Ketschke House stands at 12 Humboldt Street.

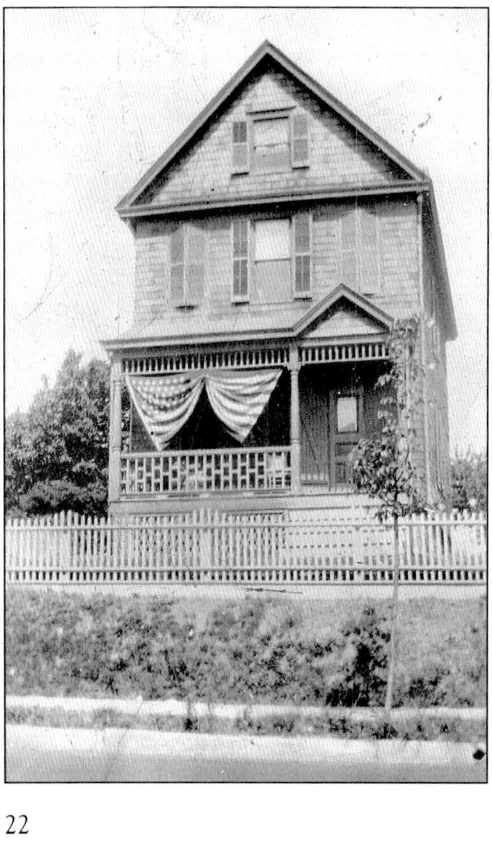

This is the home of the Palmer family, at 73 Hackensack Street, c. 1900.

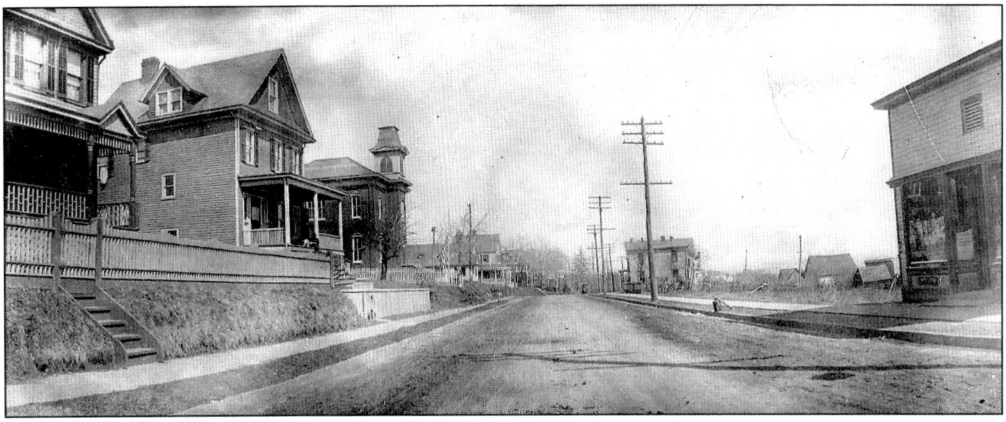

This view, looking north toward Union Avenue, shows Hackensack Street. On the east side of the street is Grabe's Ice Cream Parlor, later Schiesswohl Bakery. The houses to the left belong to the Palmer and Kenny families. The third building on the left is Mount Pleasant School.

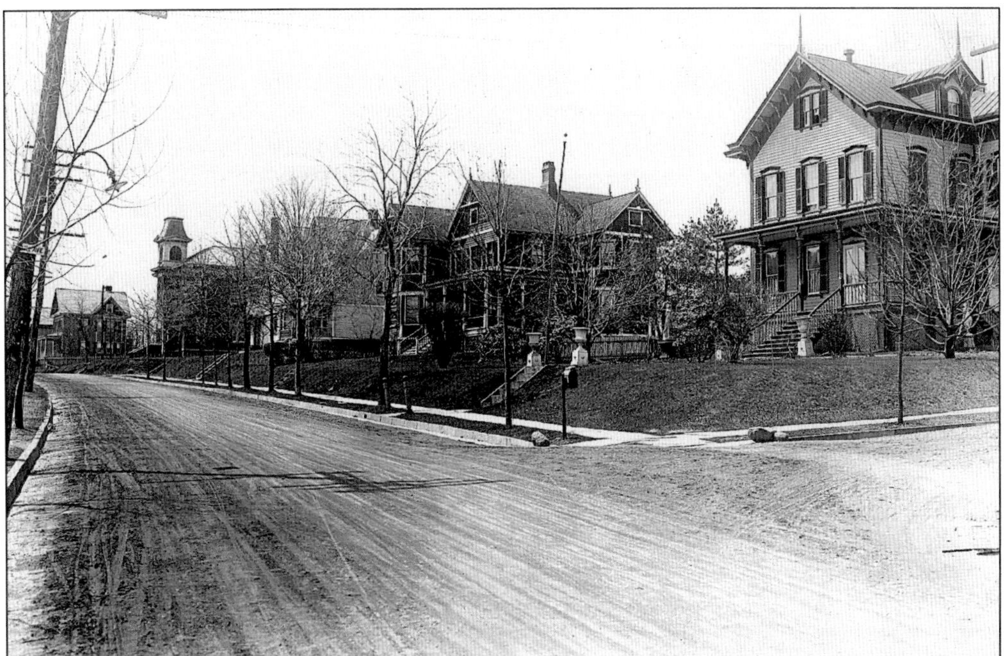

Looking south from Main Avenue, this view shows Hackensack Street. Mount Pleasant School is down the road; its bell tower is visible.

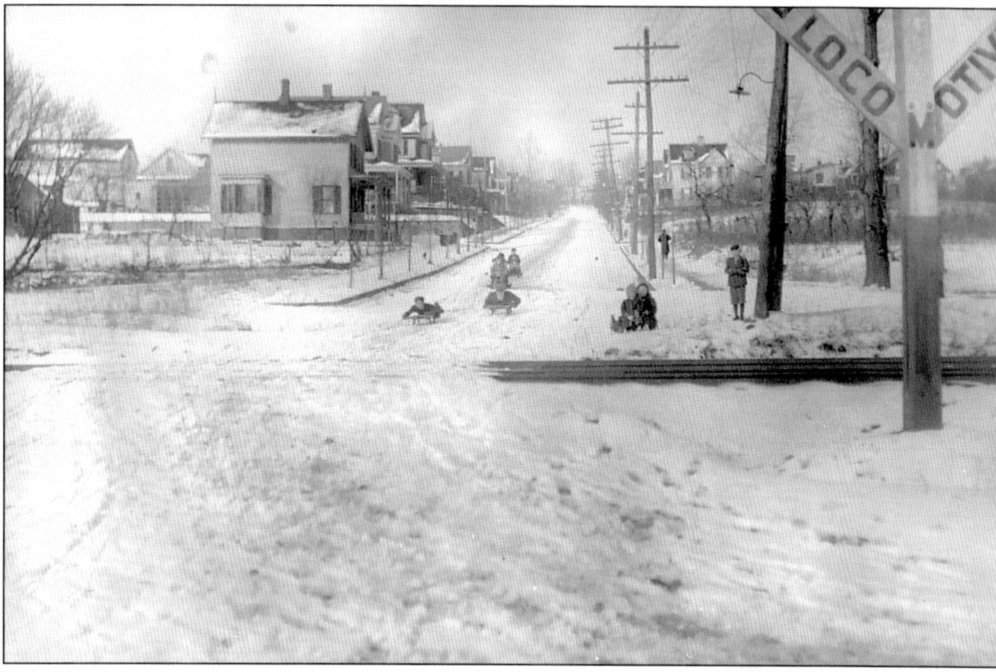

Sledding down Anderson Avenue by Park Place East was a wintertime pleasure. This photograph was taken in January 1911.

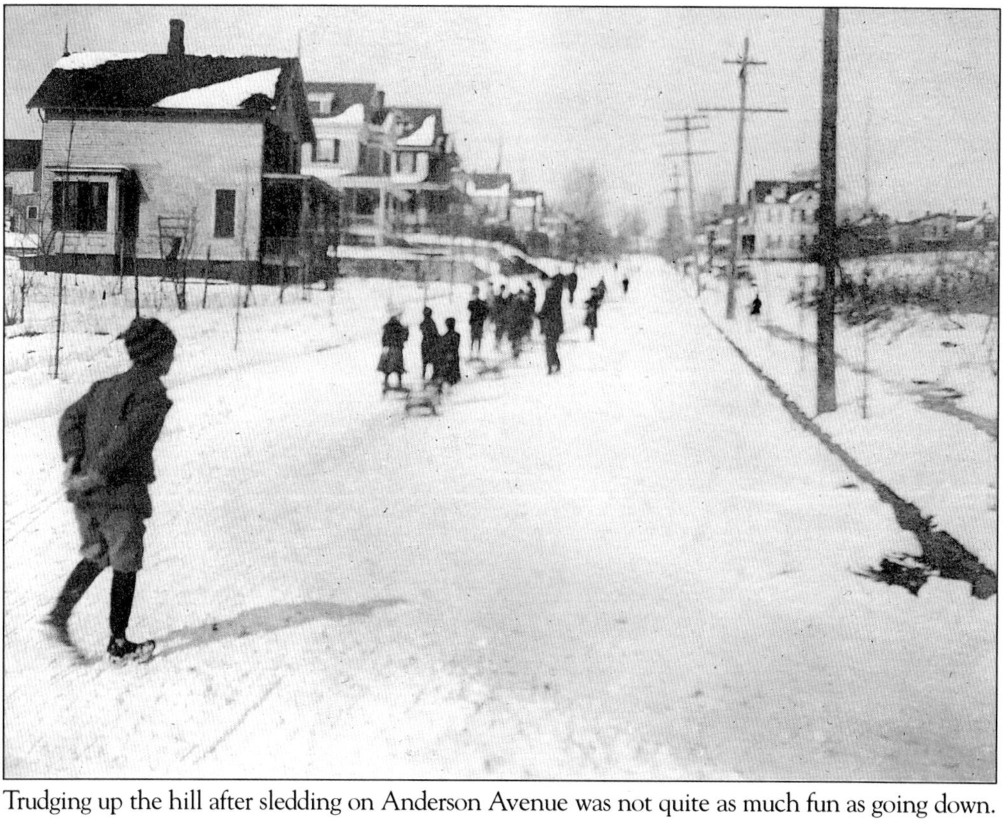

Trudging up the hill after sledding on Anderson Avenue was not quite as much fun as going down.

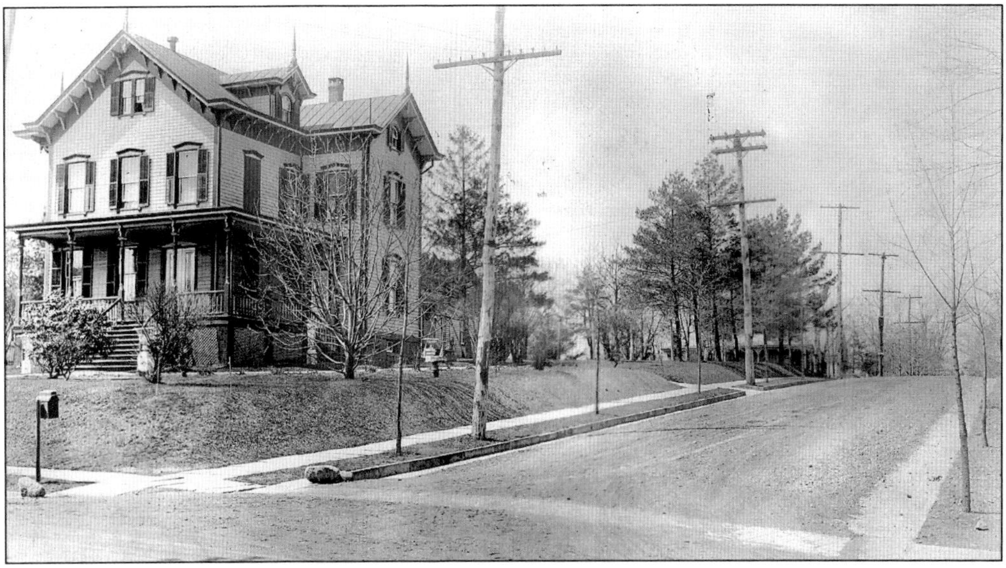

The Zumkley (Zumpkley) House, on the corner of Main Avenue and Hackensack Street, was the home of the Kohbertz family after the mansion became too large for them.

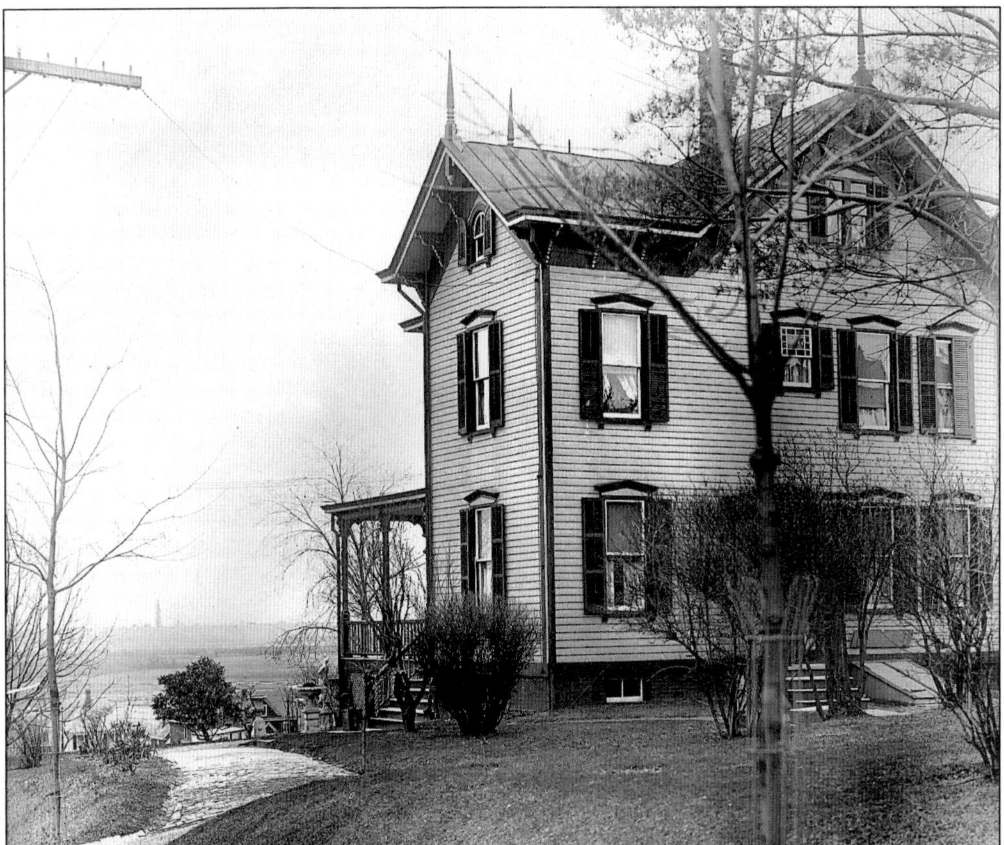

This rear view of the Zumkley House includes a view of New York City and the Metropolitan Life Insurance Building.

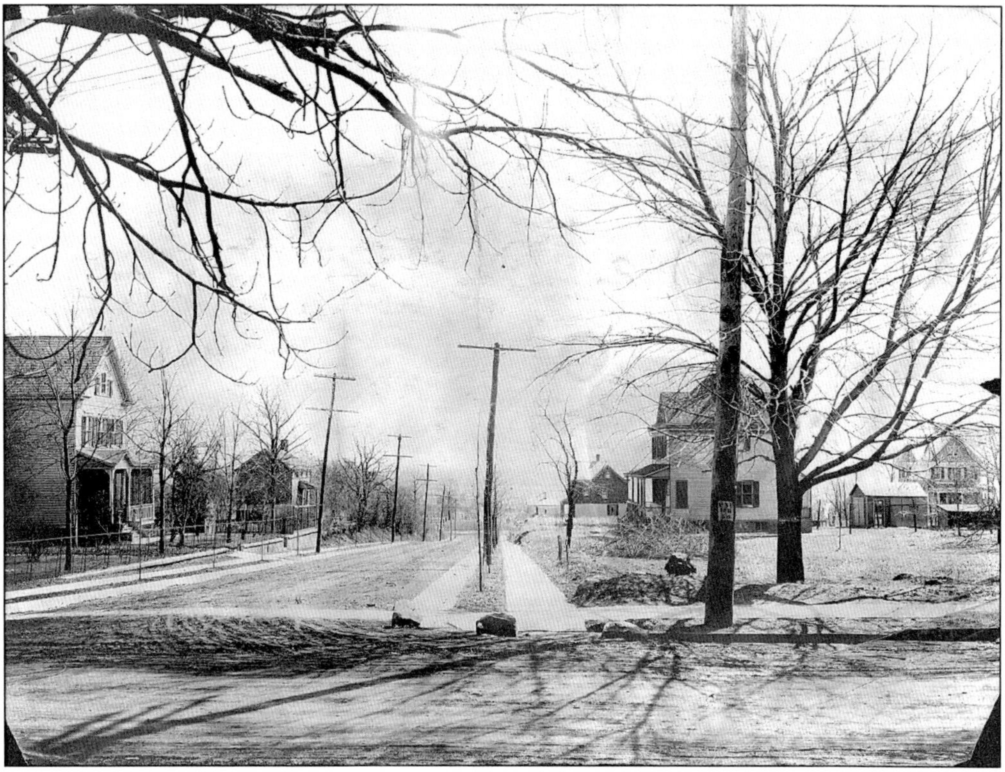

Moonachie Avenue is seen in this *c.* 1910 photograph, taken looking east from Hackensack Street.

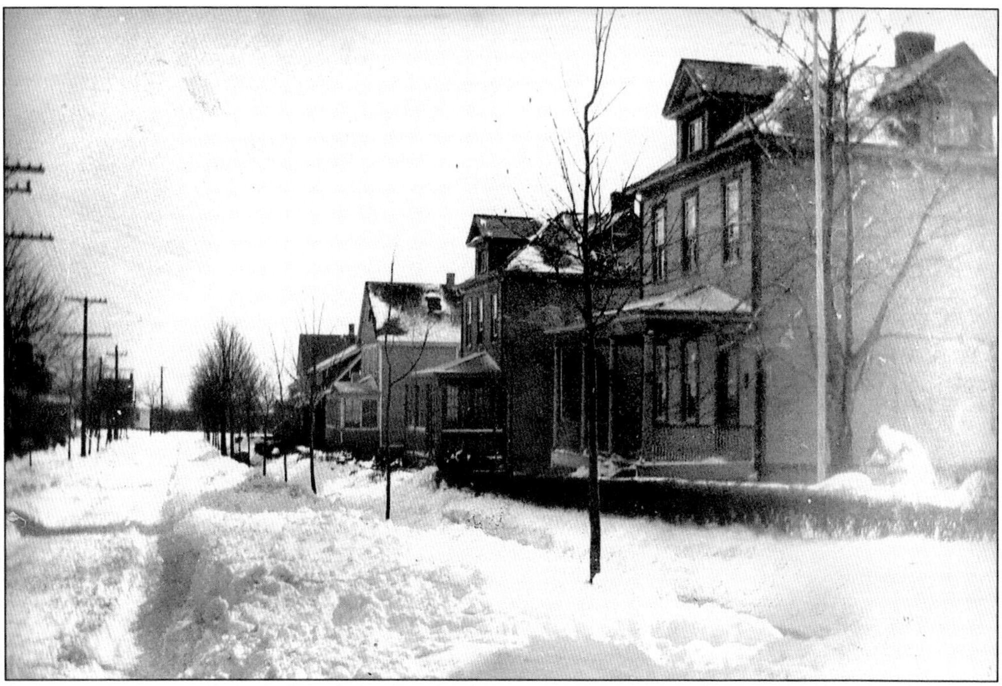

Ryerson Avenue is pictured in this view, looking toward Wood-Ridge Street from Hackensack Street in 1924.

Three

Business and Transportation

Farming was the main occupation in Wood-Ridge in its early years. Aside from farming, owning a tavern and keeping an inn were also early businesses. The Windisch Hotel, noted on the map of 1876, was located on old Polifly Road. With the coming of the railroad, John Adelung built his hotel opposite the depot before 1887. Retail shops began to make their appearance *c.* 1890. A bakery was established in the 1880s on Hackensack Street, as well as a butcher shop. When the railroad depot was built, some businesses sprang up nearby. John Bloom owned a dry goods store and shoe emporium. A grocery and candy store stood next to the Adelung Hotel. A tobacco shop near the railroad was an outlet store for the Lobravico Tobacco Factory. Drugstores, delicatessens, grocery stores, an ice-cream parlor, and a dry goods store were located on Hackensack Street, along with a tinsmith and harness repair shop and a feed and hay store at the southern end of town.

Transportation in Wood-Ridge evolved over the years. At first horse-drawn wagons were used to transport materials to the waterways. As automobiles became more popular, they began to be widely used in town. Trains came through Wood-Ridge, as did the trolley and, later, buses. Although the trolleys are gone, the train and bus services still exist.

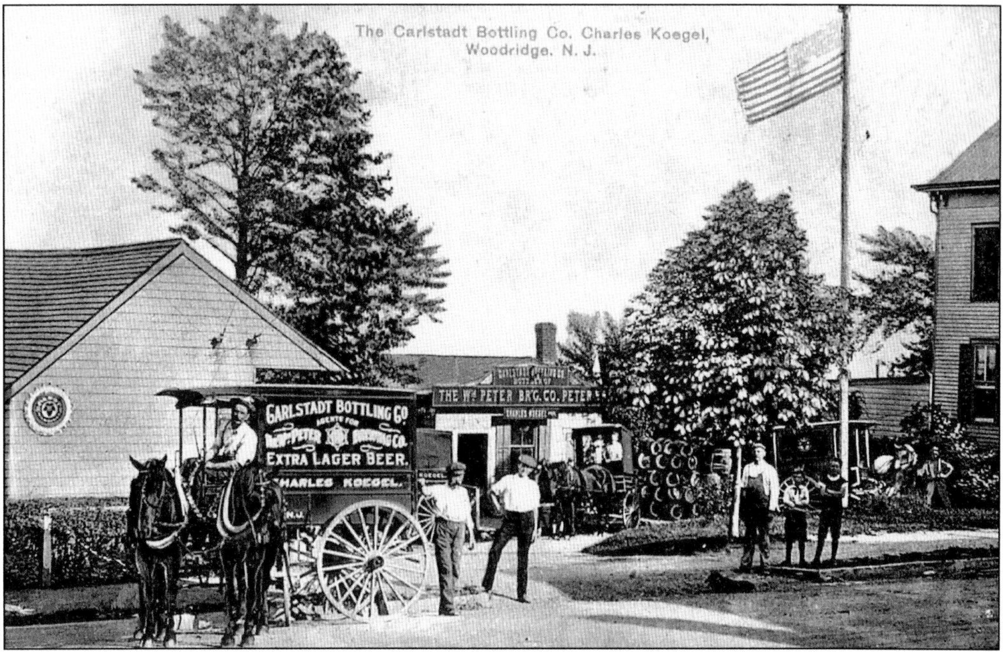

The Carlstadt Bottling Company was located near the Carlstadt line near the site of the present-day Jehovah's Witnesses building, owned by Charles Koegel.

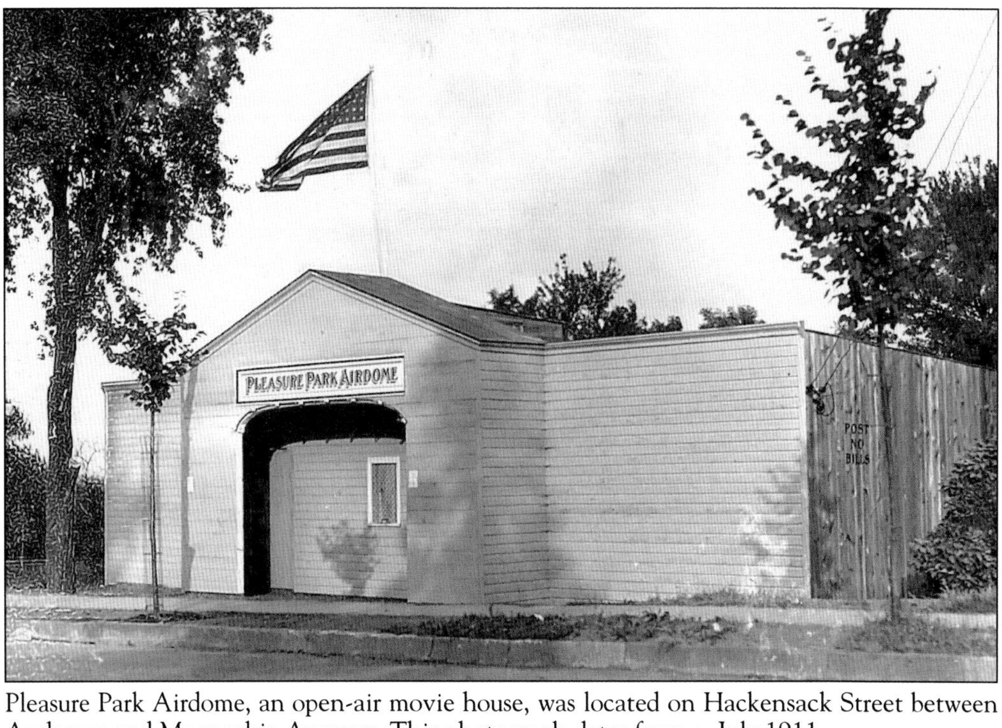

Pleasure Park Airdome, an open-air movie house, was located on Hackensack Street between Anderson and Moonachie Avenues. This photograph dates from *c.* July 1911.

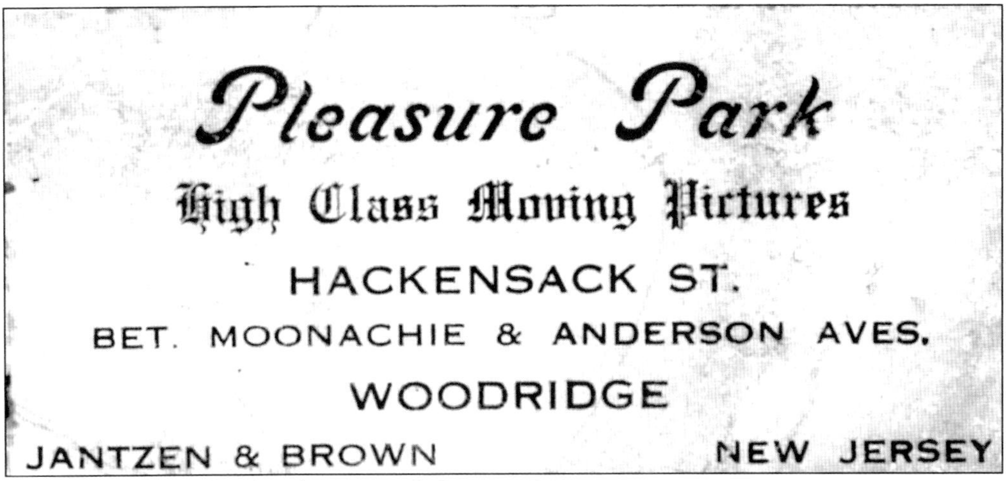

Shown here is a ticket for Pleasure Park from c. 1911.

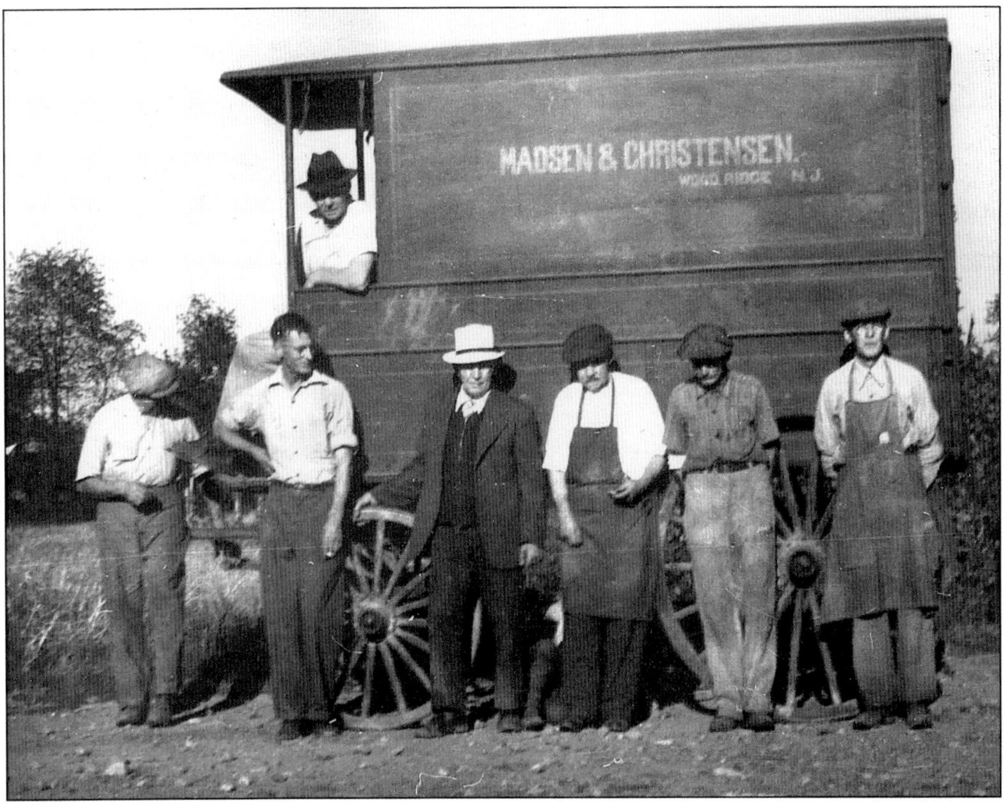

Madsen & Christensen greenhouses started using wagons in 1905. Posing by the company wagon, from left to right, are Henning Gustafson, Willy Eilert, owners Knud Christensen and Christian Madsen, Henry Madsen, and Nils Ebersen. John Peterson is in the cab. In 1975, the greenhouses were destroyed by fire, and in the late 1970s and early 1980s, the 96-unit West Ridge Mews condominiums were built on the site of Madsen & Christensen.

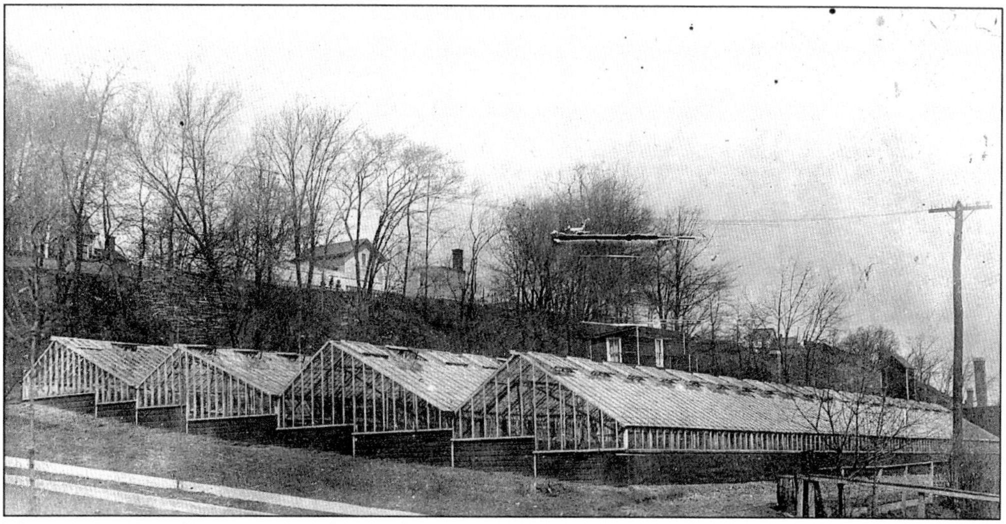

Numerous greenhouses were located in Wood-Ridge, including Fischer's, on Moonachie Avenue near the location of Terminal Construction Company.

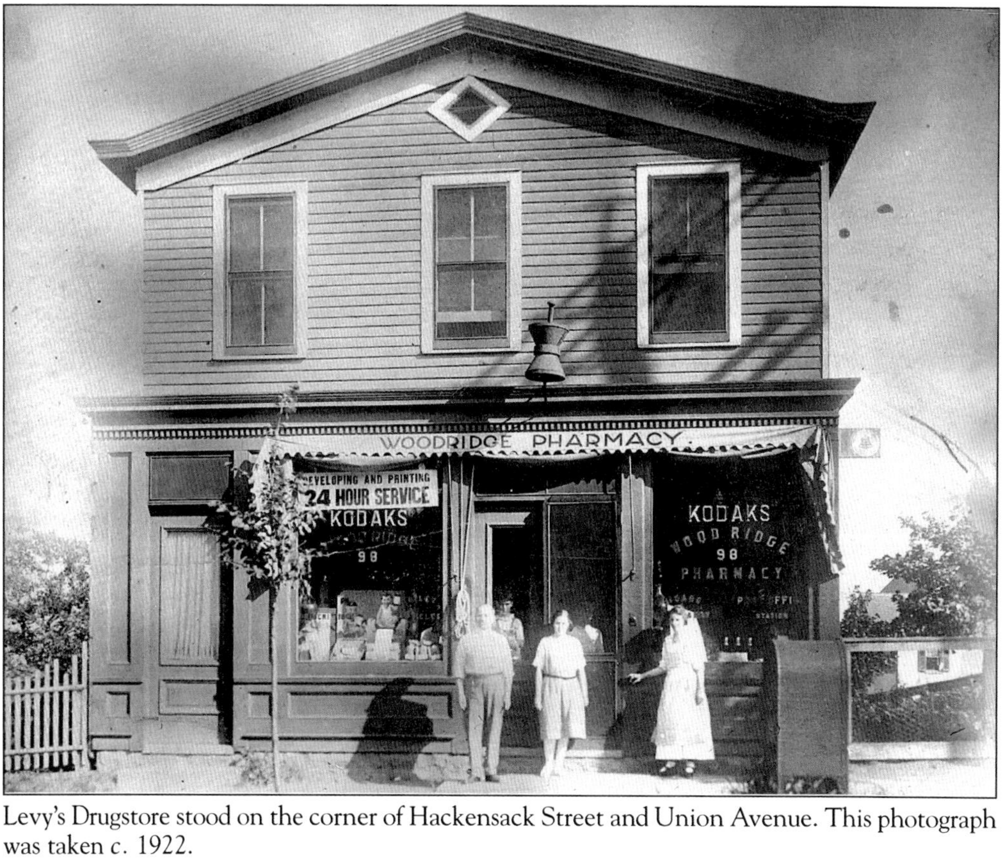

Levy's Drugstore stood on the corner of Hackensack Street and Union Avenue. This photograph was taken *c.* 1922.

Franz Fritsch's tavern stood on Hackensack Street. This photograph dates from c. 1898.

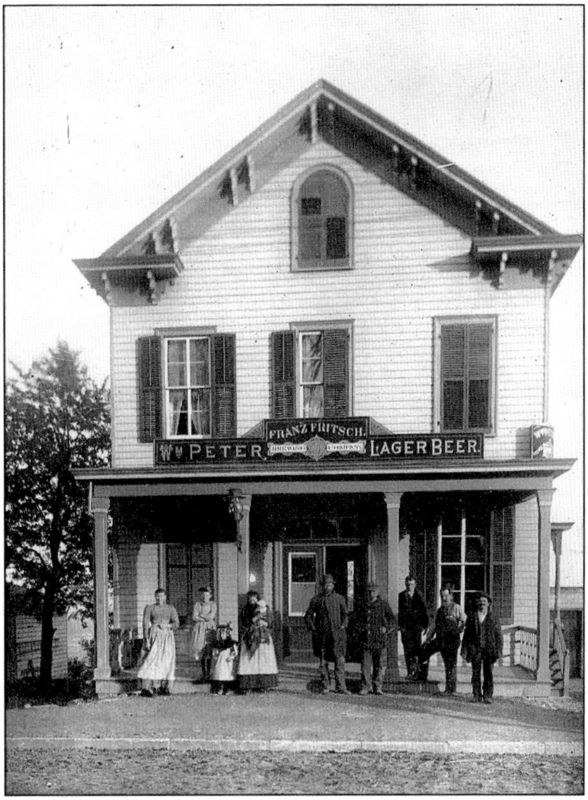

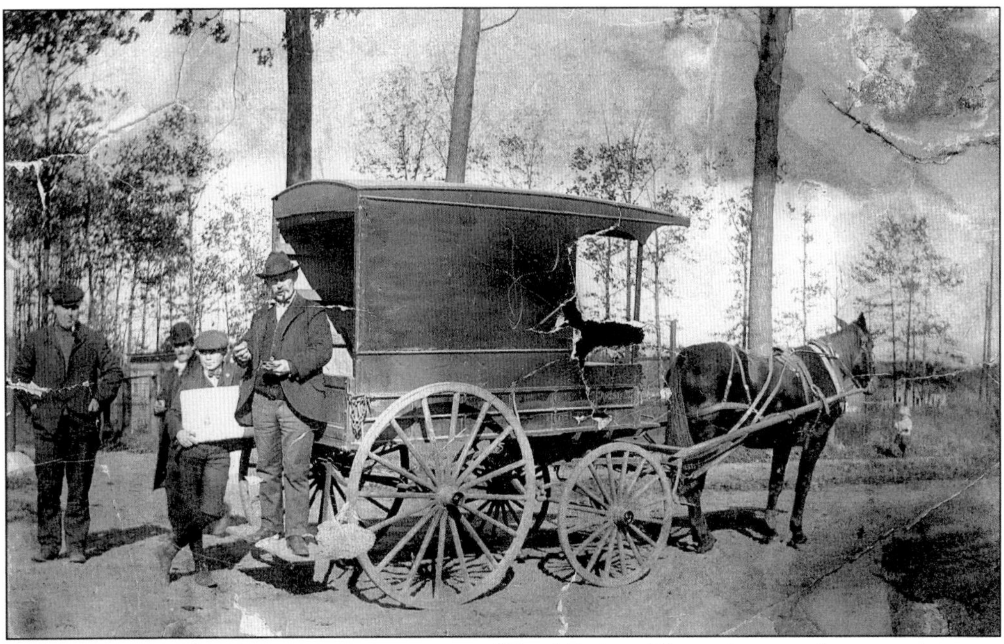

Mr. Wisse was the first newspaperman in Wood-Ridge. This photograph was taken on Humboldt Street c. 1903.

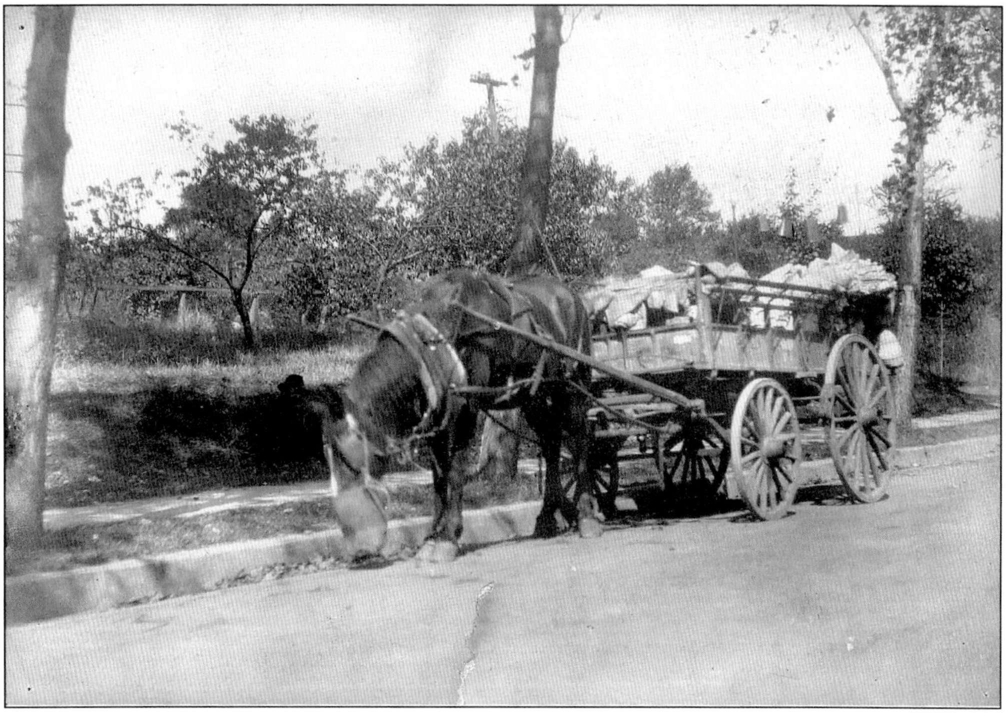

Here, the junk wagon makes its way along Hackensack Street.

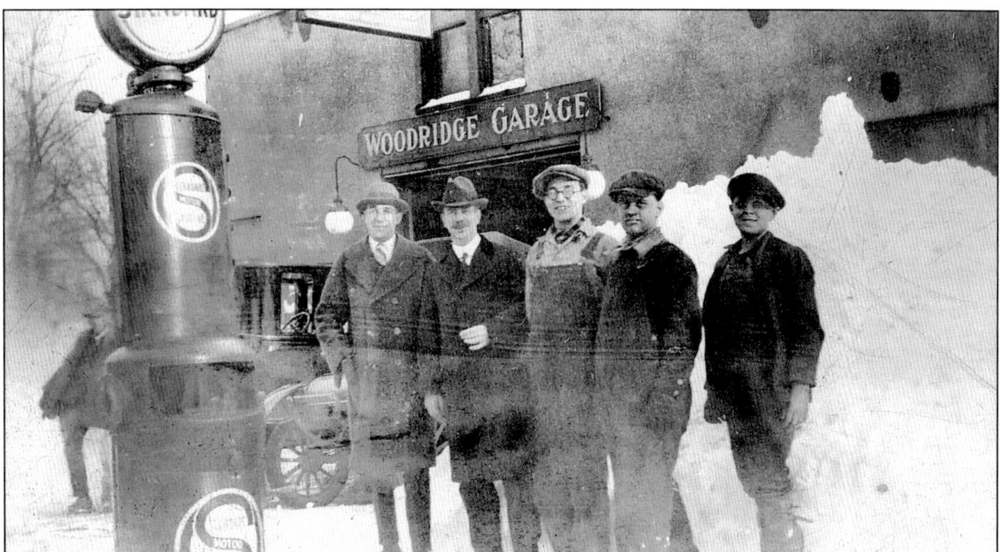

The Wood-Ridge Garage was located at the corner of Hackensack Street and Moonachie Avenue. This building is still in use today.

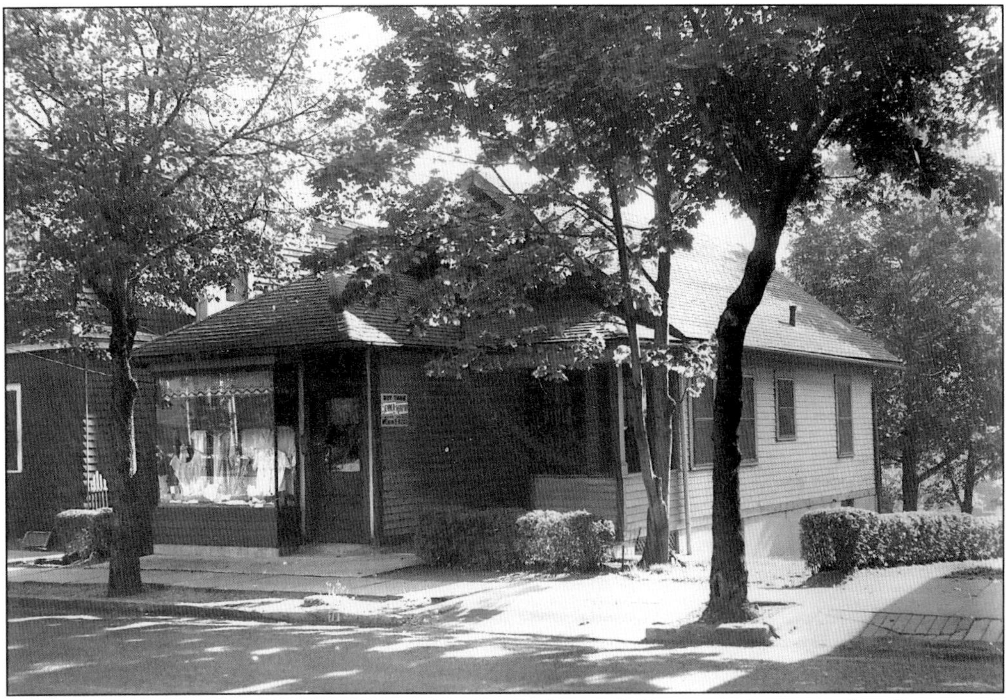

Anna Bartsch's Dry Goods Store, located at 78 Hackensack Street, is shown in this photograph taken *c.* 1921.

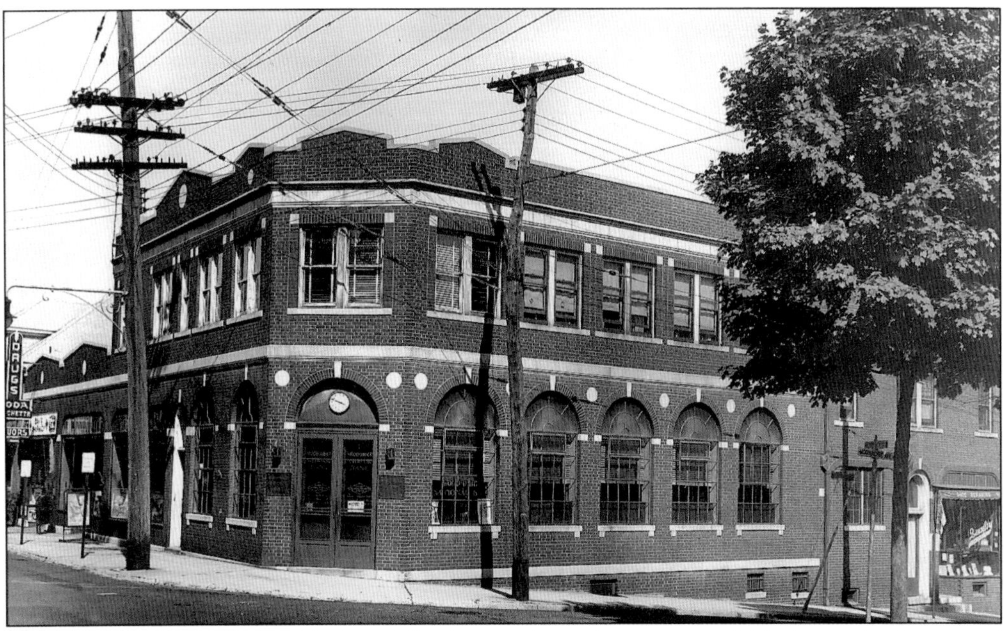

The original Wood-Ridge National Bank stood on the corner of Hackensack Street and Moonachie Avenue. Note Davis Drugs to the left and the shoe repair shop to the right on Moonachie Avenue. Murray Ludmer's offices were on the second floor. The borough offices and post office were located between Davis Drugs and the bank. This was the business center of town before Sunshine City was built.

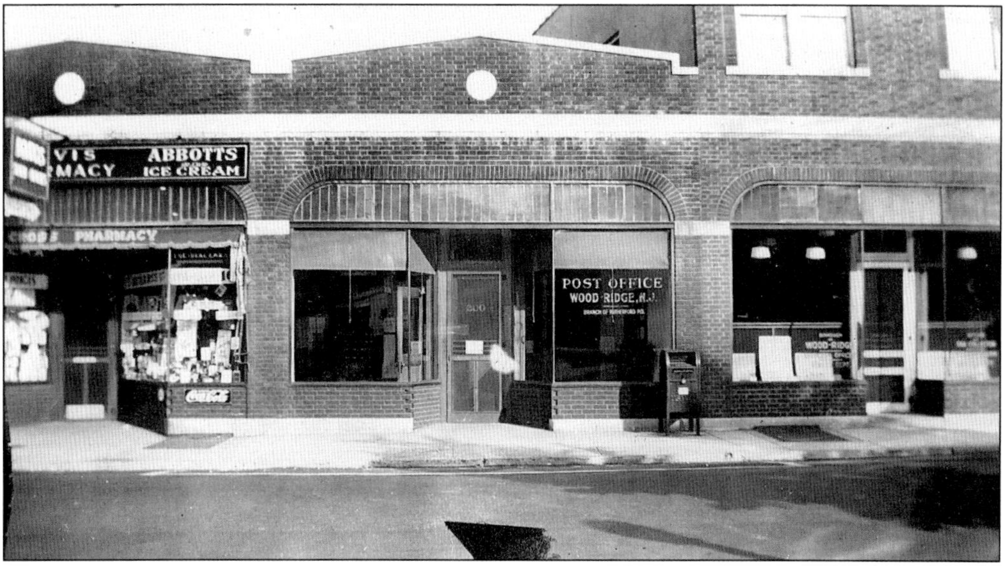

This *c.* 1934 photograph shows Davis Drugs, the post office, and the borough of Wood-Ridge's offices on Hackensack Street.

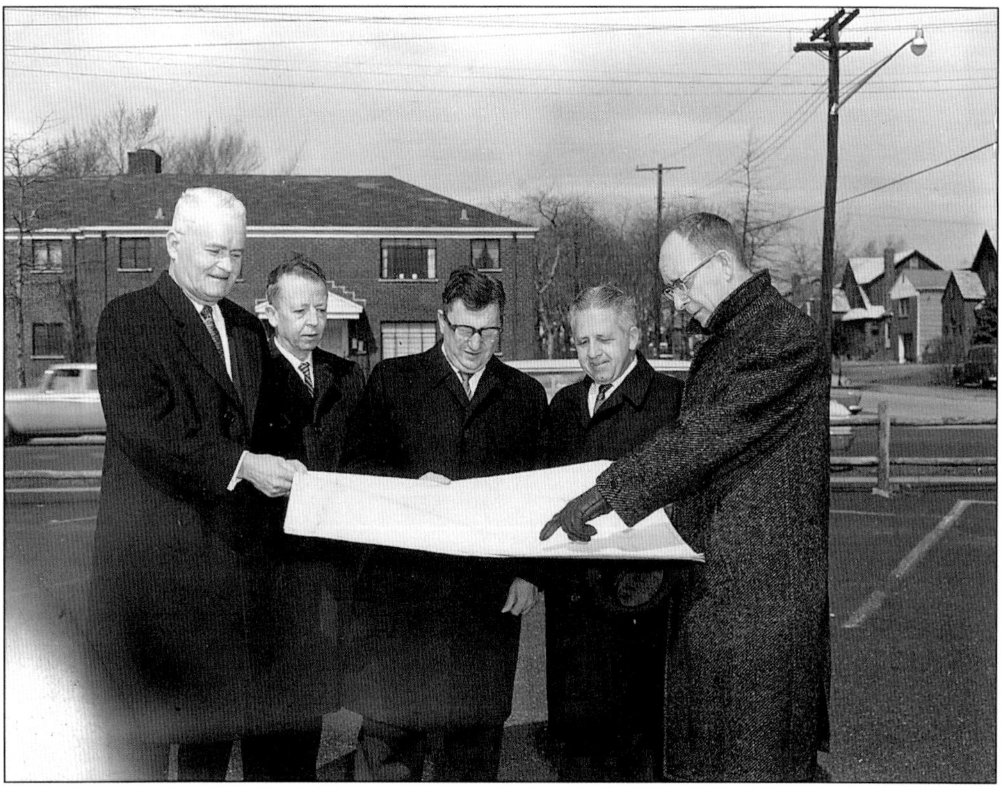

Shown is the groundbreaking for the current post office. Identified are Robert Stoesser, borough clerk, second from left, and Ignazio LaRosa, mayor, third from left. LaRosa died in office.

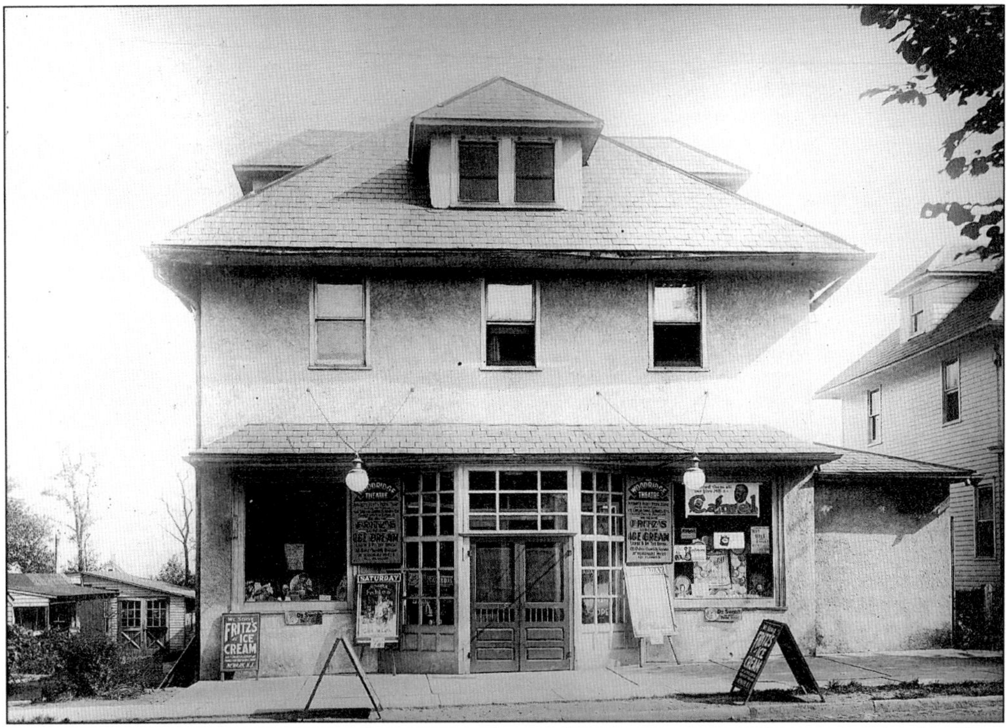

The Wood-Ridge Theatre, located at 178 Hackensack Street, is pictured *c.* 1923. This building replaced Pleasure Park. Numerous drinking establishments have been located here as well, most notably the Rainbow's End. The building was torn down in the 1980s.

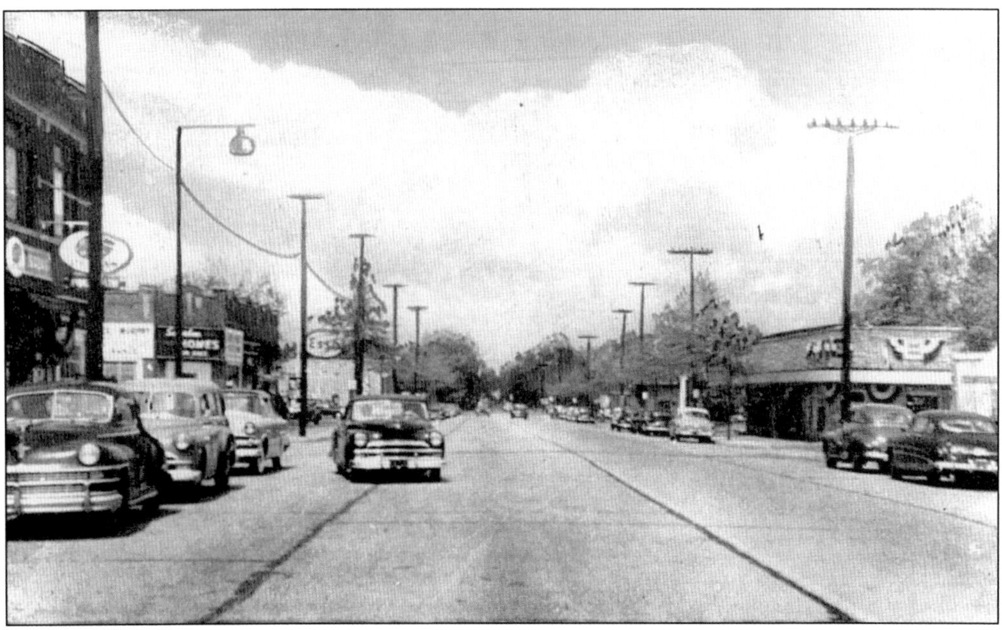

Looking north toward Windsor Road, this photograph shows Valley Boulevard *c.* 1950.

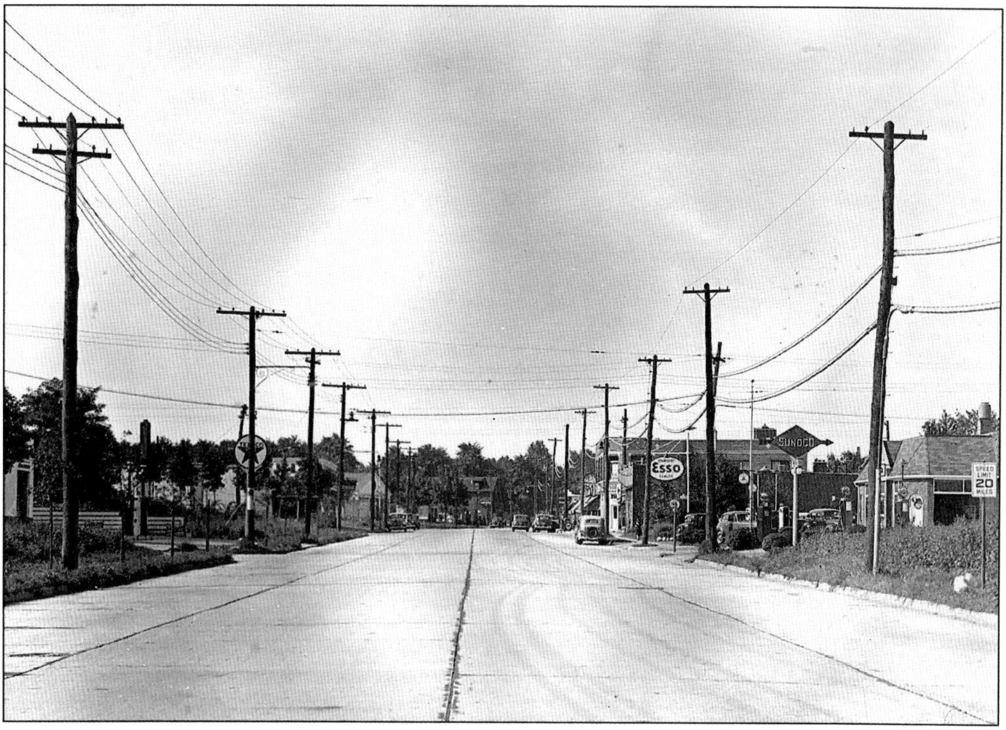

Looking south, this view shows Valley Boulevard near Innes Road *c.* 1940.

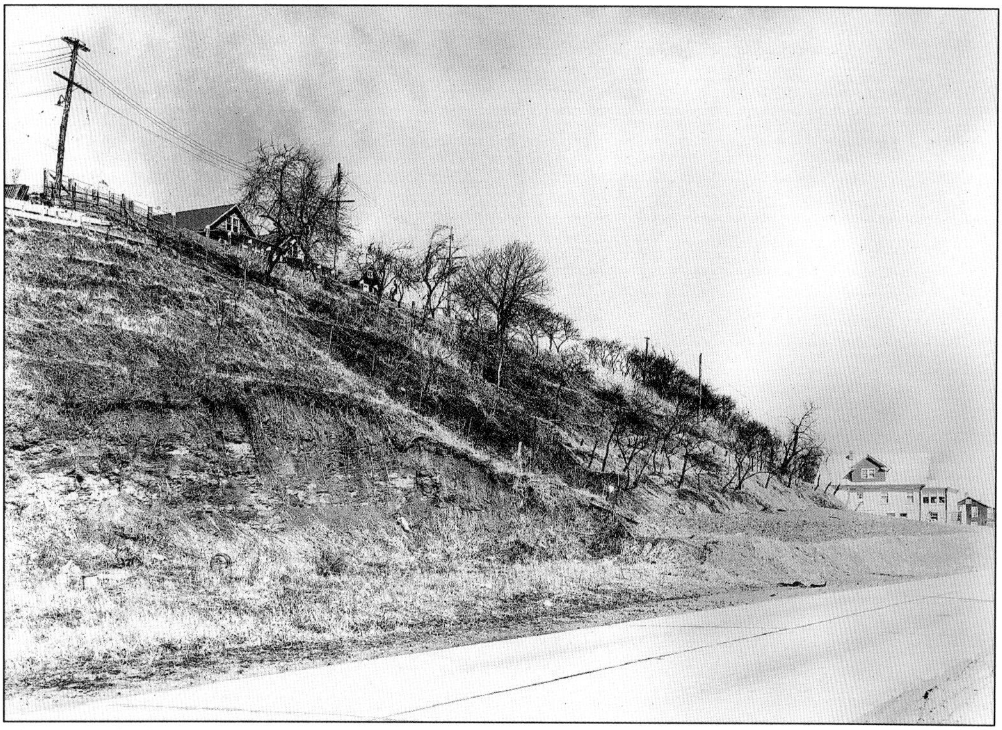

This view looking north from Route 2 shows the highway that is now Route 17. Today, the Fiesta Banquet Facility sits here on the side of the hill.

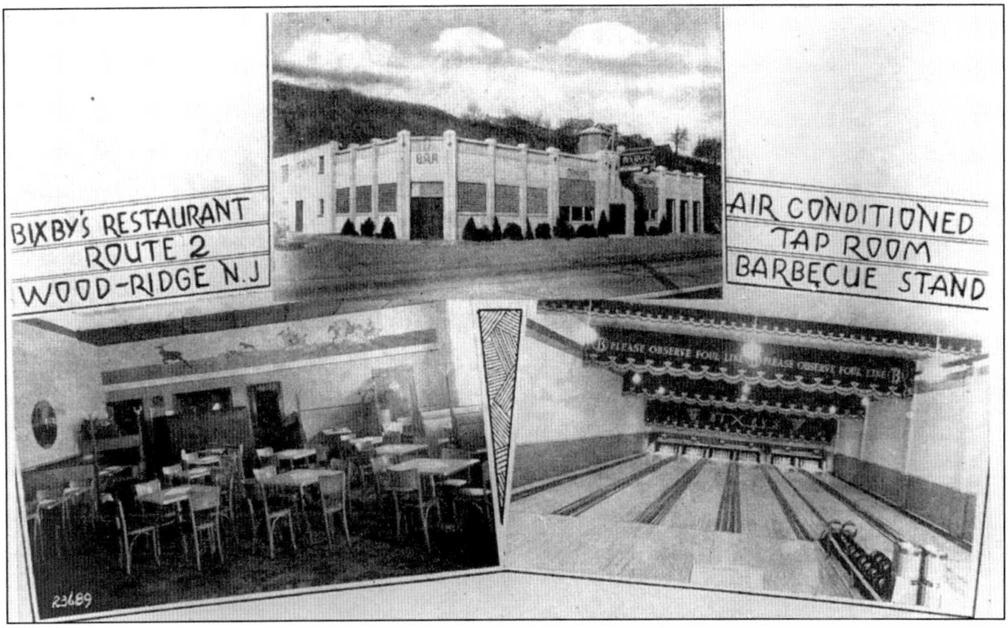

Bixby's Restaurant once stood where the Fiesta is now located.

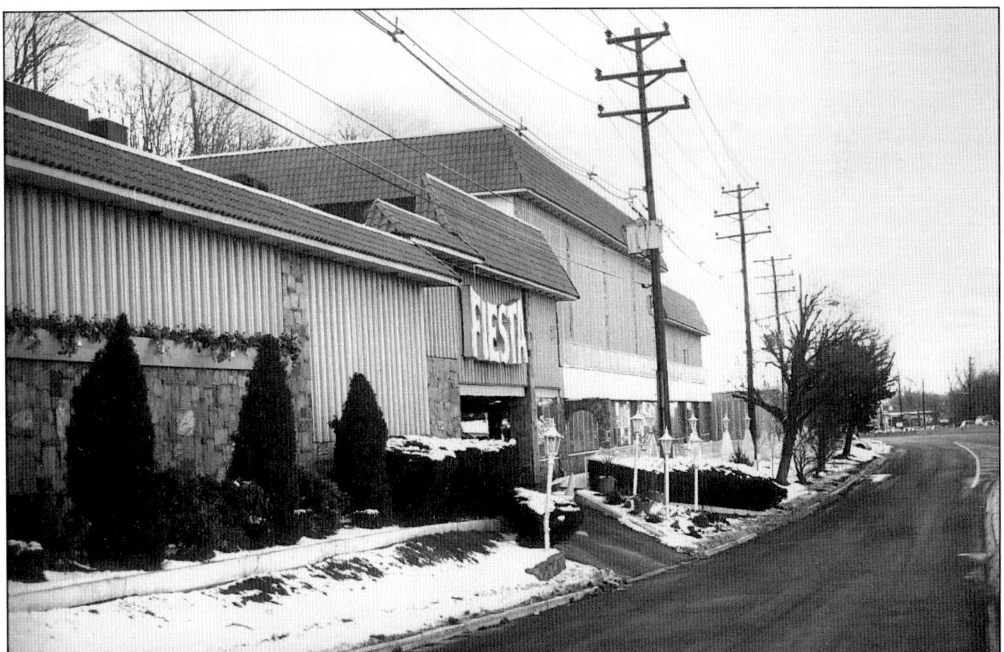

The banquet facility known as the Fiesta is pictured here.

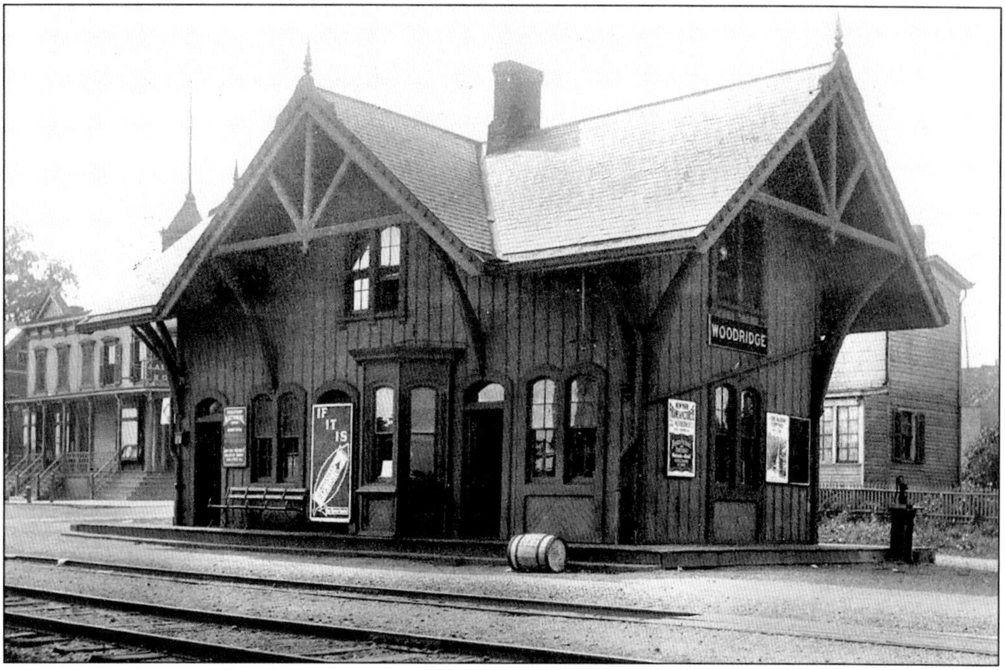

This is how the Wood-Ridge Train station looked *c.* 1909. Mrs. Hart was the station agent. The Adelung Hotel is visible to the left.

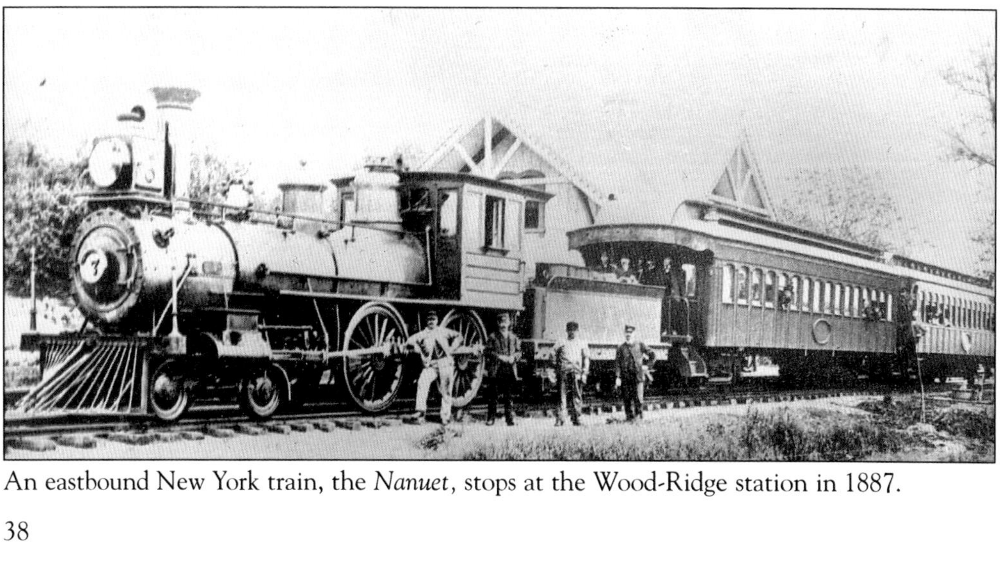

An eastbound New York train, the *Nanuet,* stops at the Wood-Ridge station in 1887.

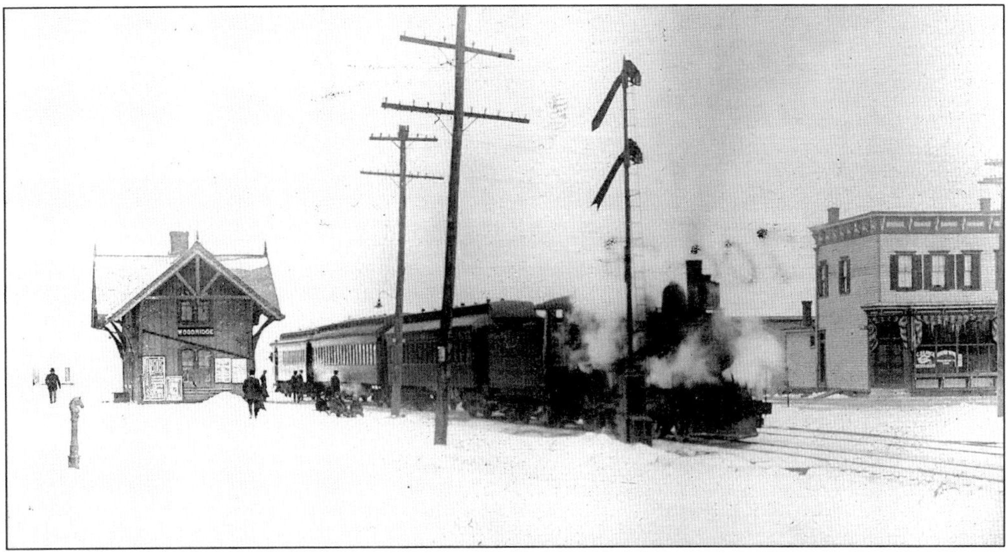

Another eastbound train pauses at the Wood-Ridge station in January 1912.

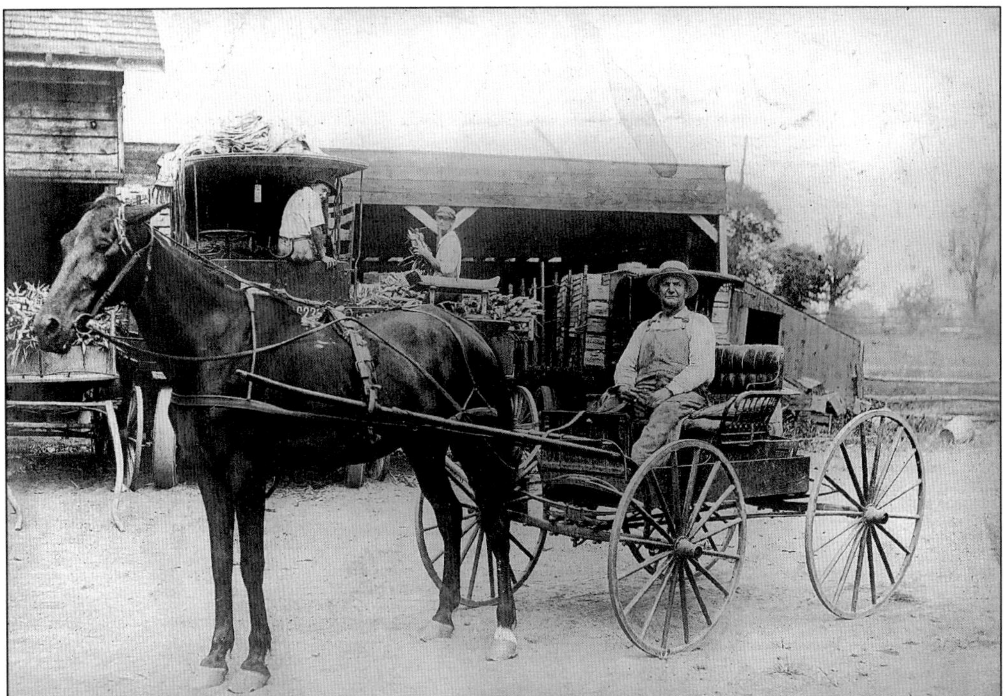

Leopold Brandenburg is pictured on his farm after the corn harvest. His mode of transportation was a popular one in the days before the automobile arrived.

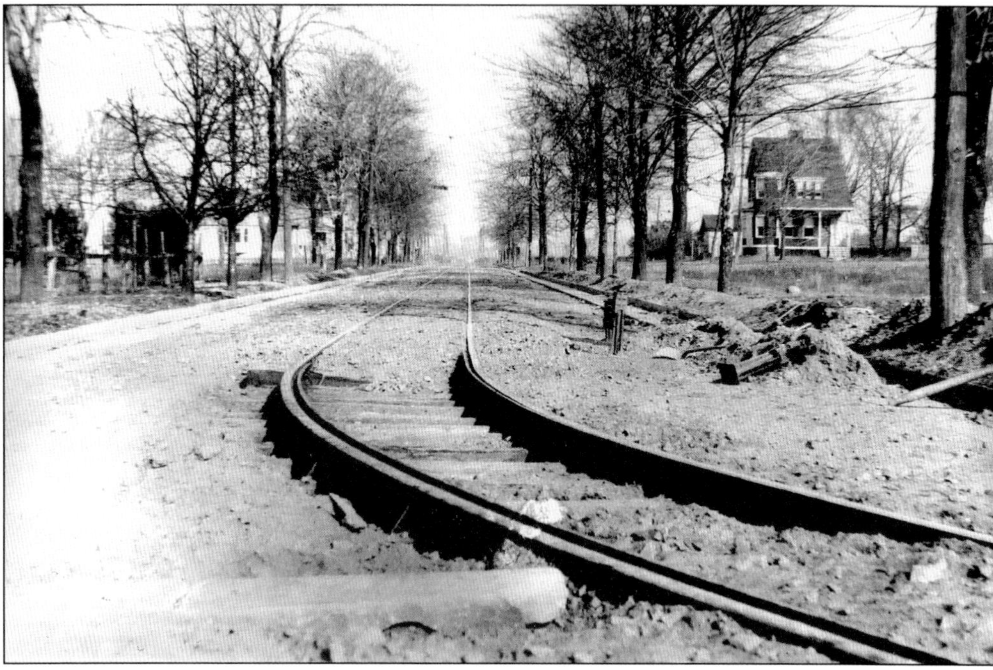

The trolley was another popular form of transportation in the early 1900s. Shown are the tracks on Fourth Street running north toward Union Avenue *c.* 1912. The house to the right still stands.

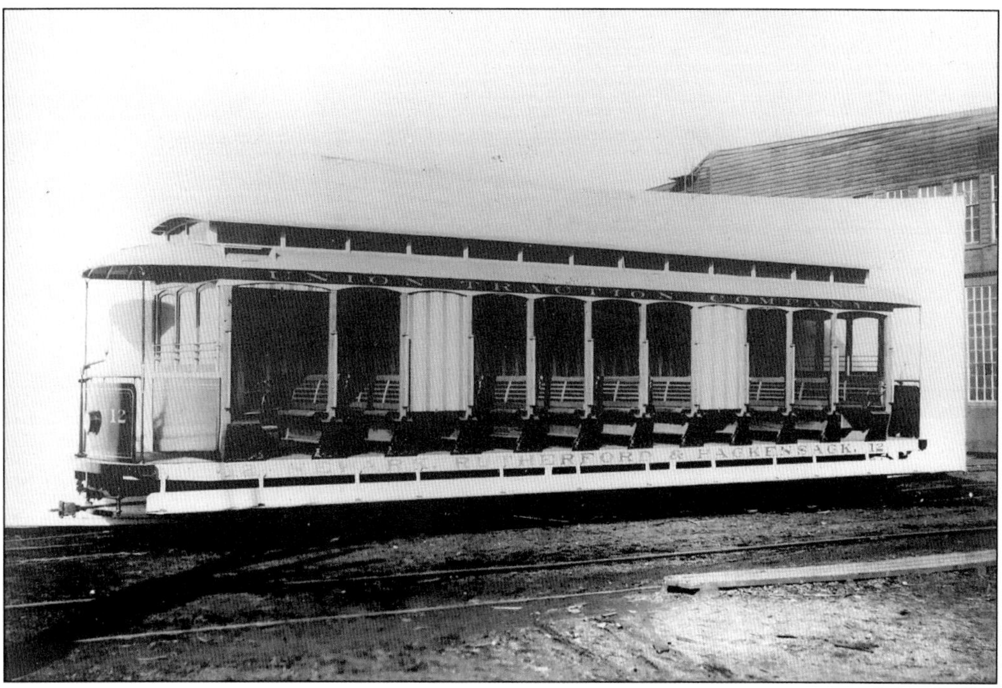

This trolley was the Union Traction Company 12-bench, open-type car No. 12. Built in 1897, it was destroyed by fire in 1906 at the Cleveland Avenue turnout in Hasbrouck Heights.

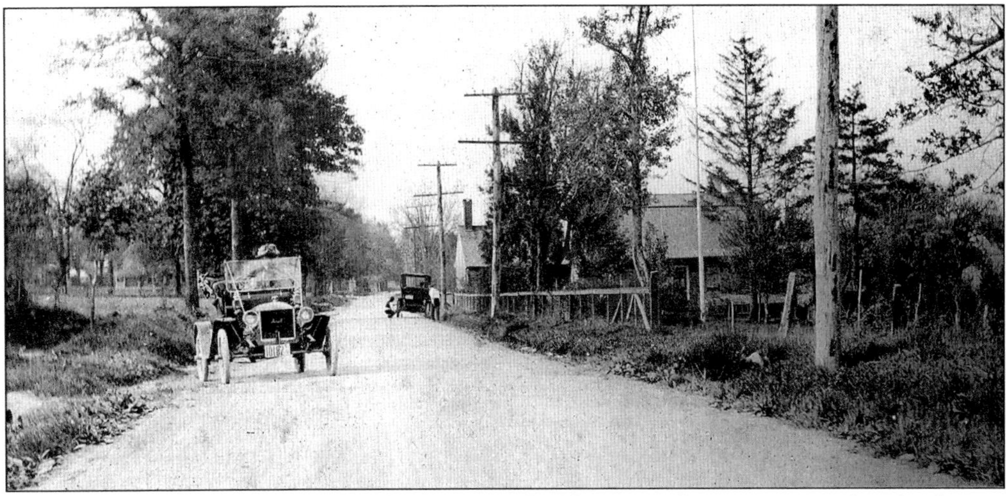

Shown is Harry Bringman's Maxwell in 1912. Lulu Obermeyer Bringman is at the wheel.

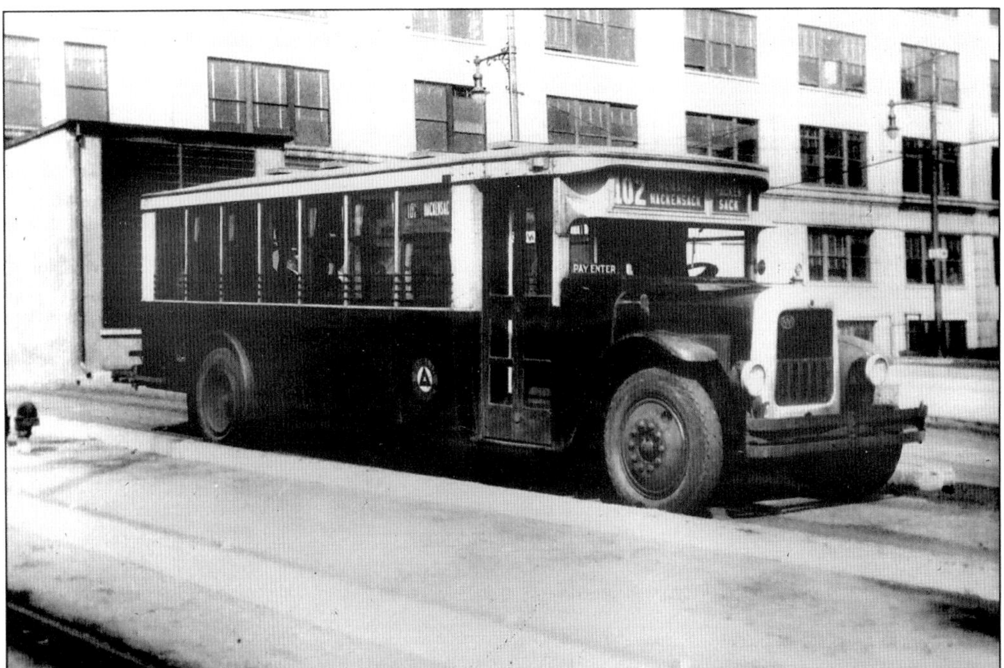

The No. 102 bus traveled between the cities of Hackensack and Newark along Hackensack Street and made numerous stops in Wood-Ridge. The bus number was later changed to 76. Today, bus No. 76 continues to follow the same route.

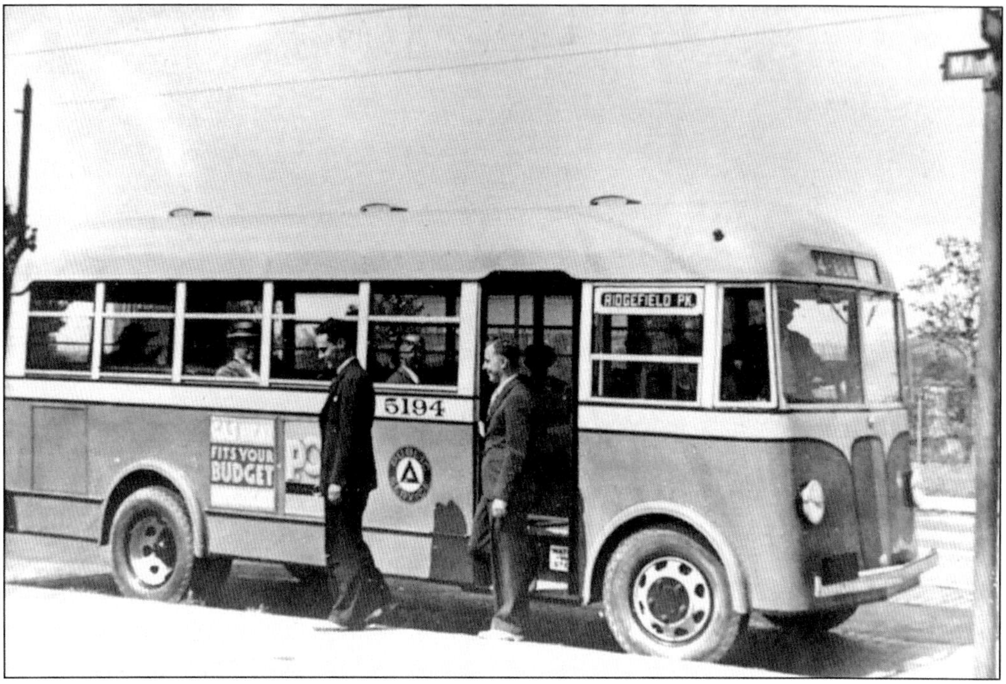

The Grandview bus traveled between Hackensack and East Rutherford.

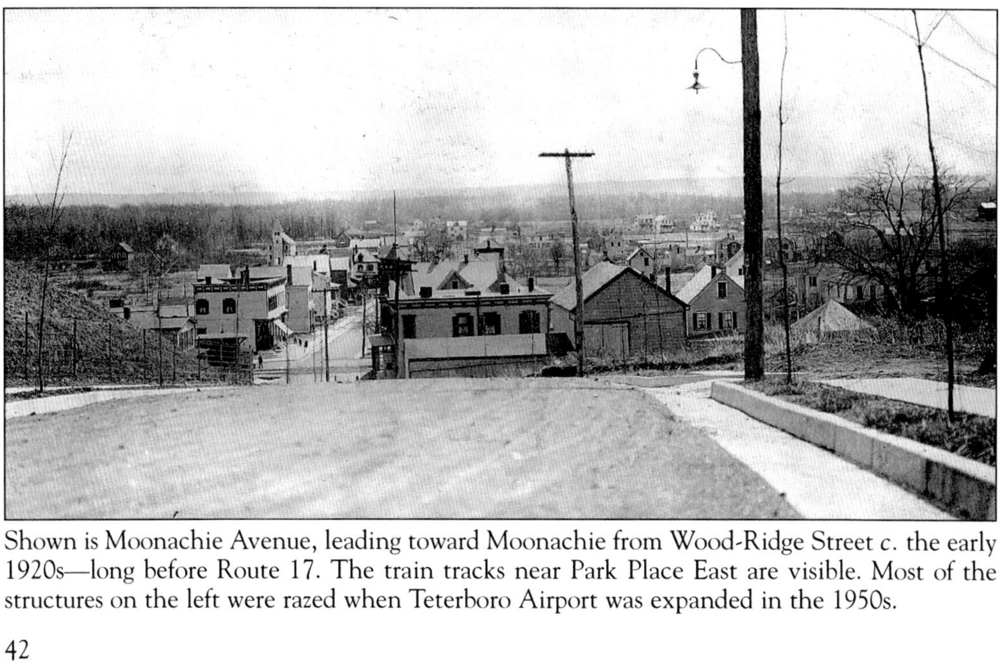
Shown is Moonachie Avenue, leading toward Moonachie from Wood-Ridge Street *c.* the early 1920s—long before Route 17. The train tracks near Park Place East are visible. Most of the structures on the left were razed when Teterboro Airport was expanded in the 1950s.

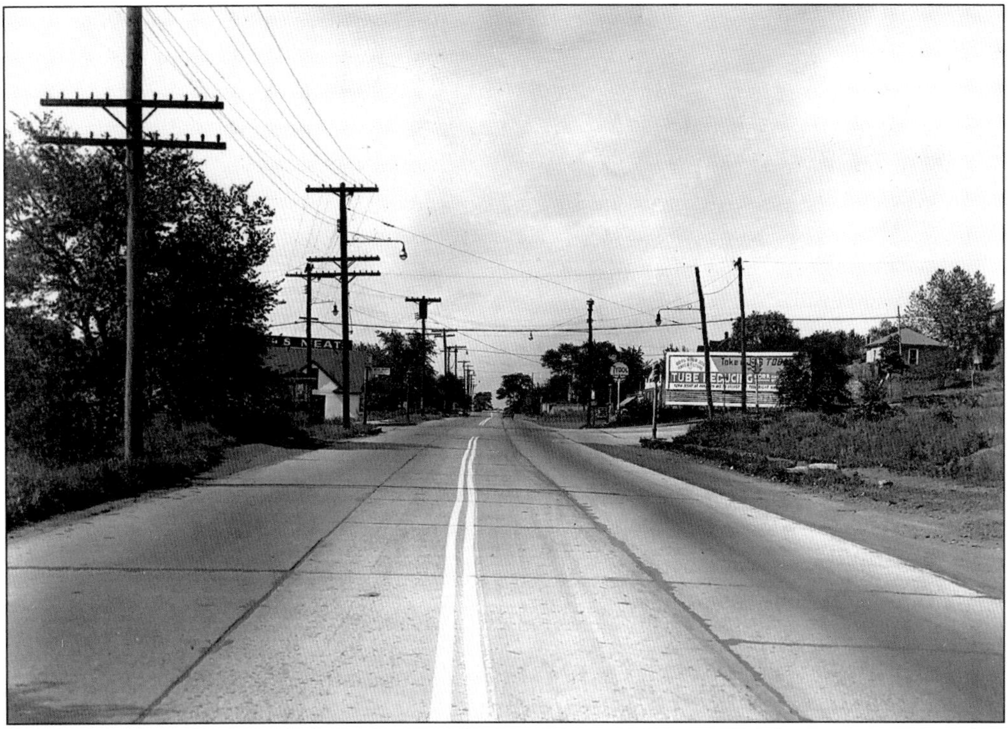

This late-1940s photograph shows Route 2 before it became Route 17. The intersection is that of Route 2 and Moonachie Avenue.

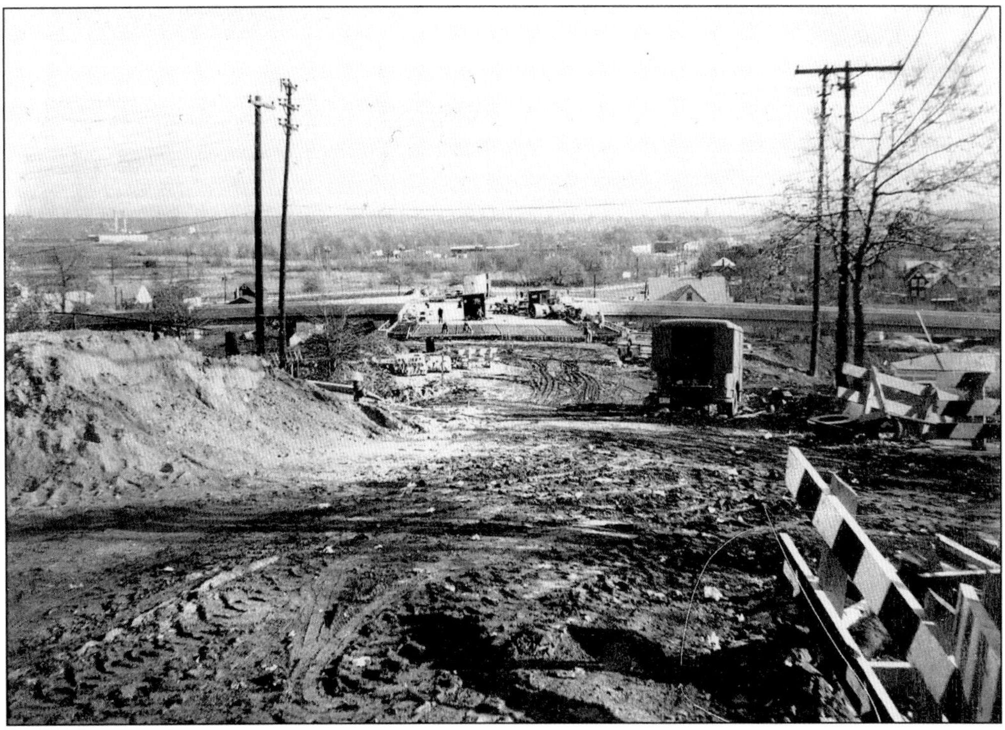

In this photograph from the late 1960s, construction of the Route 17 overpass is under way.

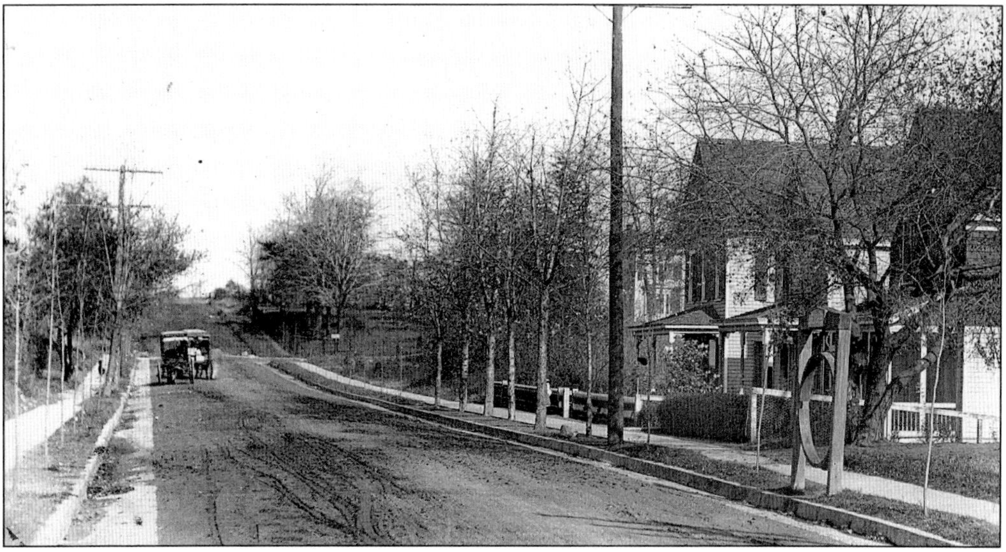

This photograph, looking north from Anderson Avenue, shows Wood-Ridge Street in September 1911.

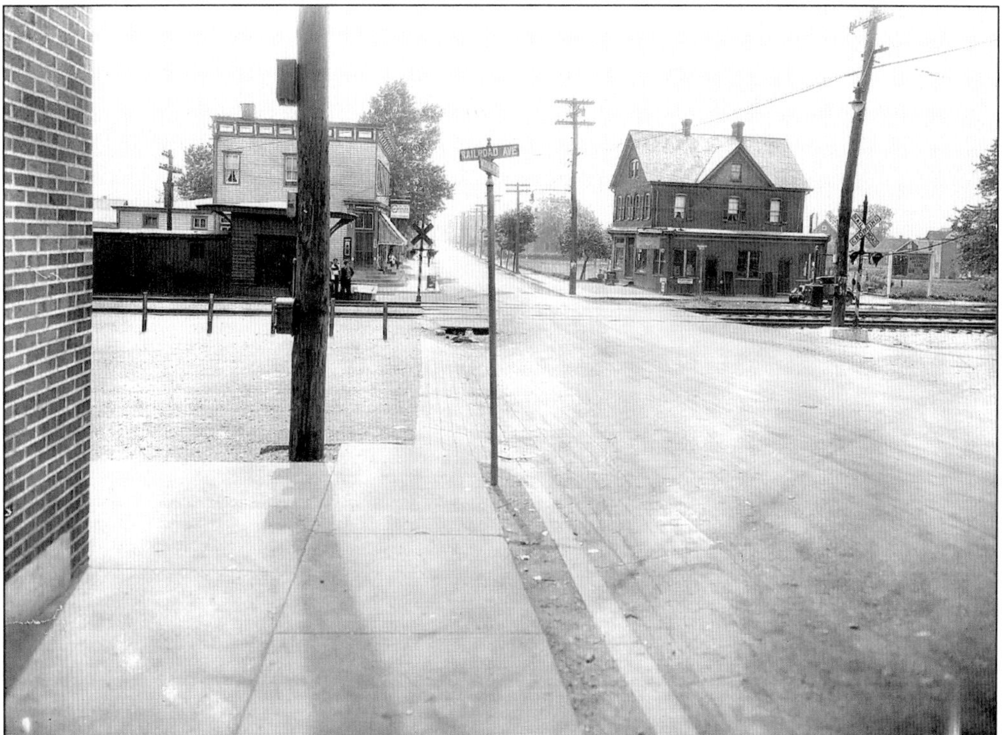

Spina's Grocery Store and the Delmonico building are visible in this *c.* 1930 view of Moonachie and Railroad Avenues.

Four

Churches, Schools, and Civic Activities

The earliest school was built in the southern part of town by a descendant of Capt. John Berry in 1801. Named Mount Pleasant School, it was a one-story structure about 25 feet by 20 feet. Although records do not show what happened to the first building, they do confirm that a second school was built in 1845. The second school was a frame building about the same size as its predecessor. It stood on Hackensack Street near Fritsch Avenue. In the early 1900s, the building was moved a few blocks away to Hill Street, where it is still part of a residential dwelling. The cornerstone of a new larger school was laid in 1872 on the corner of Hackensack Street and Union Avenue. The red brick two-story building had four classrooms and a bell tower in front. It was the first four-room school house in Bergen County. An addition to the new Mount Pleasant School was built in the early 1900s. The original section of Mount Pleasant School still stands today but is extremely modified from its original form. School No. 2, which at first was a junior high school and is now the high school, was built in 1922. Increased enrollment from the building of the Wood-Ridge Heights development below Twelfth Street prompted the building of an elementary school in the 1950s. After a hard-fought battle, the referendum calling for the school to be built finally passed, and construction started soon after. Located on Wood-Ridge Avenue, the school was named for longtime borough educator Catherine E. Doyle. Currently, the second addition to Doyle School is being constructed. In the early 1960s, another elementary school was built on to the high school. Named Windsor School since it faced Windsor Road, it was later renamed in honor of Wood-Ridge school district administrator and teacher Gretta Ostrovsky. The Assumption School was built in 1938 with eight classrooms and an auditorium. It was expanded in 1965.

Churches played an important role in Wood-Ridge. Although a small town, Wood-Ridge hosted Protestant, Catholic, Baptist, and Jehovah's Witnesses congregations. The First Presbyterian Church was formed in 1889, and its first service was conducted at Mount Pleasant School. On land donated by Frederick Kohbertz, a one-story building was erected in 1890 at the corner of Hackensack Street and Union Avenue. A new church was constructed on Valley Boulevard in 1952. In 1977, between Passover and Easter, a fire devastated the building. Our Lady of the Assumption Church offered the use of its building for services.

St. Paul's Episcopal Church was founded in 1913, and the first services were held at a private house. In 1916, a church was constructed on the corner of Humboldt and Center Streets. One of the founders of the church, resident Joseph Briggs, the president of Tiffany Glass in New York City, created a stained glass window in memory of his son. The church was enlarged in the late 1950s, with the first service held in the new building in 1962.

The Church of the Assumption of Our Blessed Lady, also known as Our Lady of the Assumption Church, was organized in 1926. The original wooden church stood on the corner of Main Avenue and First Street. A new church was constructed in the 1950s.

In 1928, the First Baptist Church found its home in Wood-Ridge. It was located on Highland Avenue. When the congregation moved to a new site in Hasbrouck Heights in 1957, the structure became the civic center. In 1974, a new building was constructed. It was named in honor of Robert Stoesser in 1991.

The Jehovah's Witnesses came to Wood-Ridge in 1964. Kingdom Hall is still located on Hackensack Street.

Wood-Ridge civic activities include borough-sponsored commissions and many organizations that enhance the lives of citizens of all ages. Wood-Ridge plays host to three senior citizen clubs, Veterans of Foreign Wars, the American Legion, and numerous recreational programs for children. Additional parks have been constructed, and renovations have been made at existing play areas.

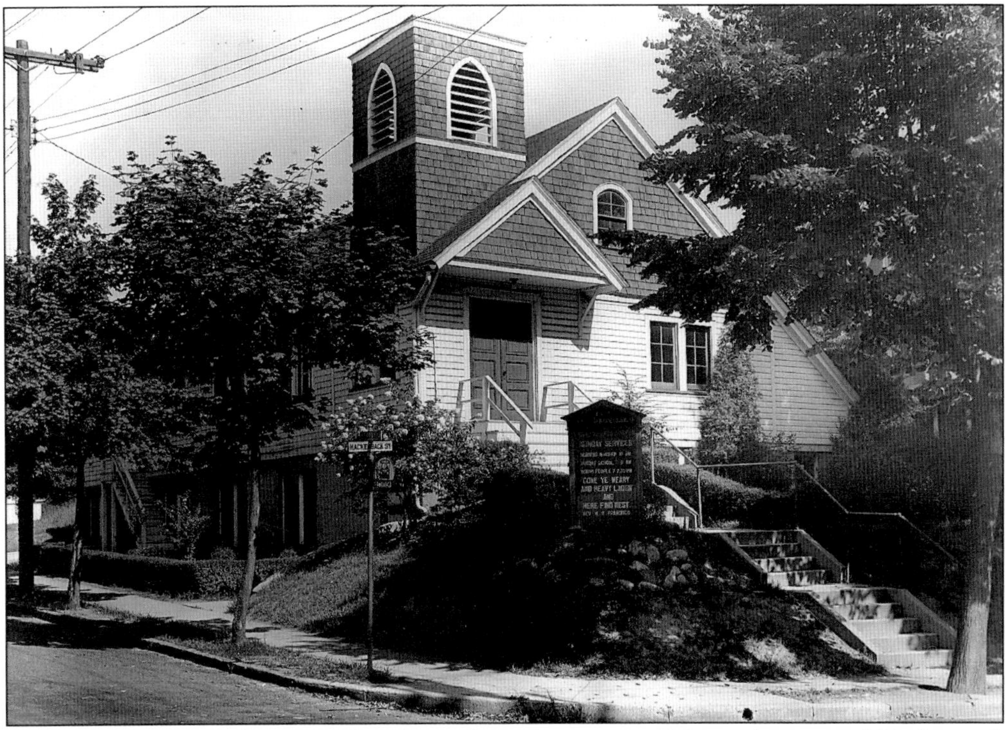

The original First Presbyterian Church stands on the corner of Union Avenue and Hackensack Street, now the site of a borough parking lot.

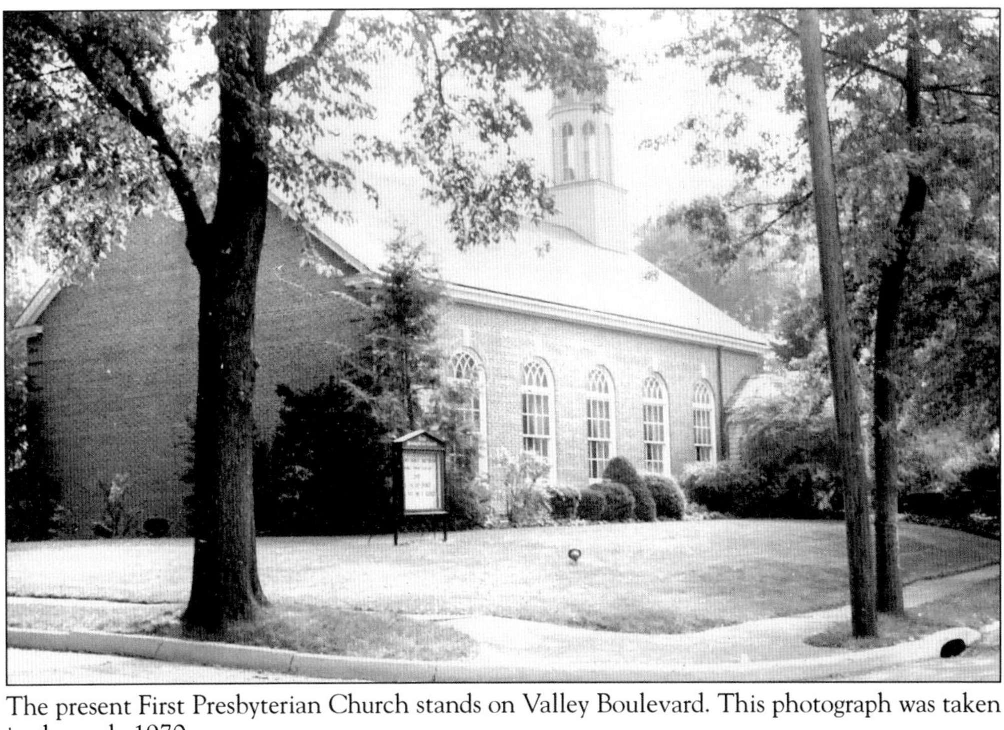

The present First Presbyterian Church stands on Valley Boulevard. This photograph was taken in the early 1970s.

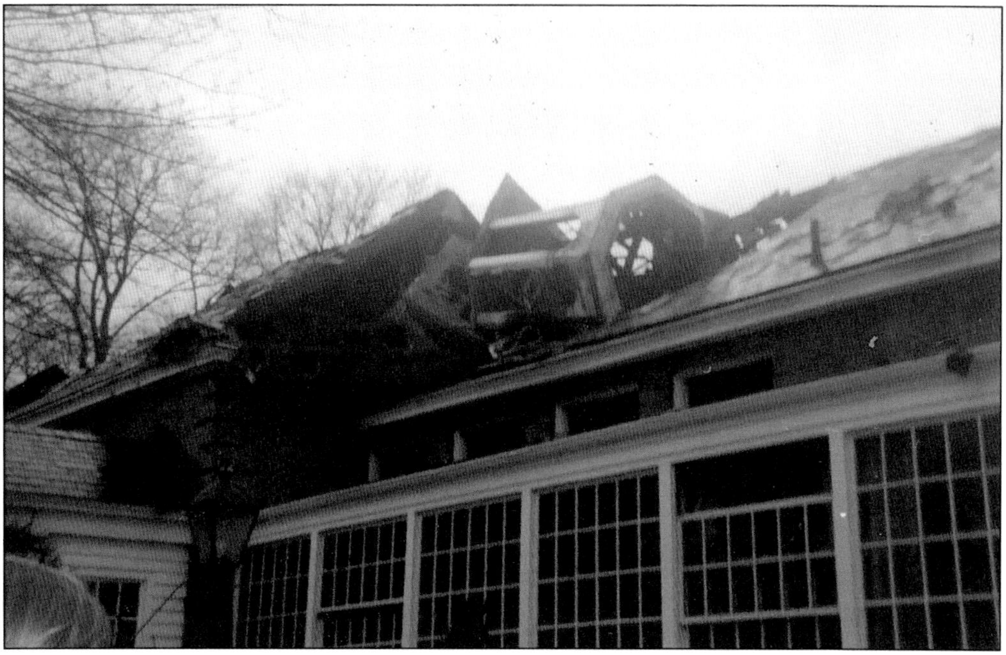

In April 1977, the Presbyterian church suffered a serious setback when it was engulfed in fire right before the Easter holiday. The church was later restored to its original condition. Our Lady of the Assumption Church had one less Sunday Mass so that the Presbyterians could use the facilities for worship. (Photograph courtesy of Catherine Cassidy.)

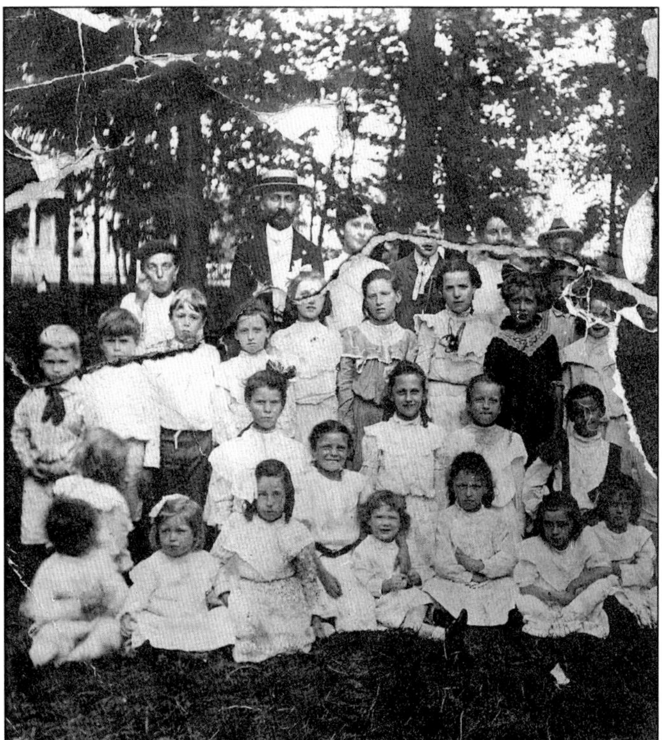

A Sunday school picnic is held in Gwinn's woods, in the area of Charter Oak Street, c. 1905. From left to right are the following: (first row) two unidentified youngsters, Cora Nelson, Florence Kofahl, and Miriam Edward; (second row) Emma Limbeck, Mabel Walsh, Edna Kofahl, Ida Wichoff, and Jennie Bassett; (third row) Howard Nelson, ? Newman, ? Gwinn, Elsie Ruhle, Lulu Edward, Gertrude Ruhle, Lulu Obermeyer, and Cecelia Walsh; (fourth row) Karl Limbeck, Emile Pirovano, Edith Pirovano, unidentified, and Ethel Pirovano.

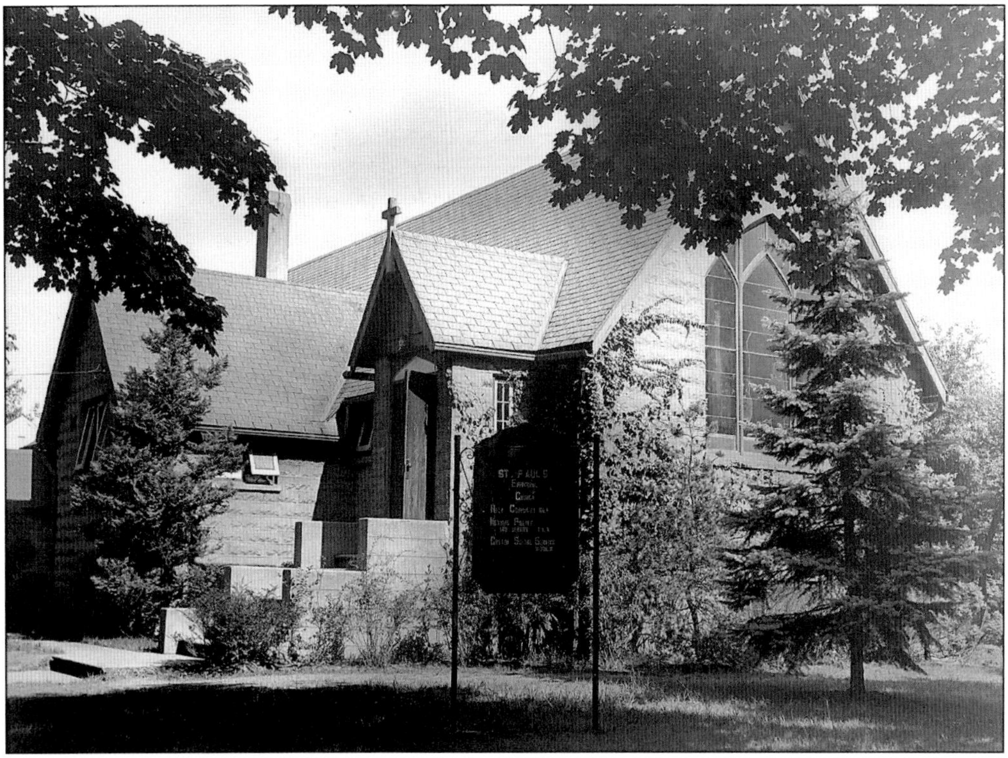

Shown is St. Paul's Episcopal Church. The large Tiffany window, to the right near the fir tree, was created by resident Joseph Briggs in memory of his young son.

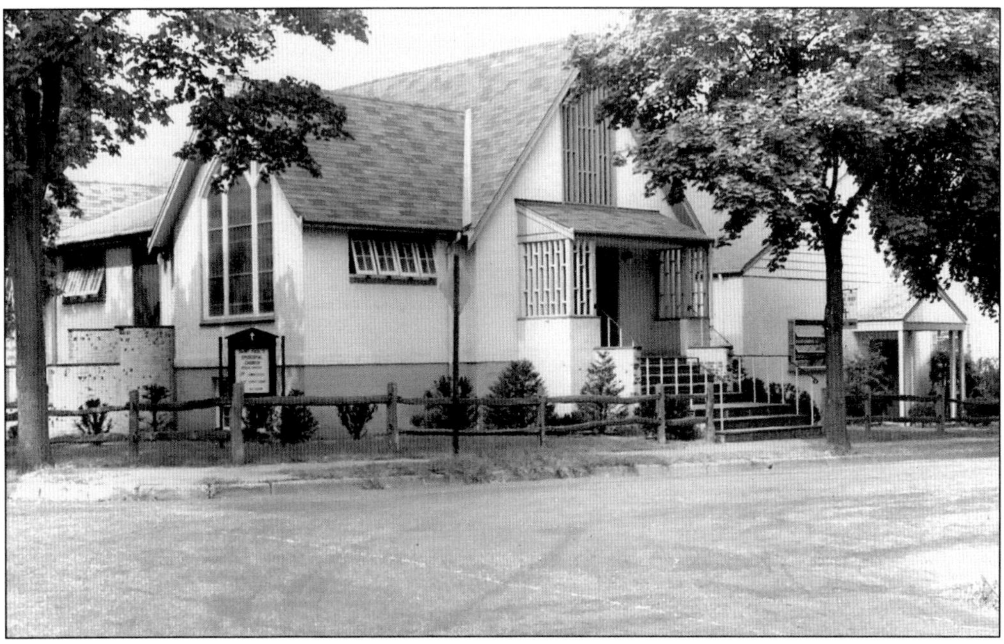

Here is St. Paul's as it looked in 1975. The Tiffany window was moved after an addition was constructed. It is located to the left in the photograph. To the right is Cosbey Parish Hall, named in memory of the church's longest serving pastor, the Reverend Edward Cosbey.

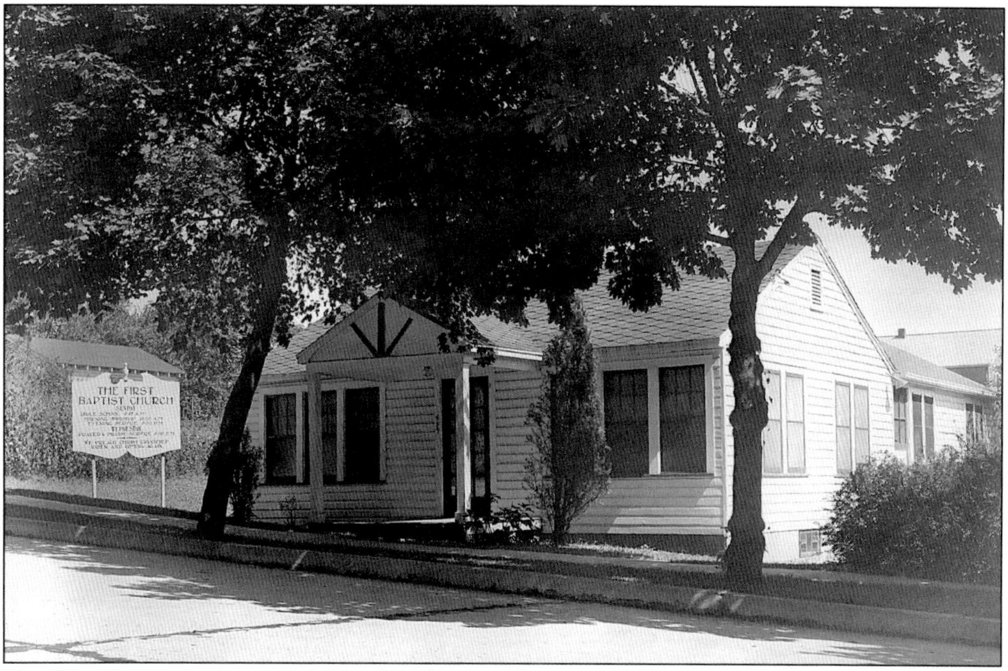

The First Baptist Church of Wood-Ridge stands on Highland Avenue. This building later became the civic center. The current civic center, built in 1974 and later dedicated in the memory of Bob Stoesser, now stands at this location.

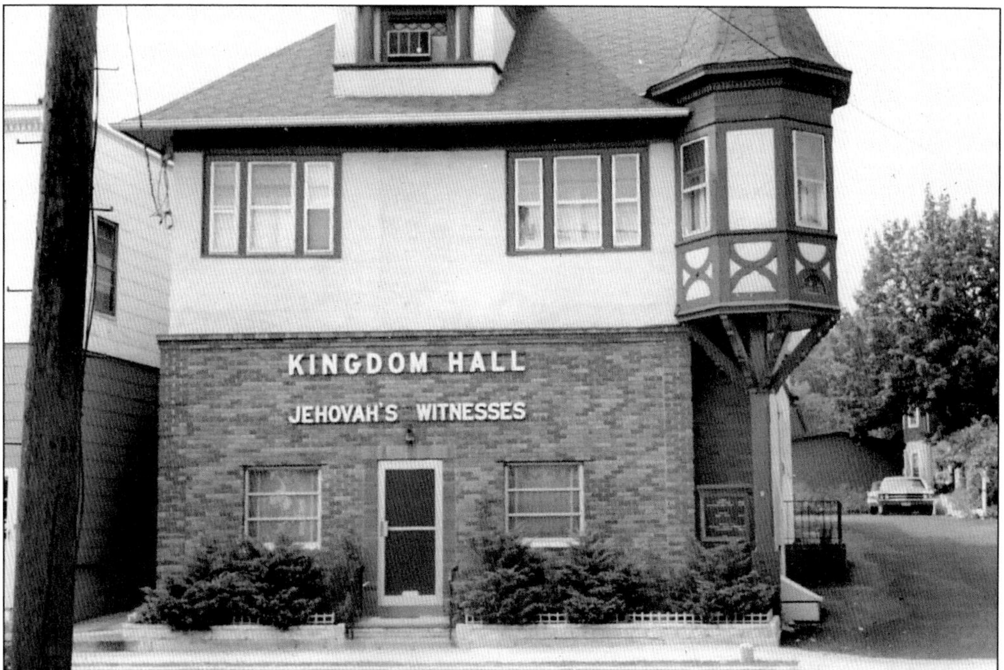

Kingdom Hall of Jehovah's Witnesses is located on Hackensack Street. The congregation of Jehovah's Witnesses formally dedicated the building in July 1964. The building has remained relatively the same as it appears in this 1975 photograph.

The original Our Lady of the Assumption Church stands at Main Avenue and First Street.

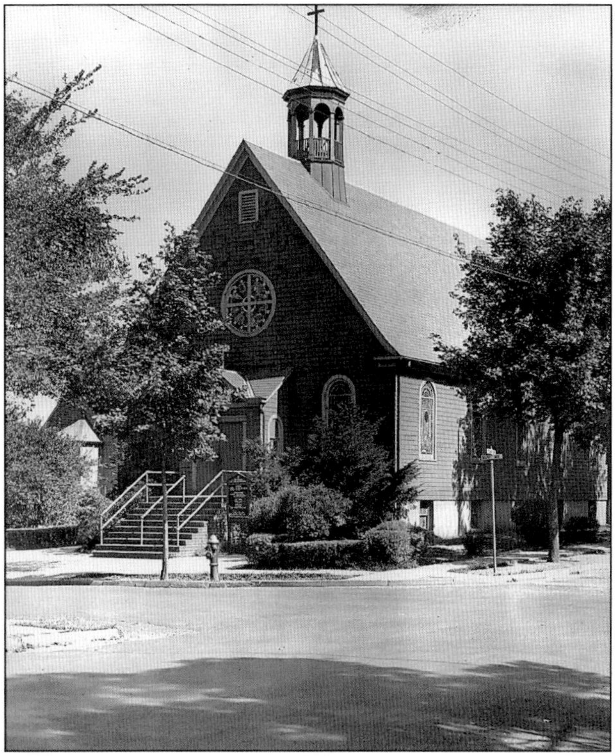

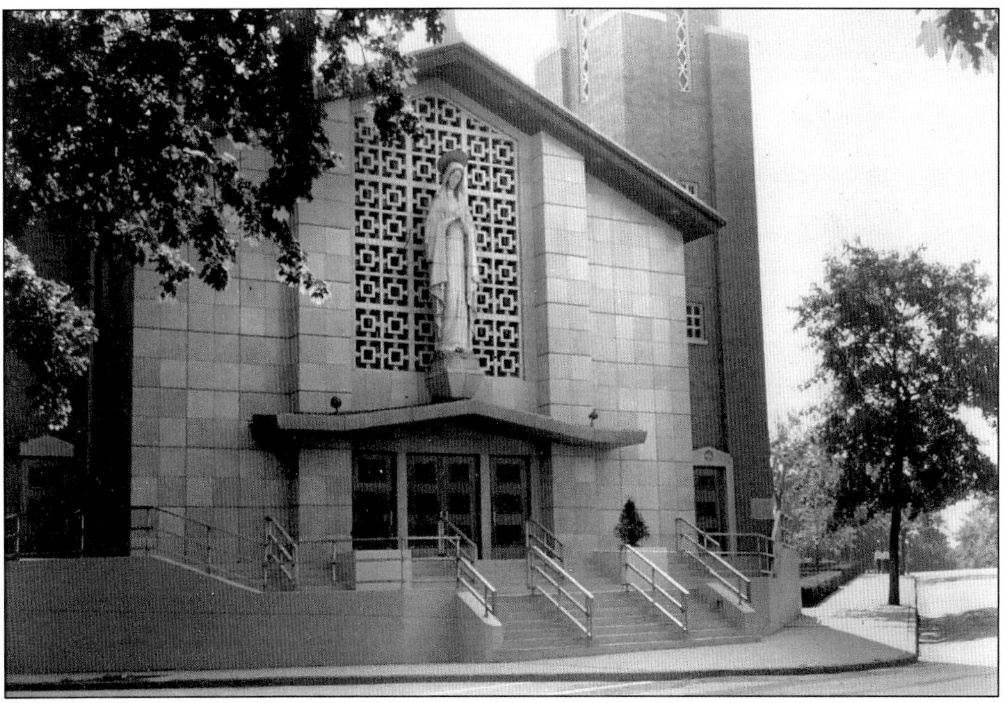

The new Our Lady of the Assumption Church was constructed in 1958. Fire destroyed part of the interior in 1995. Services were held in the church hall until parishioners were welcomed back to the restored church on Christmas Eve 1995.

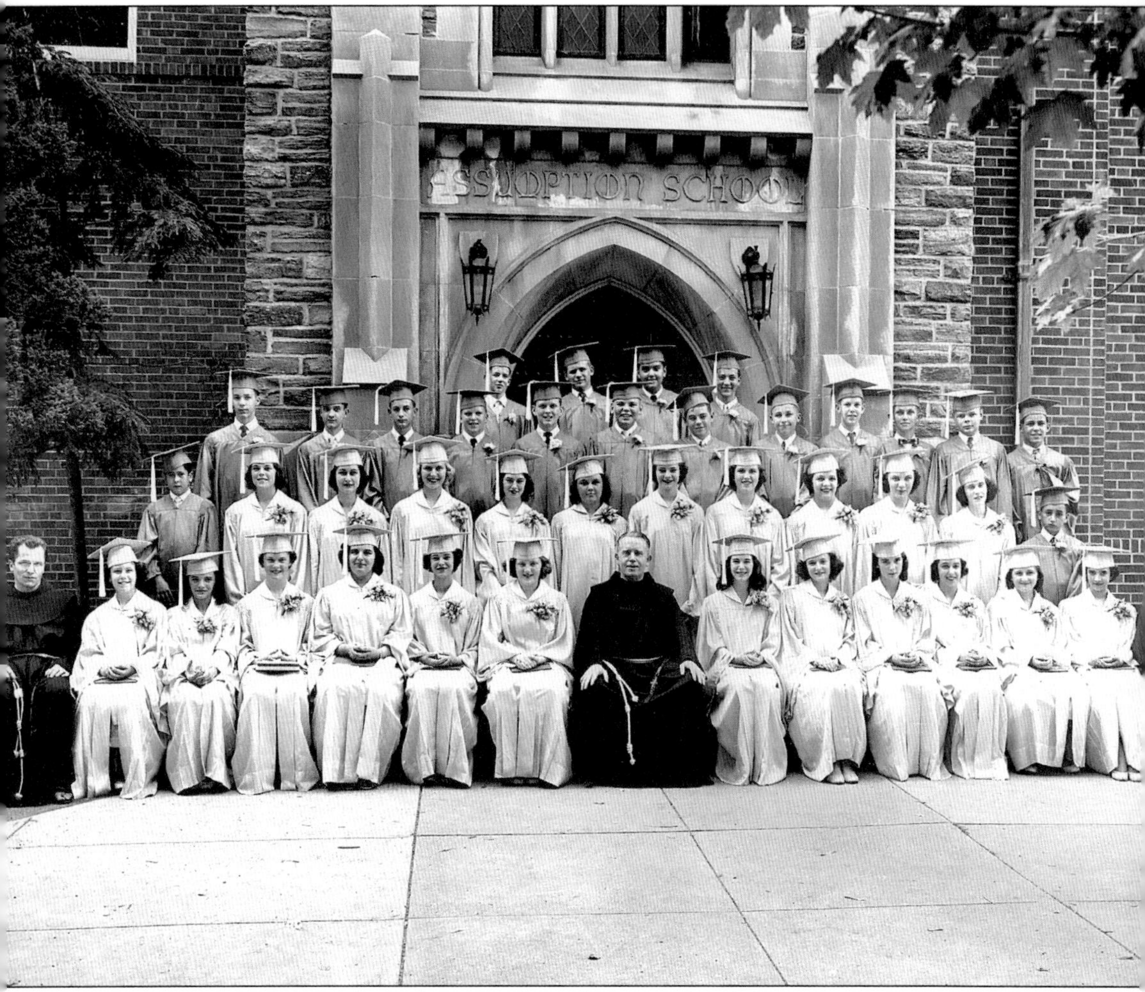

This is the eighth-grade graduation class of Our Lady of the Assumption School in 1956. Fr. William Hayes, center, spearheaded the construction of the new church. John Keenan, now Fr. Christopher Keenan, chaplain of the New York City Fire Department, is in the third row, fourth student from the right. (Photograph courtesy of Eileen Helbig Toughill.)

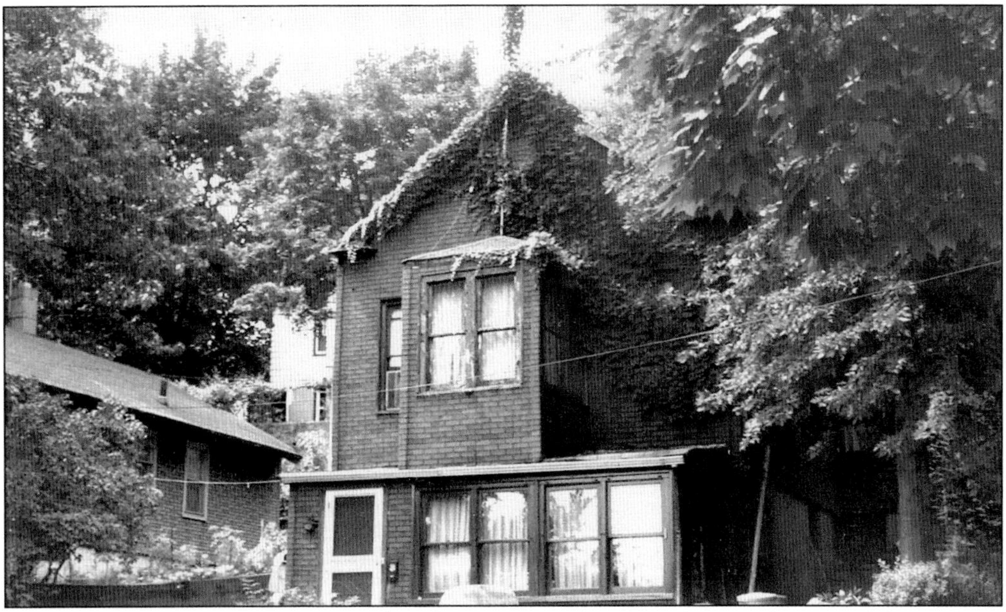

The first school to be built in Wood-Ridge was moved and made into the second floor of this house, which stands on Hill Street. The photograph was taken in 1975.

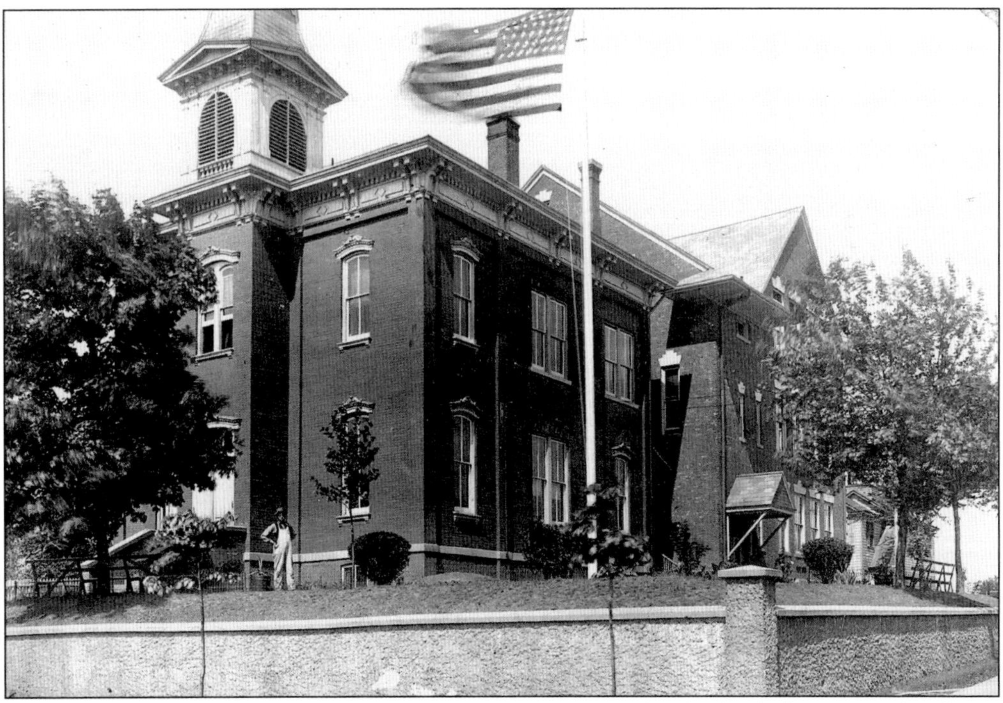

Shown is School No. 1, better known as Mount Pleasant School. The bell tower and addition are no longer there. Holmes Robinson (standing in front) doubled as a school crossing guard and school custodian. He was a favorite among the students.

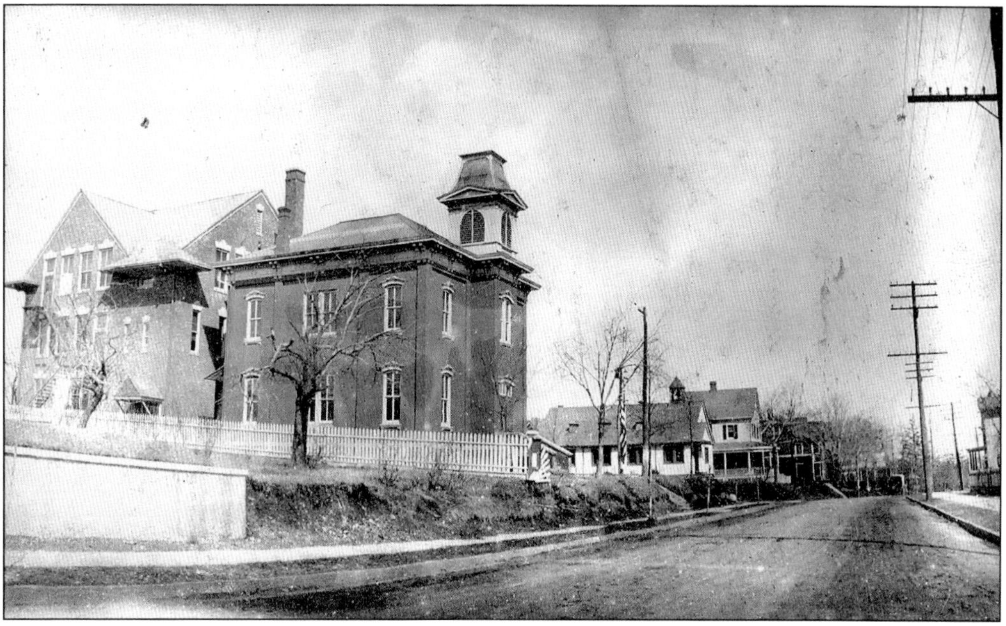

This view of Mount Pleasant School was taken looking north *c.* 1900.

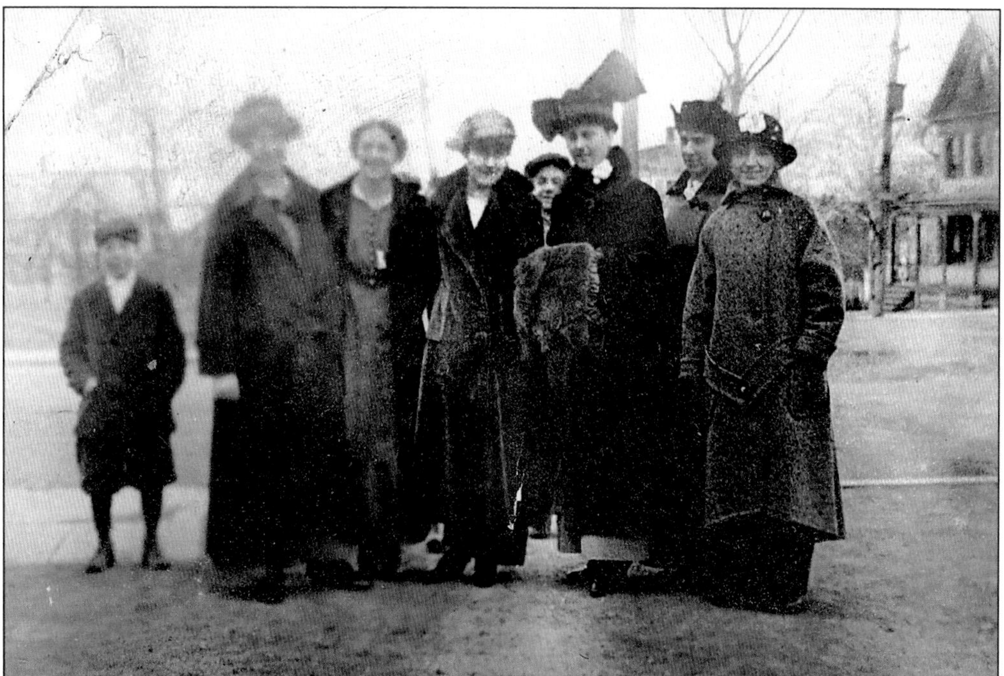

Pictured in 1913 at Mount Pleasant School, from left to right, are ? Cuneo and teachers E. Hamlin, C. Barritt, M. Klock, M. Mooney, A. Elias, and A. Kriegal.

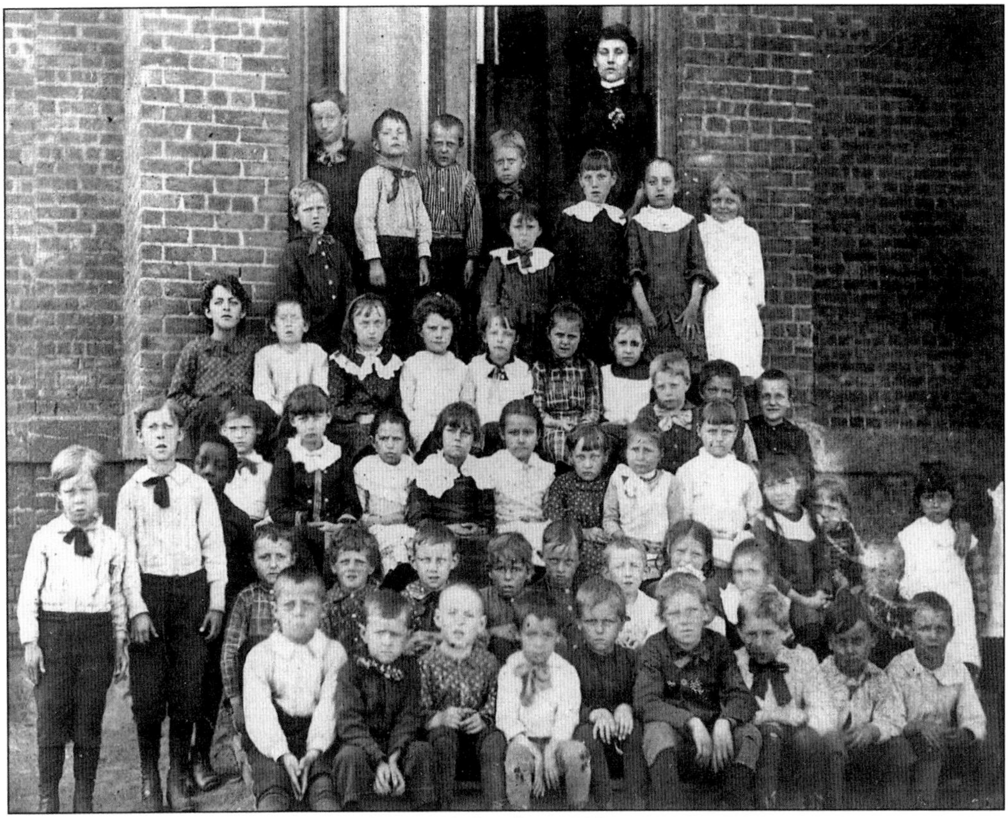

These students attended Mount Pleasant School *c.* 1885.

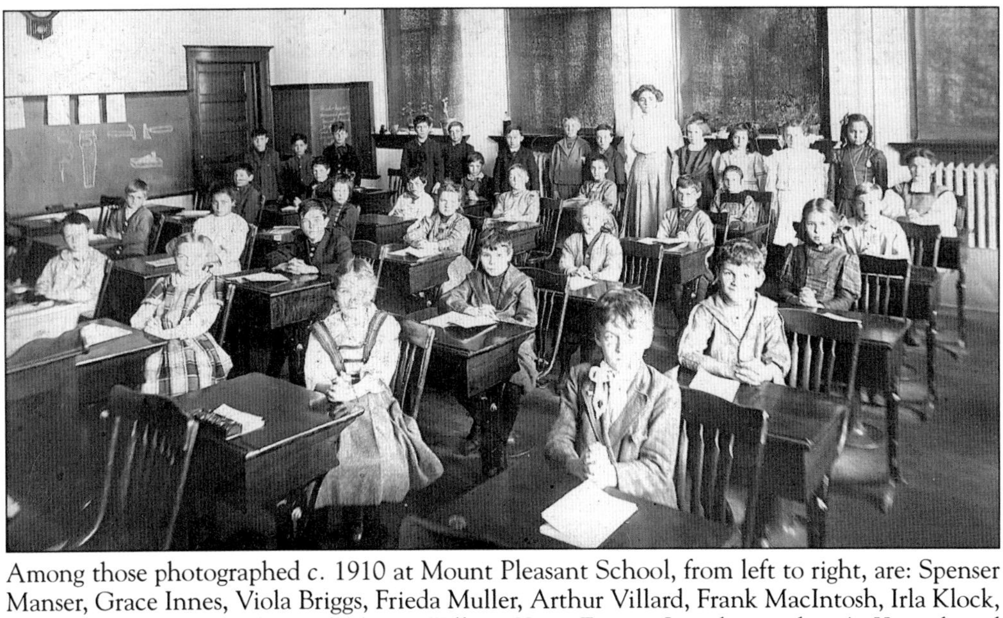

Among those photographed *c.* 1910 at Mount Pleasant School, from left to right, are: Spenser Manser, Grace Innes, Viola Briggs, Frieda Muller, Arthur Villard, Frank MacIntosh, Irla Klock, Walter Brightly, Wilfred Brandenburg, William Kour, Francis Janeski, teacher A. Kriegal, and Carrie Backus, Florence Carsten, Frank Keogh, Julius Distel, ? Meyer, Ida Marzorati, John Bringman, and Alex Gwinn.

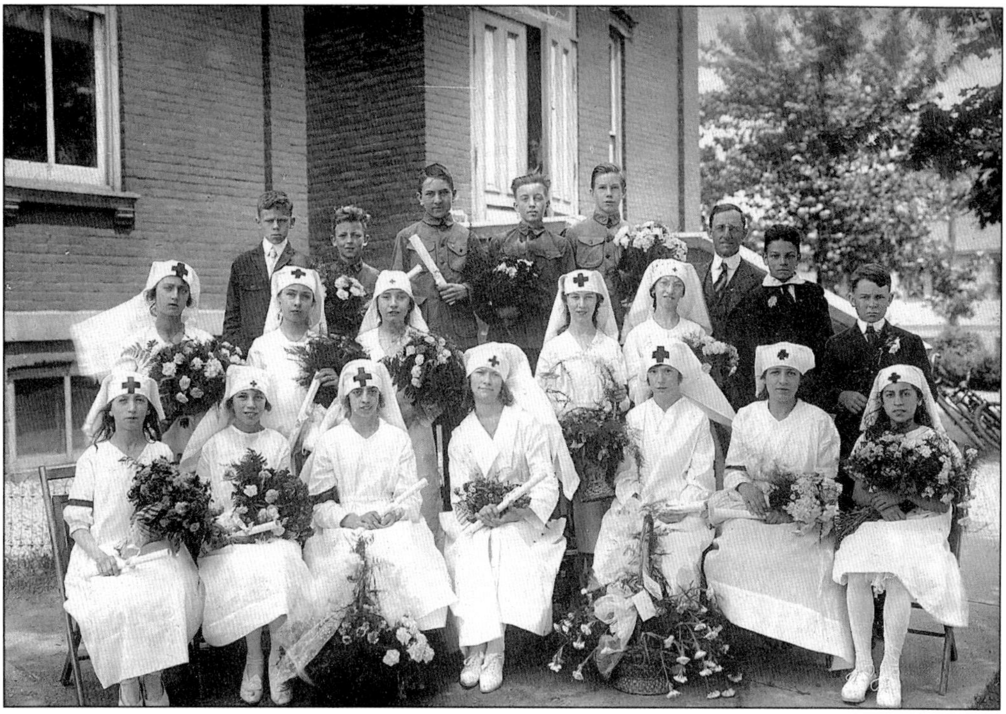

Shown is the 1918 eighth-grade graduation class. Bob Stoesser is in the back row, second from the left. Mr. Dixon, the principal, is to the right. Note the dress of the students during the period of World War I.

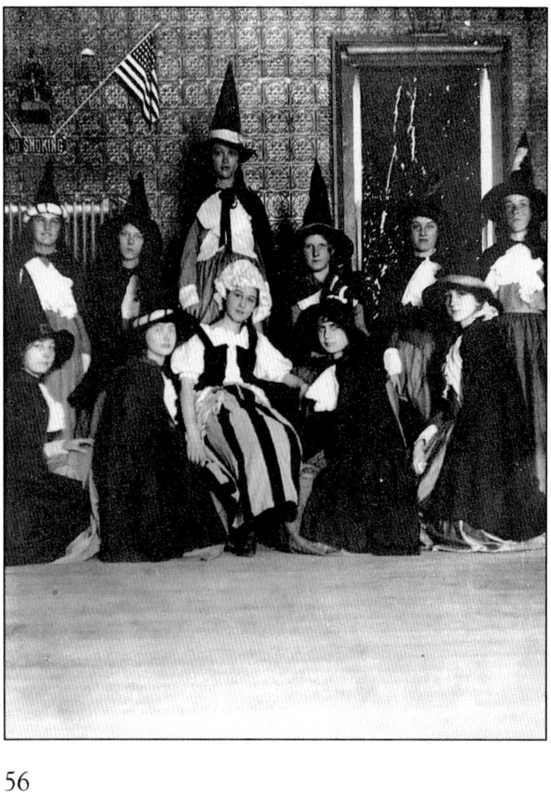

The 1919 play at Mount Pleasant School was *Florinda*. In the back row, from left to right, are Bertha Palmer, unidentified, Jane Manser, unidentified, Minnie Salzer, and Abby Aldam.

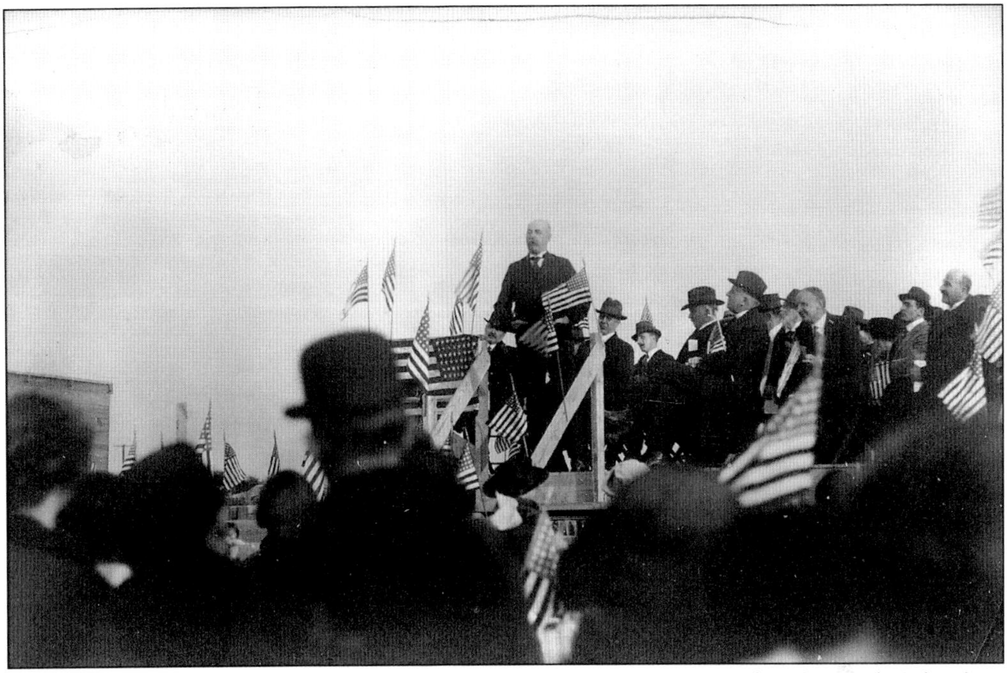
School No. 2 was dedicated in 1922. This building later became Wood-Ridge High School.

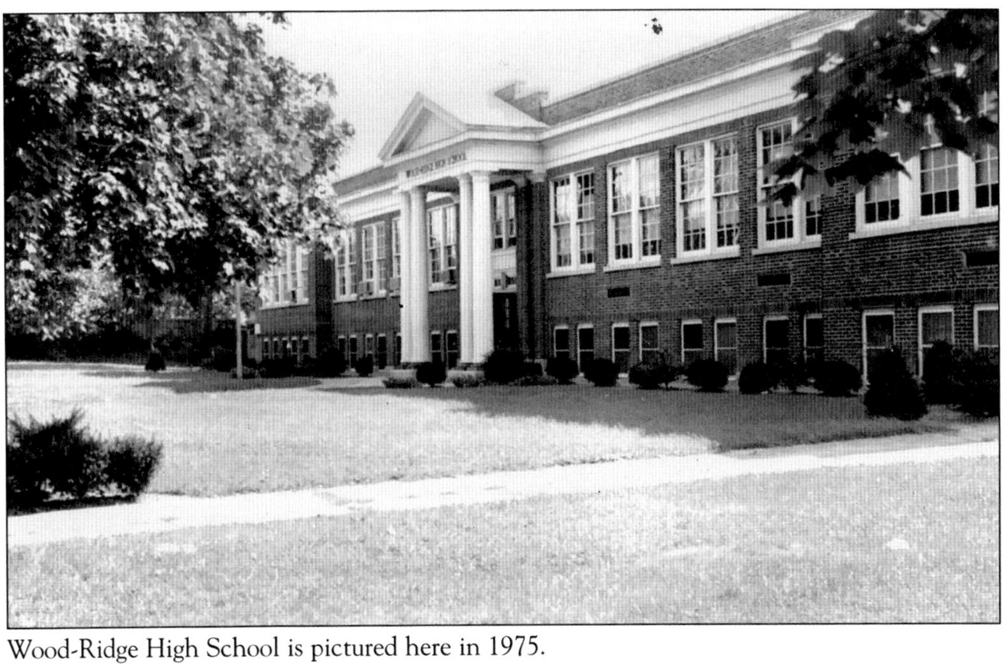
Wood-Ridge High School is pictured here in 1975.

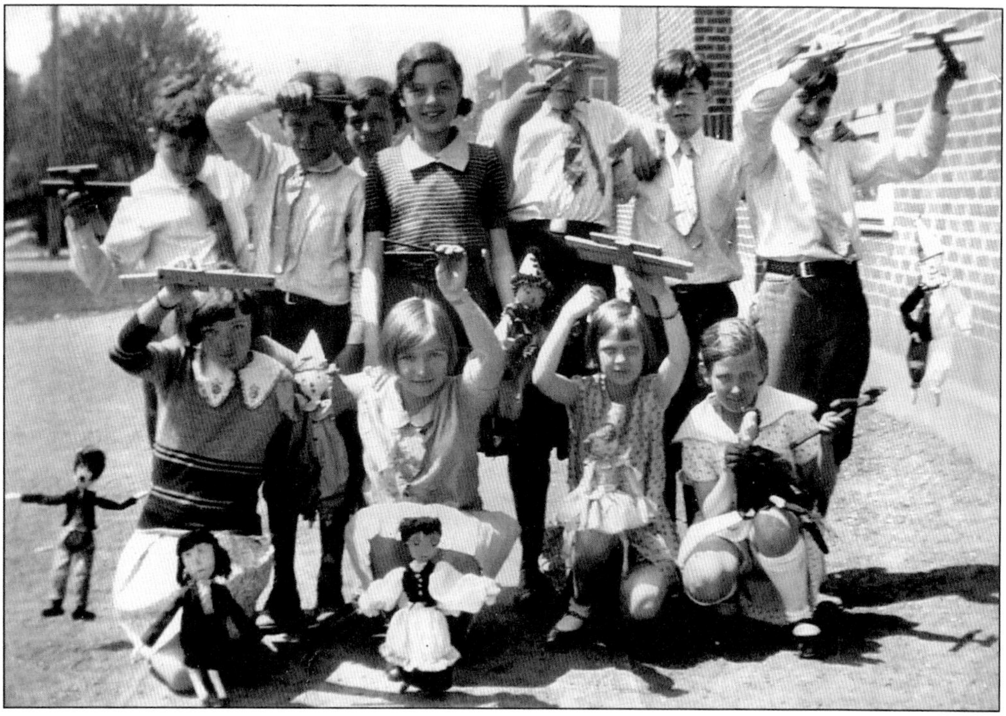

Students show off their class project c. 1931. From left to right are the following: (first row) unidentified, Mabel Heathwood, Eleanor Christmann, and Ruth Stumm; (second row) Billy Wesp, unidentified, Robert Schreiber, two unidentified students, Phillip Sottong, and Robert Hyland.

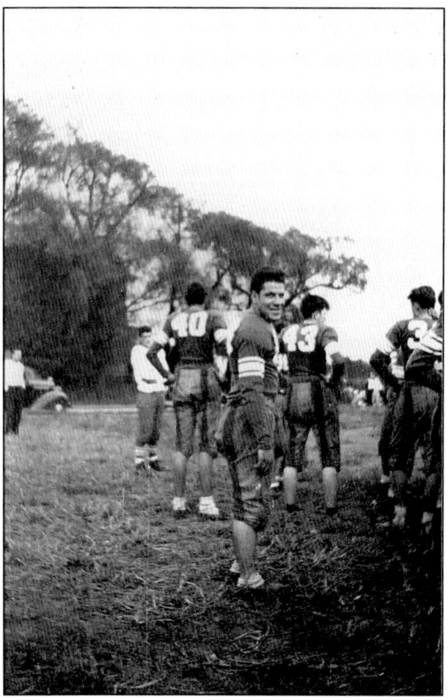

Donato Greco gets ready to go into the game for Wood-Ridge. The photograph was taken in 1940–1941.

Danny Moderelli poses during a football game during the 1940–1941 season.

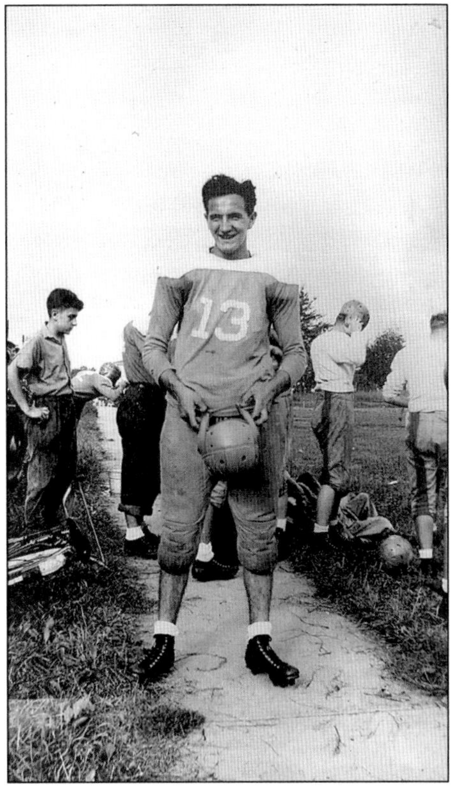

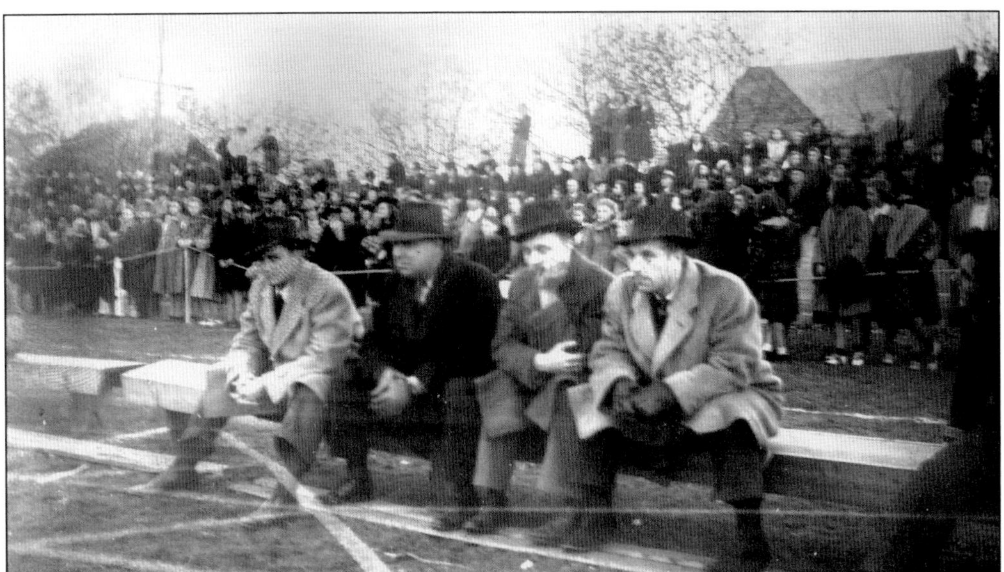

Sitting on the sidelines, from left to right, are coach Carl Muller, principal Fremont Donley, and coaches Will Lemmerz and Eugene Luongo.

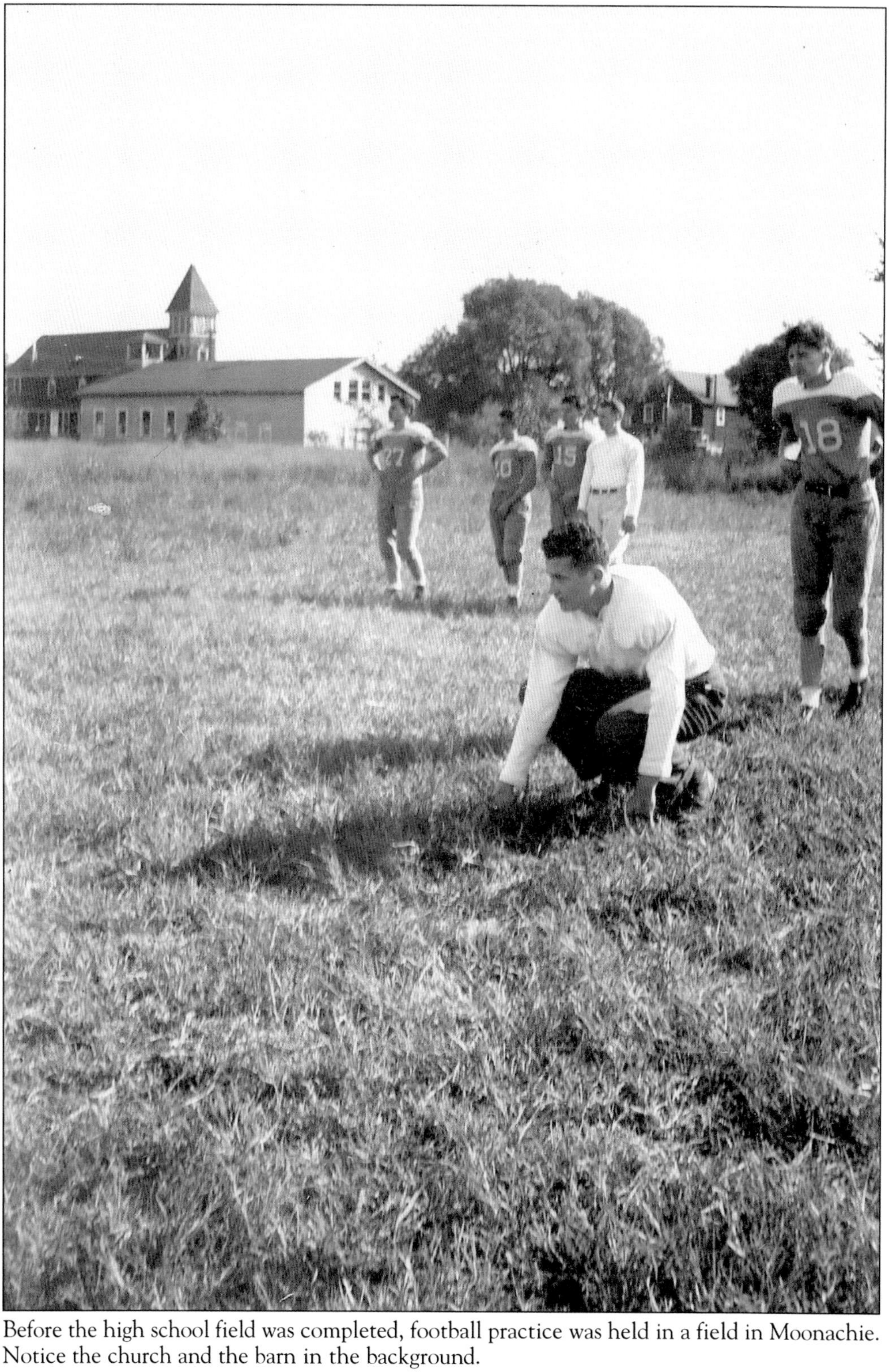

Before the high school field was completed, football practice was held in a field in Moonachie. Notice the church and the barn in the background.

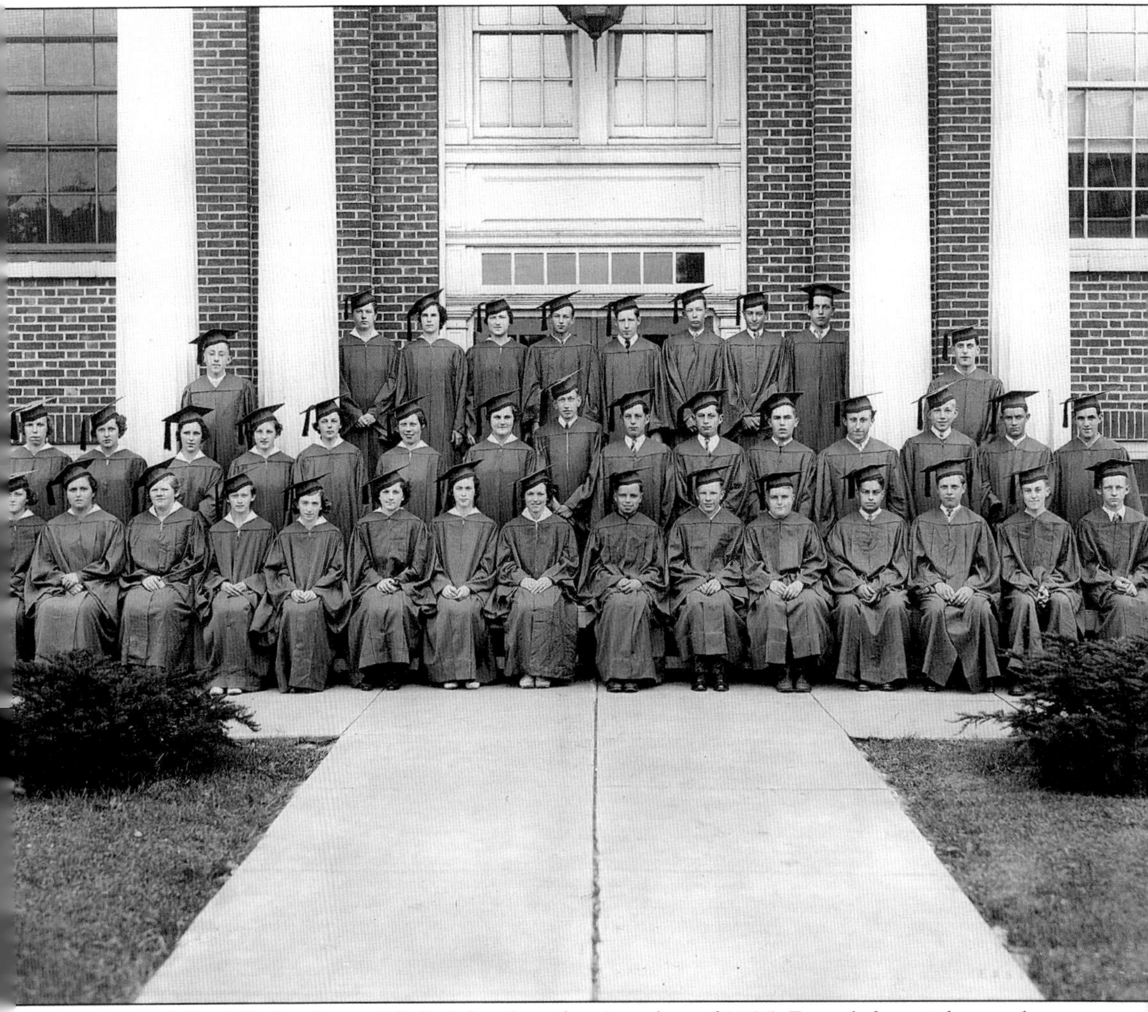

Here is the Wood-Ridge Junior High School graduation class of 1935. From left to right are the following: (first row) Eleanor Spies, Edna Haese, Helen Frank, Aurelia Schneider, Catherine Metzger, Antoinette La Rosa, Dorothy Clayton, Virginia Herman, Morgan Loesch, Harold Traber, Stephen Ferriol, Raymond Asmar, Robert Gustafson, Arthur Wakeling, and Robert Neidhardt; (second row) Marie Smith, Edna Prince, Agnes O'Leary, Elsie Martin, Harriet Kuhl, Anna Weiss, Marjorie Heger, Francis Steinburger, Edward De Appolonio, Mario De Appolonio, Robert Kennedy, Joseph Koniar, William Glynn, Robert Simpson, and Lawrence Gage; (third row) Edward Quist, Virginia Bell, Grace Duffy, Mary Farr, Norman Raabe, Samuel Scales, Edward Baksa, William Schubart, Otto Niederer, and Robert Hyland. Absent from the photograph is Frank Maffia.

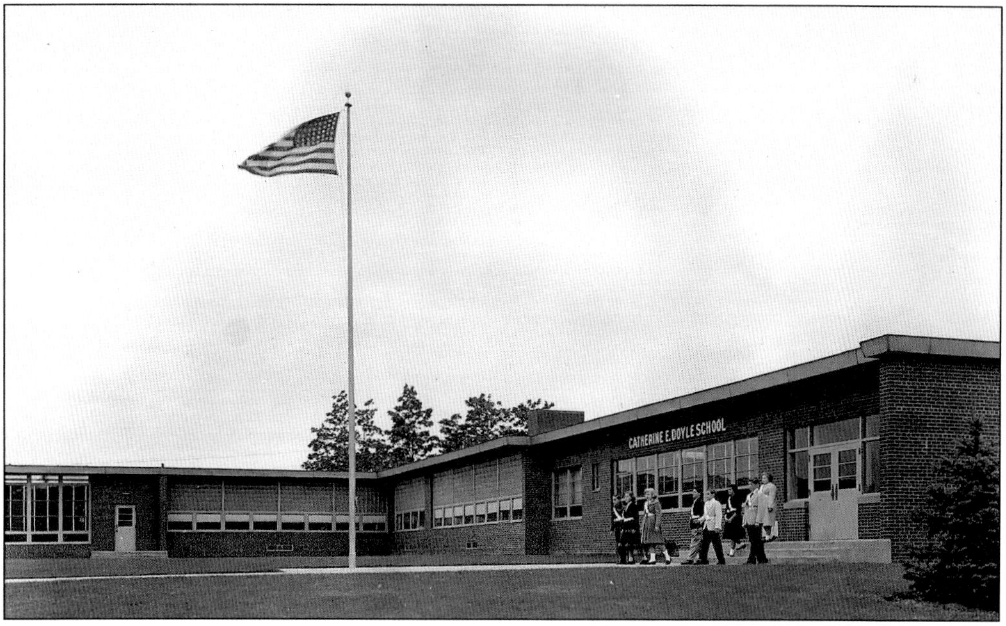

Catherine Doyle School stands on Wood-Ridge Avenue. The school was named after a longtime educator and administrator. Catherine E. Doyle was the first principal of the school, followed by Mildred Lowell, Robert Skovron, Dr. Nicholas Sardone, Marilyn Baruch, and current principal Barbara Laudicina. The photograph was taken in 1956–1957. The front of the school appears relatively the same today as it does here.

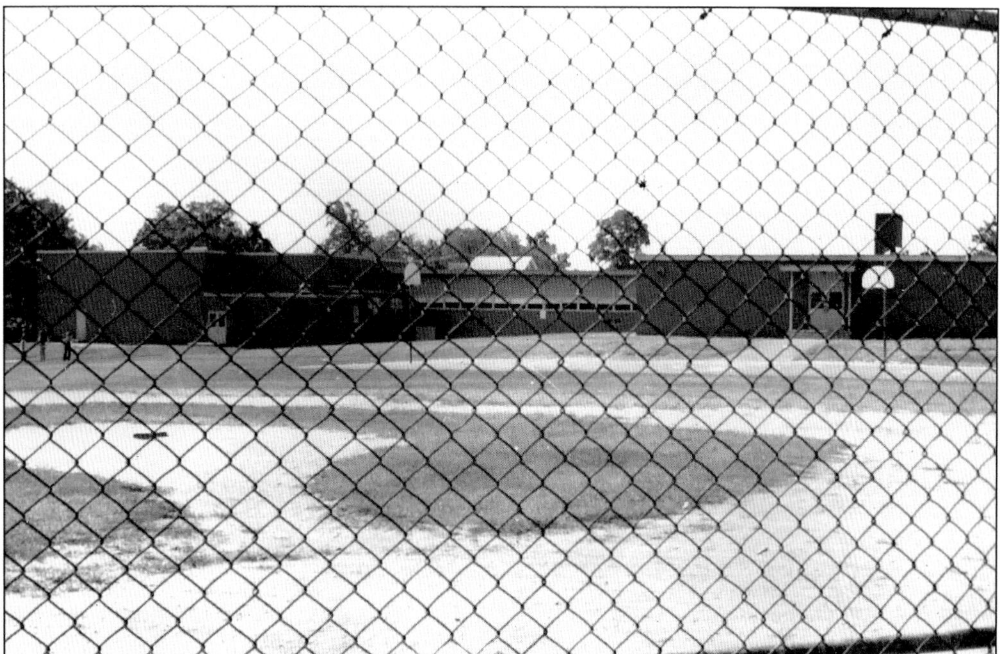

Catherine Doyle School is pictured here in 1975. Due to increased enrollments, an addition was constructed in the 1990s and a subsequent one in 2003–2004.

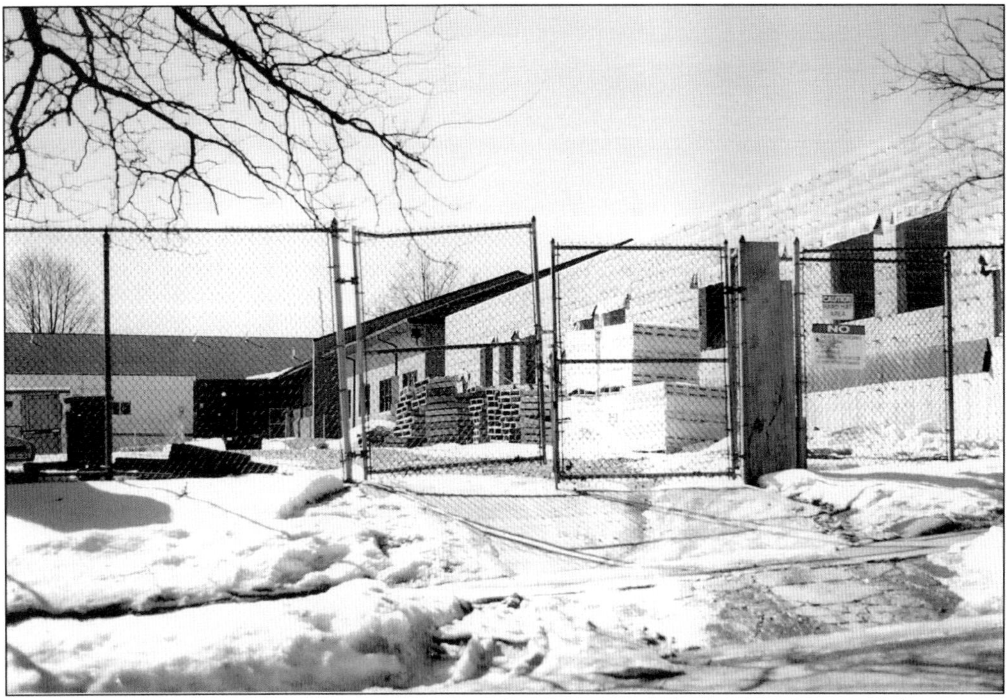

In this January 2004 view, Catherine Doyle School is seen with the foundation of the newest addition in place.

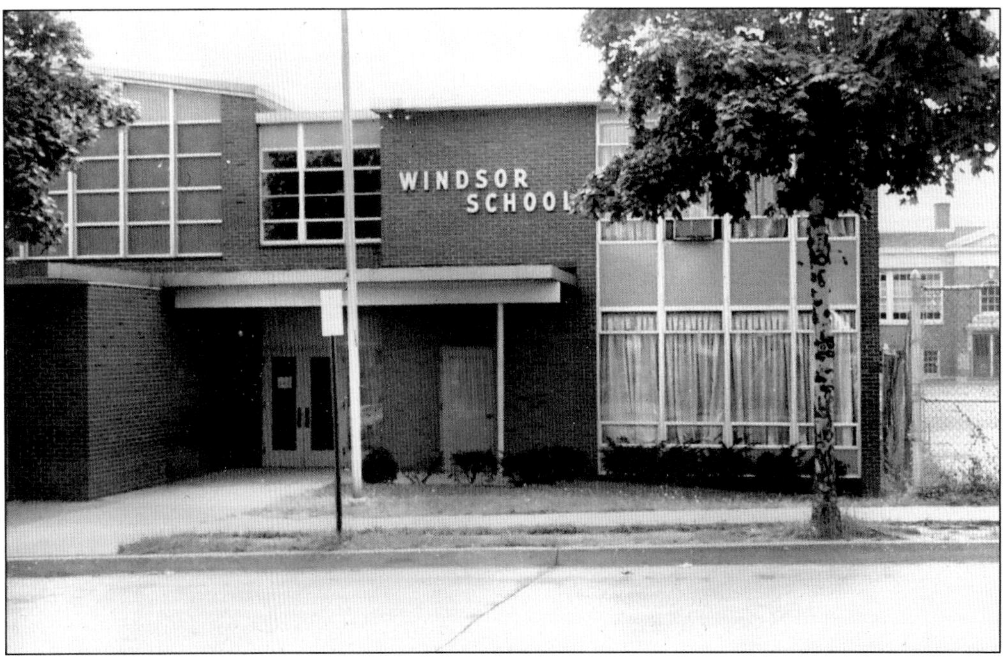

Shown is Gretta R. Ostrovsky School when it was known as Windsor School. Gretta Ostrovsky was a longtime educator and administrator for the Wood-Ridge School District. She was also a former resident, having grown up on Seventh Street. Her father was a well-known local dentist, Dr. David Roffman.

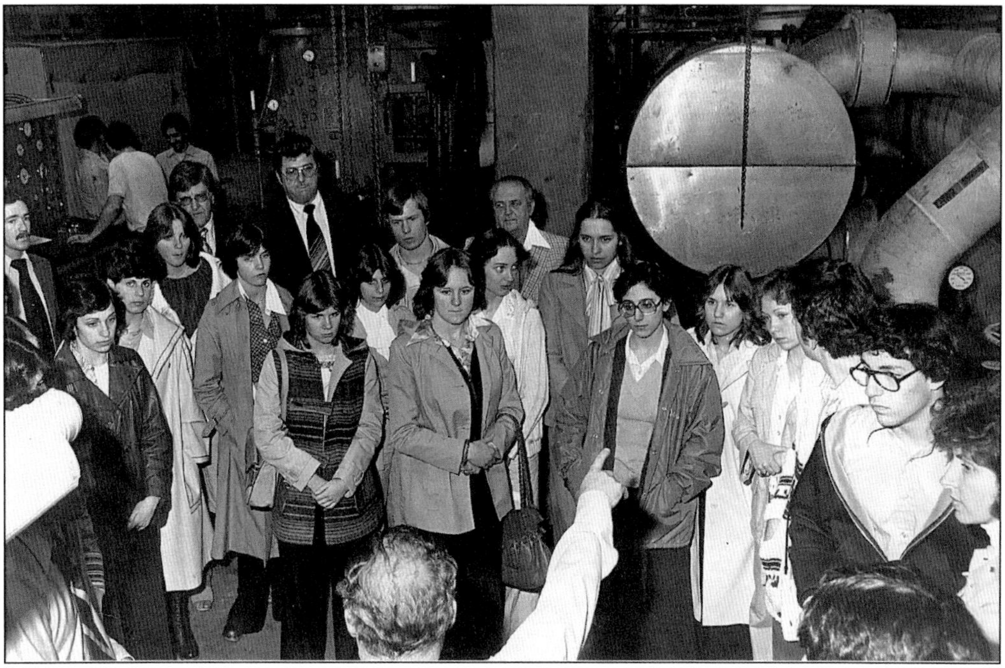

During the annual Youth Day in Government, local high school seniors role-play the part of borough officials. Students take part in a special trip. In 1978, they are shown visiting the World Trade Center. From left to right are Diane Sarlo, Jeanine Compesi, Denise Bischoff, Patricia McNamara, Susan Darragh, Susan Sarro, Kurt Zyla, Cheryl Landells, Kathleen Haggerty, Catherine Bush, Donna Senerchia, Jean Dobek, Robin Brown, Joseph Jensen, and Mark Chicketano. Councilmen Ron O'Malley and Les Cosgrove are behind the students.

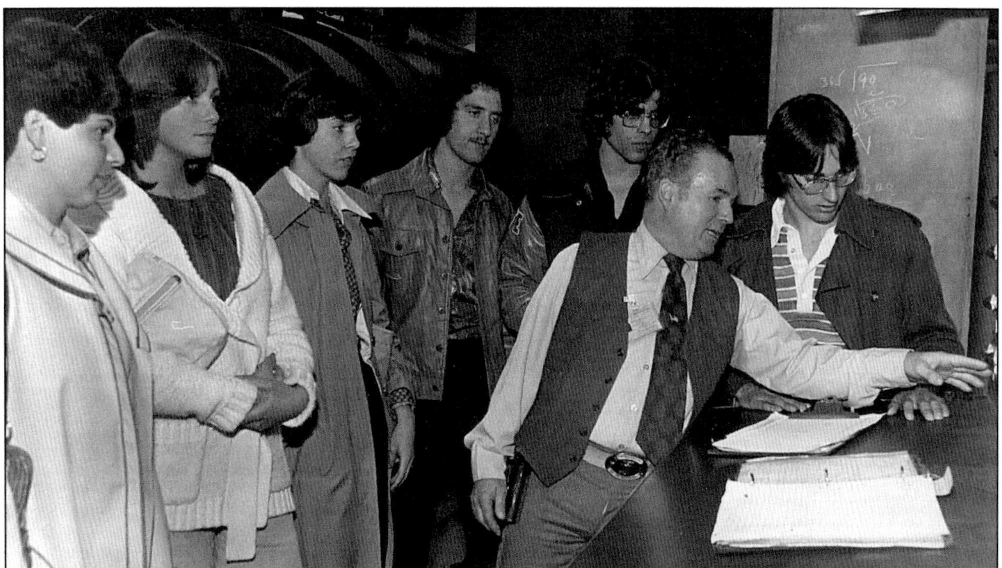

The 1978 Youth Officials view the general operation of the World Trade Center. From left to right are Jeanine Compesi, Denise Bischoff, Patricia McNamara, Gerald Salerno, Frank Marino, and Dennis Senerchia.

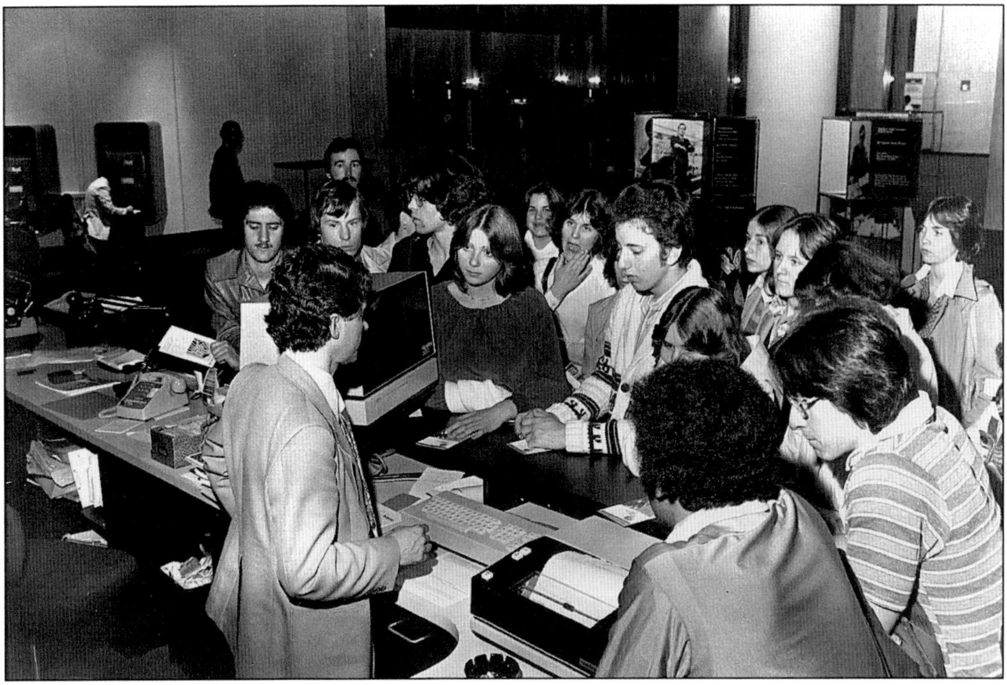

The 1978 Youth Officials visit the lobby of the World Trade Center. From left to right are Gerald Salerno, Kurt Zyla, Frank Marino, Denise Bischoff, Linda Povanda, Lorraine Izzo, Joseph Jensen, Kathleen Garvin, Cheryl Landells, Patricia McNamara, Dennis Senerchia, Raymond Kurzum, and Jean Dobek, partially obscured by Kurzum.

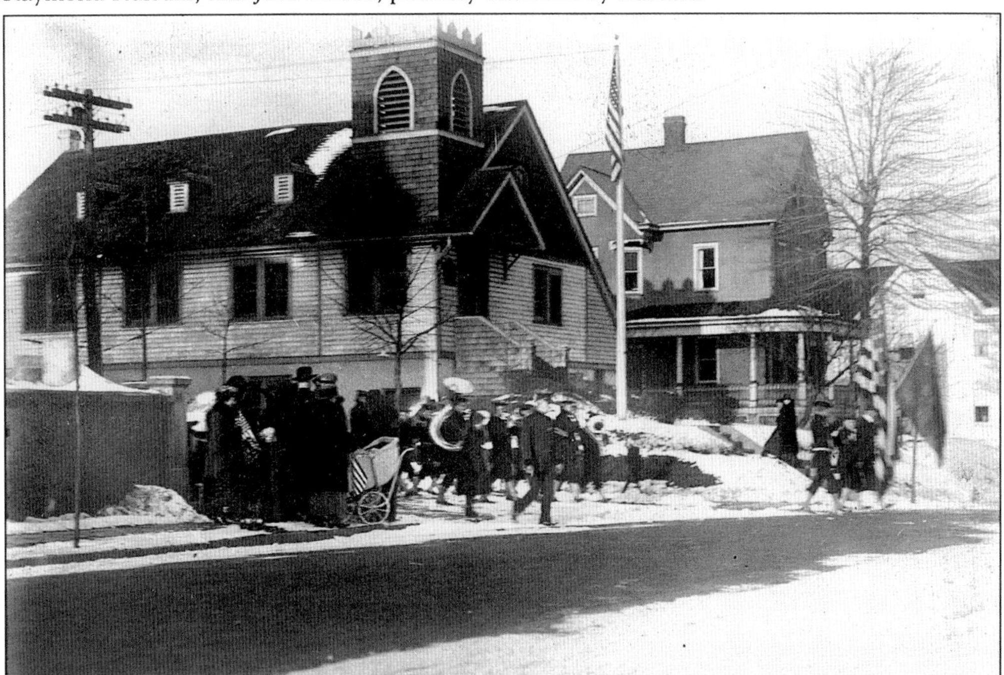

The 1916 Preparedness Day Parade is held on the corner of Hackensack Street and Union Avenue. The First Presbyterian Church is in the background.

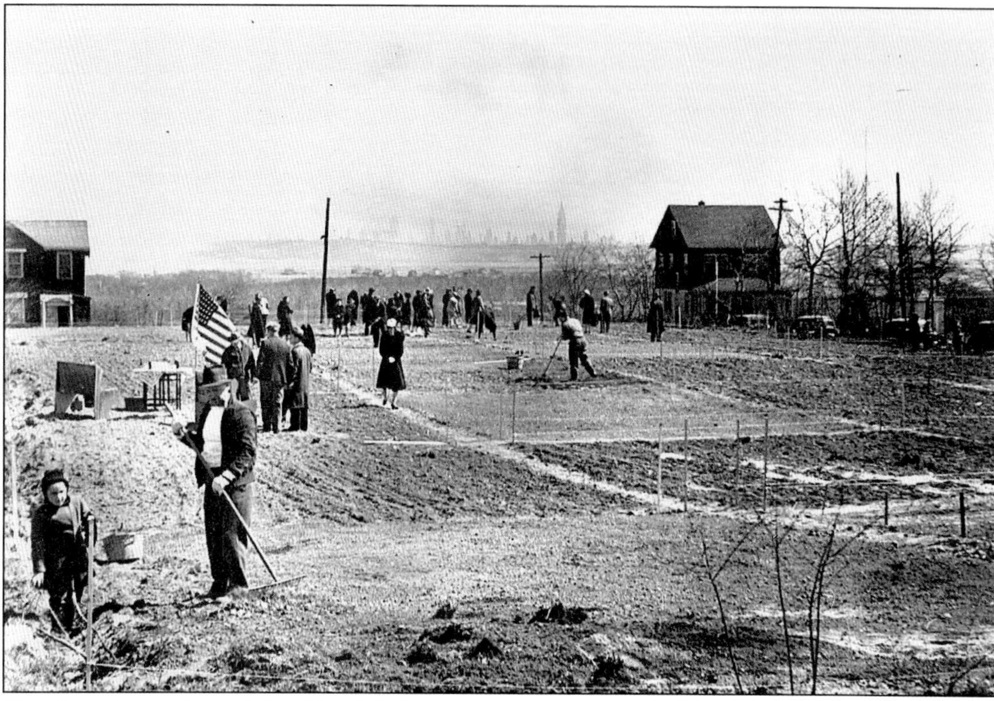

The formal opening of the Wood-Ridge victory garden was held on the property of Madsen & Christensen on April 11, 1943.

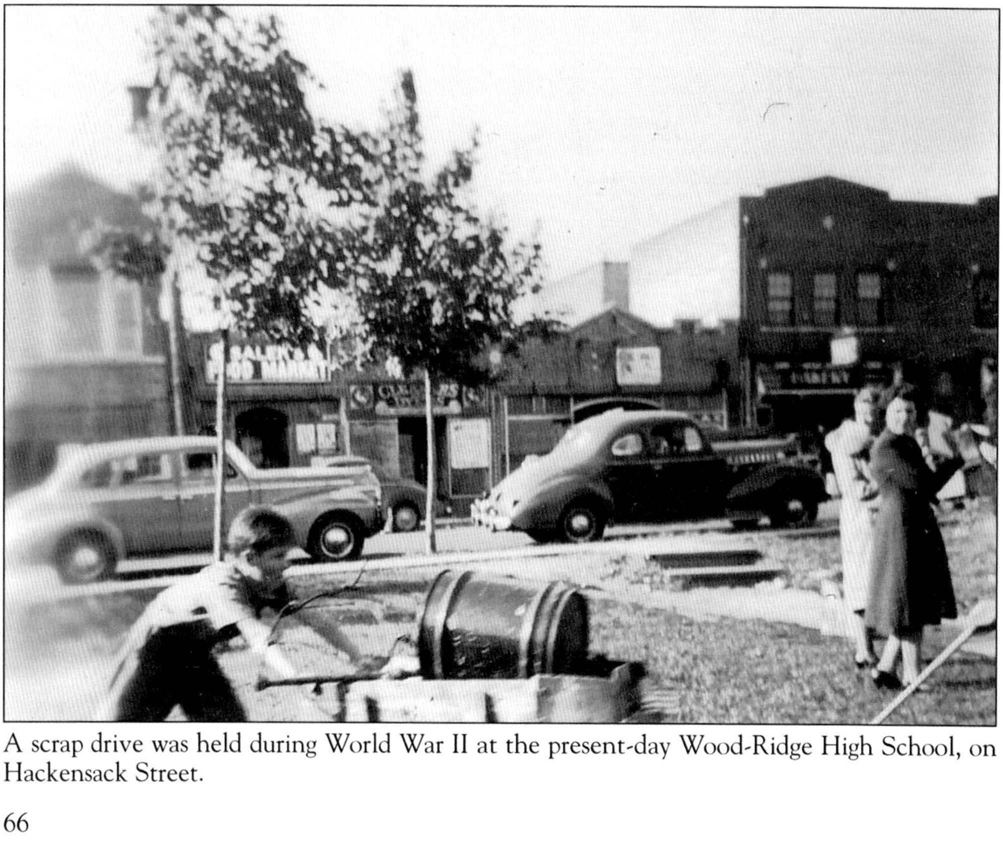

A scrap drive was held during World War II at the present-day Wood-Ridge High School, on Hackensack Street.

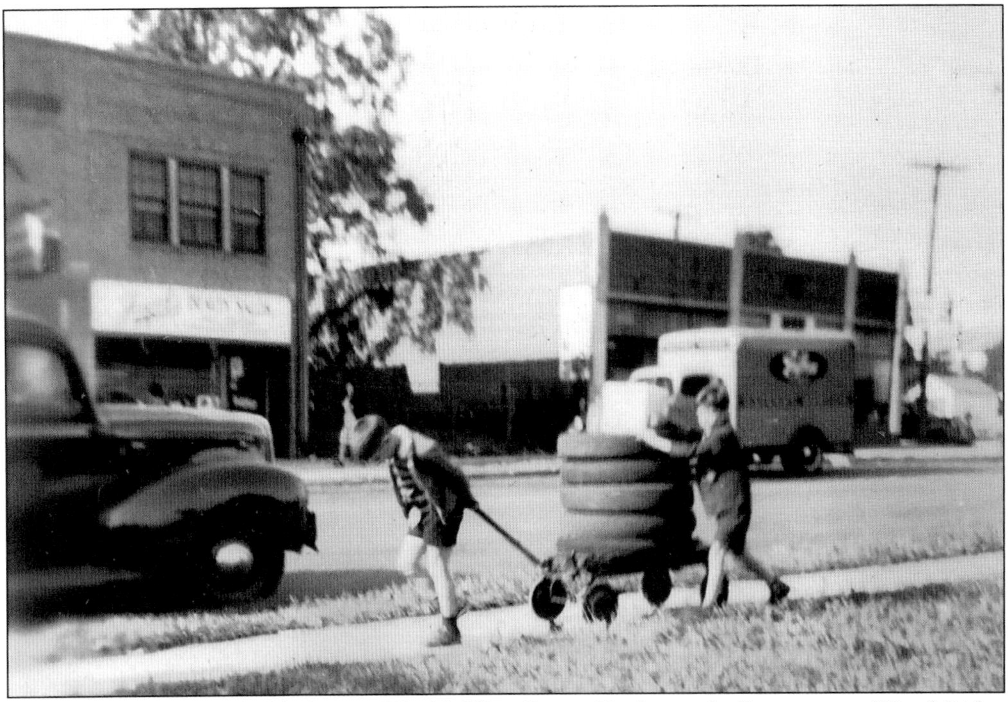

A rubber drive was held during World War II on Hackensack Street near Wood-Ridge High School.

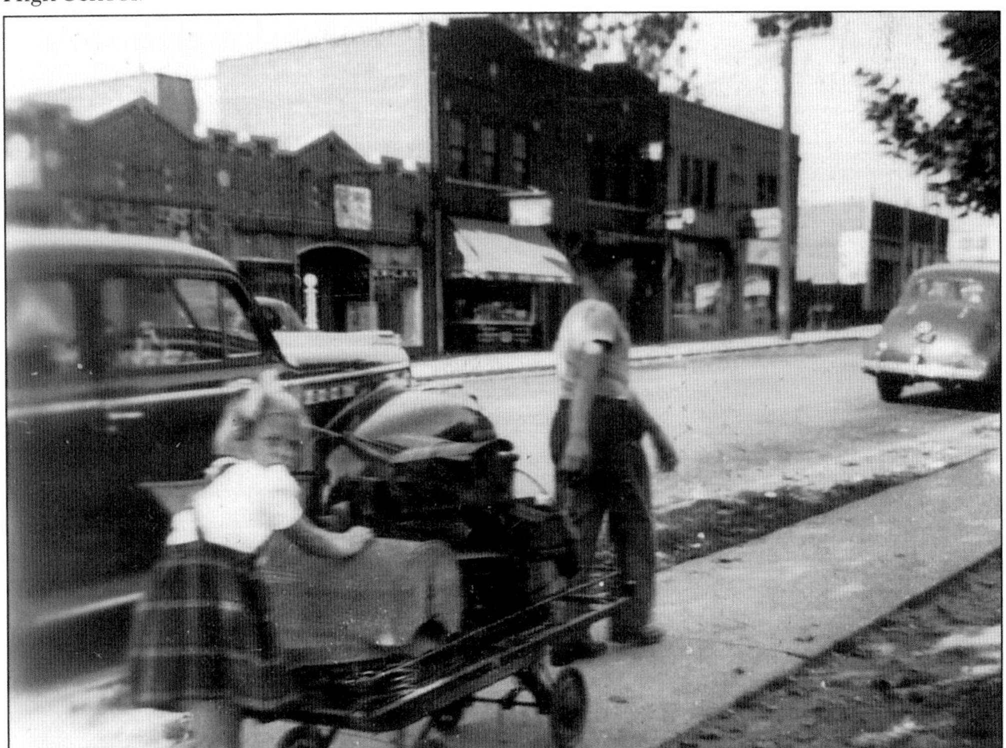

Children bring scraps for the war effort in a Radio Flyer wagon on Hackensack Street.

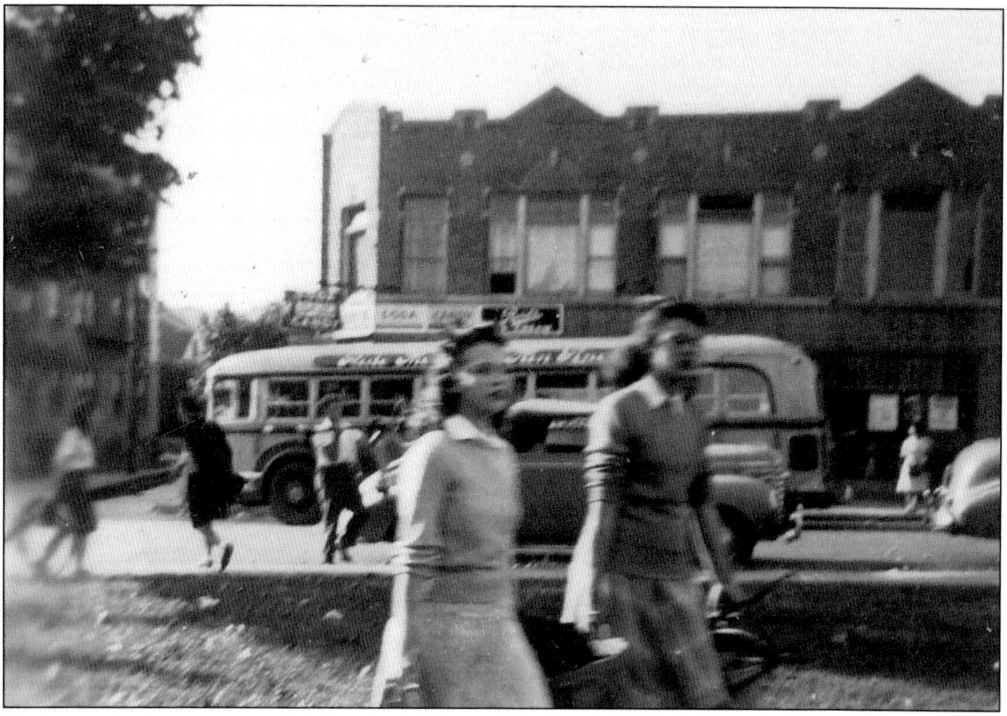

Teenagers bring in materials for a scrap drive to help the war effort. This photograph was taken in front of the high school.

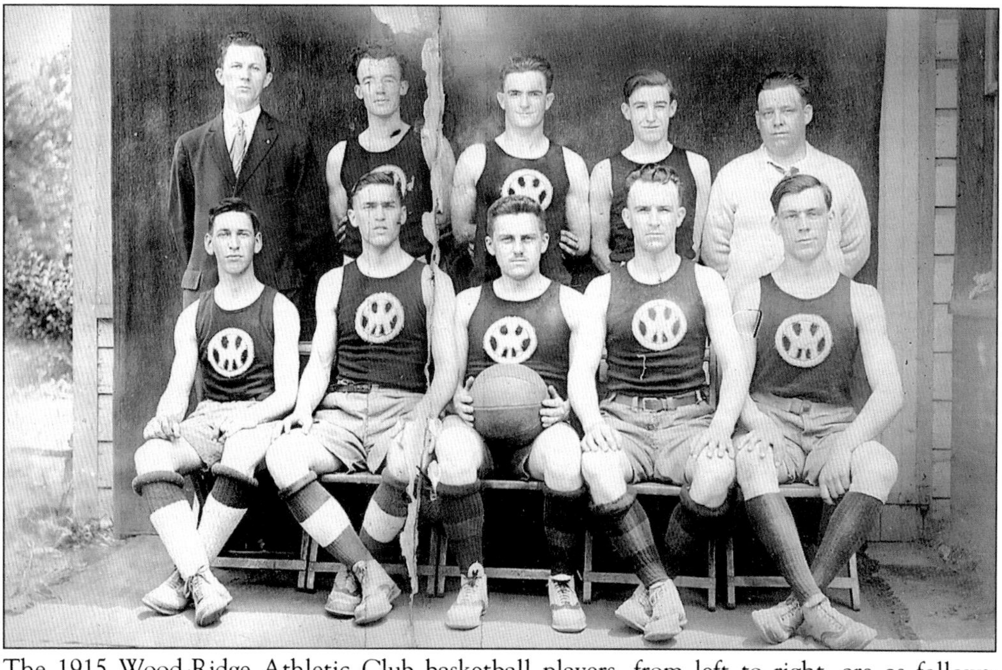

The 1915 Wood-Ridge Athletic Club basketball players, from left to right, are as follows: (first row) Charlie Gust, Fred Schiesswohl, Dick Berger, Louis Obermeyer, and Emile Bugnon; (second row) Chris Kreiling, Ray Valentine, Al Wurst, Walter Hart, and Harry Meade.

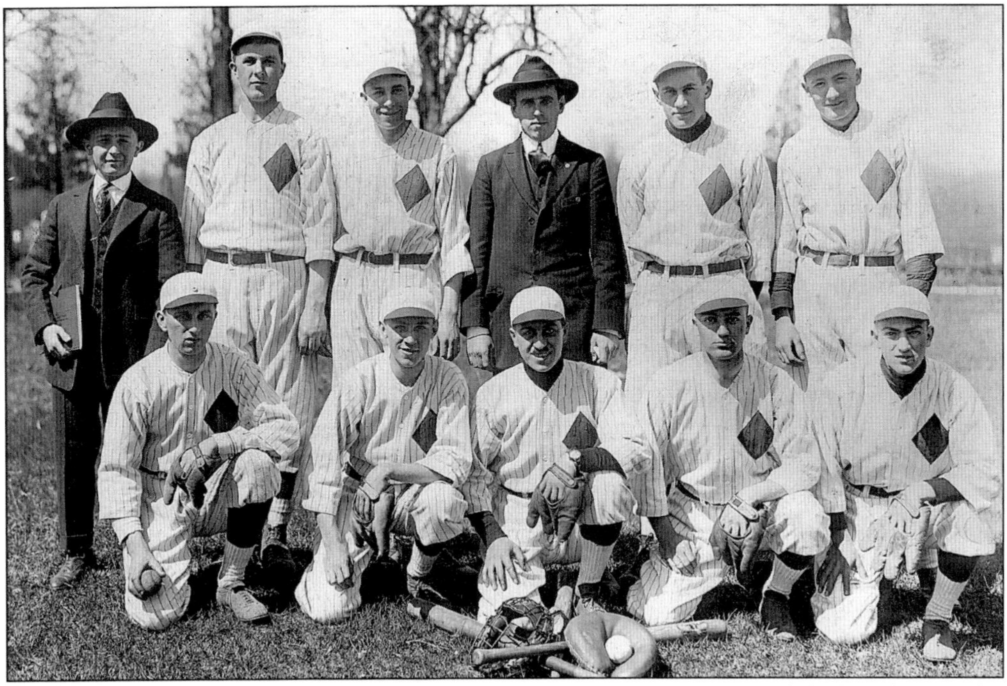

The Columbia Social Club Baseball Team is pictured *c.* 1920. From left to right are the following: (first row) William Nolan, Fred Meyers, Leo Purcaro, G. Gorab, and E. Gorab; (second row) Dominic Marconi, Wilbur Ellison, Robert Stoeffler, William Kour, Joseph Mahlbacher, and Joseph Gadda.

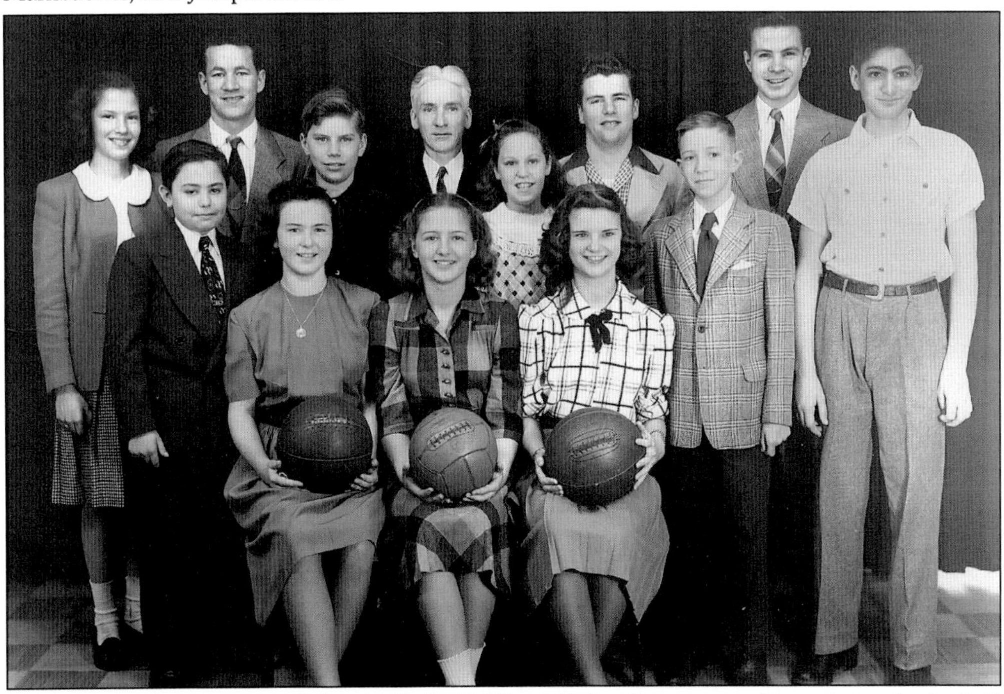

Pictured are the winners of the 1947–1948 Wood-Ridge Recreation Commission basketball foul shot contest.

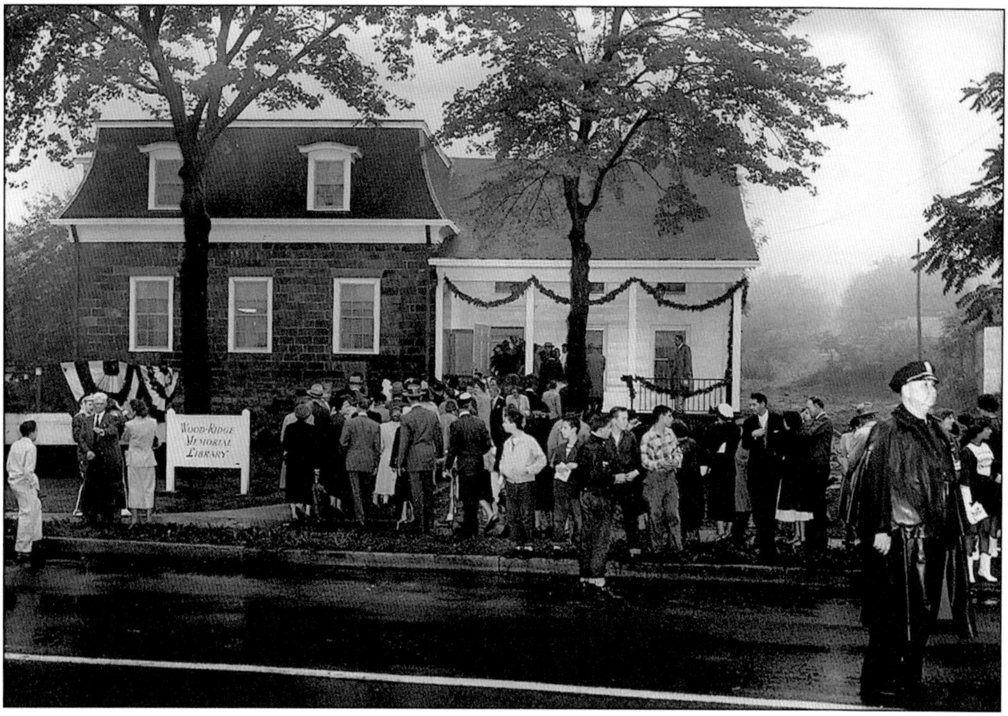

The new home of the Wood-Ridge Memorial Library is dedicated in a ceremony on September 19, 1954.

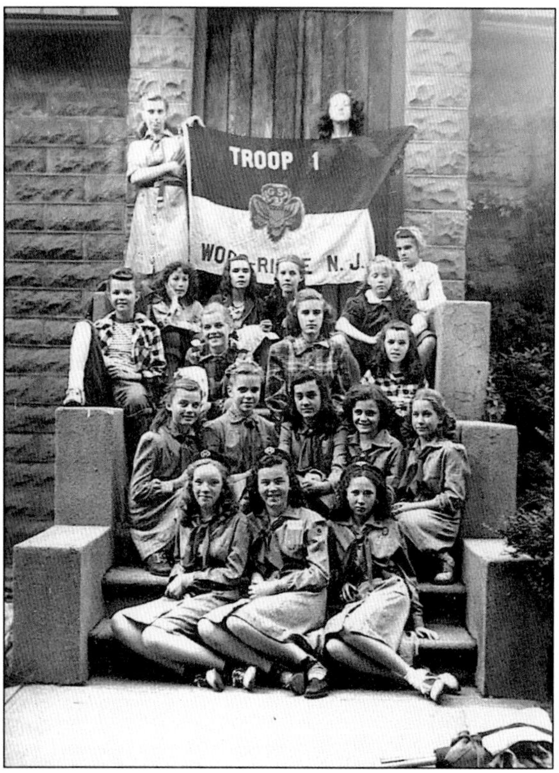

Members of the local Girl Scout troop pose in front of St. Paul's Church in 1947. The troop leader was Edith Wilkinson. From left to right are the following: (first row) Carol Doran, Dolores Rogers, and Anne Connolly; (second row) unidentified, Ruth Schnaars, Audrey Streichert, Bernice Linden, and Dorothy Suehnholz; (third row) Doris Hillenbrand, Nancy Andrews, Geraldine Ulrich, and Barbara Freeman; (fourth row) Marian Rebele, Virginia Reading, Janice Nicholson, Virginia Fair, and Claire Freytag; (fifth row)Ruth Razzetti and Joan Moran. (Photograph courtesy of Dorothy Suehnholz Dobek.)

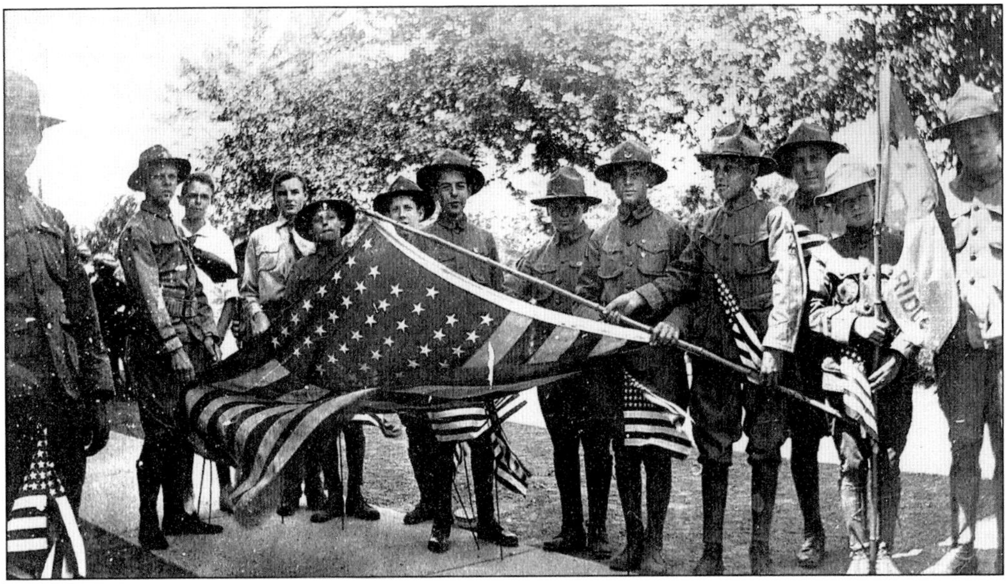

Members of the Boy Scout Troops in Wood-Ridge are pictured *c.* 1915.

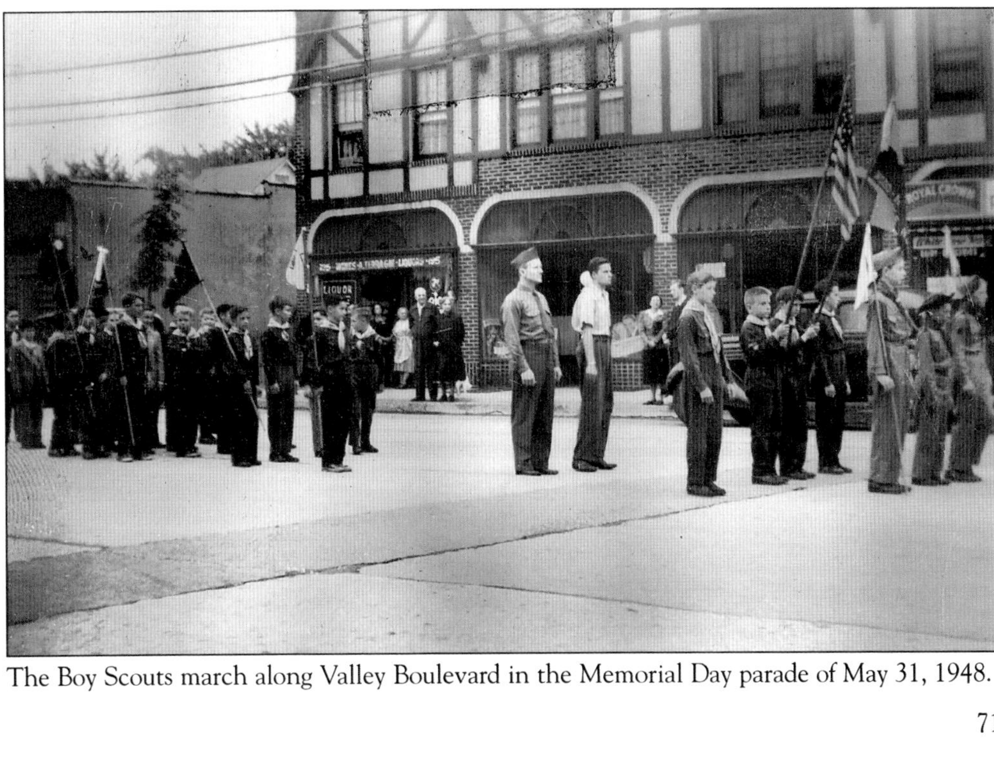

The Boy Scouts march along Valley Boulevard in the Memorial Day parade of May 31, 1948.

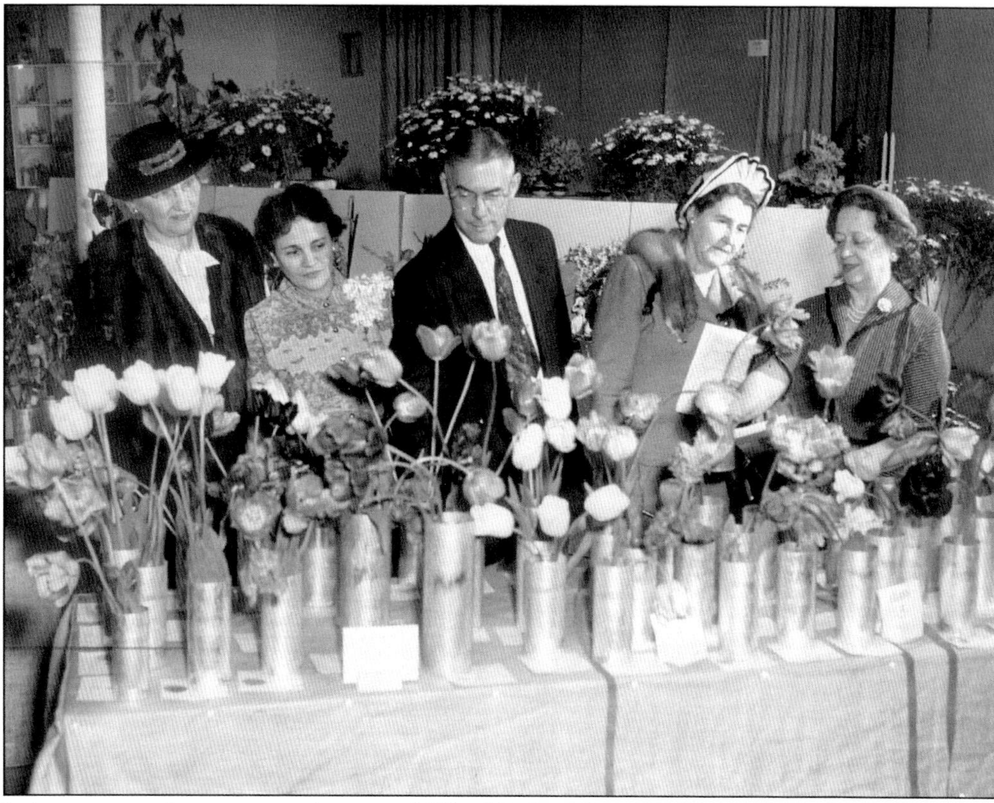

Judges inspect the entries in the annual Wood-Ridge Manor Community Garden Club Flower Show, held at Wood-Ridge High School.

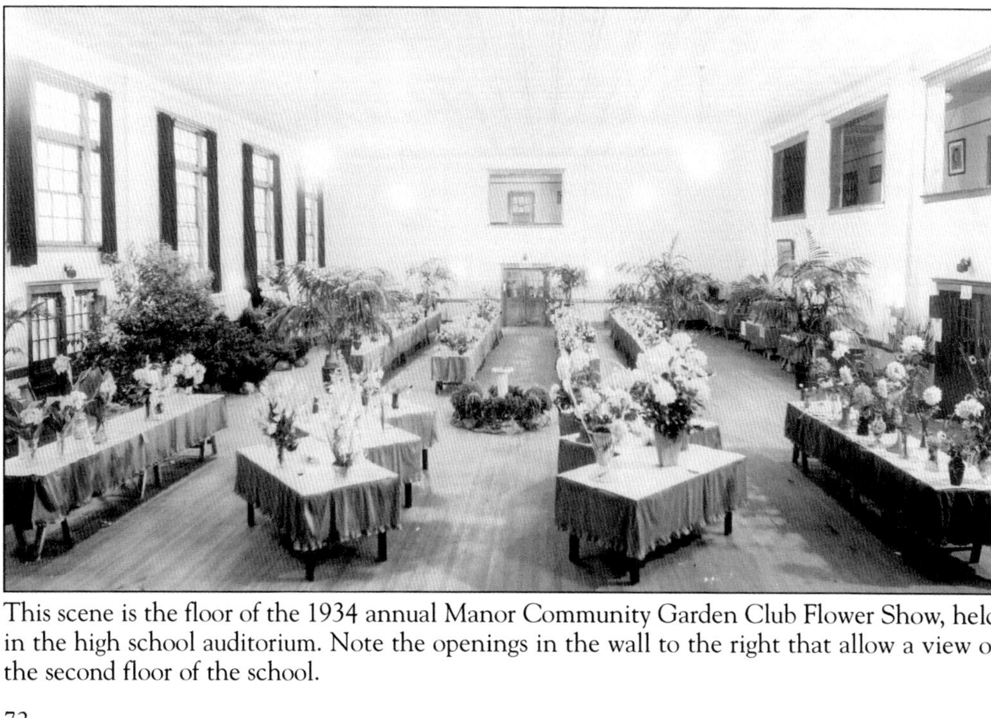

This scene is the floor of the 1934 annual Manor Community Garden Club Flower Show, held in the high school auditorium. Note the openings in the wall to the right that allow a view of the second floor of the school.

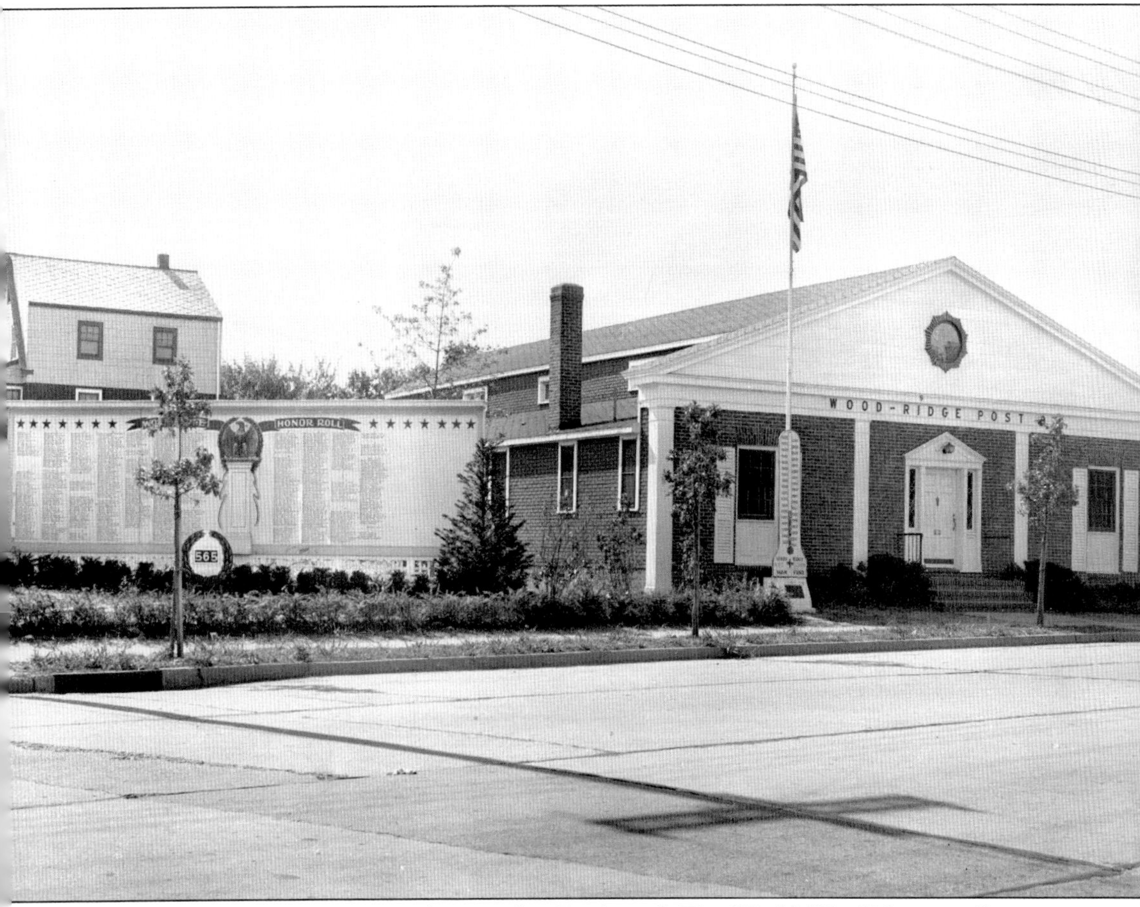

American Legion Post No. 97 stands on Valley Boulevard. The World War II honor roll is to the left, with a Sunshine City home on Marlboro Road in the background. The building burned down in 1981. The tot park is now located here.

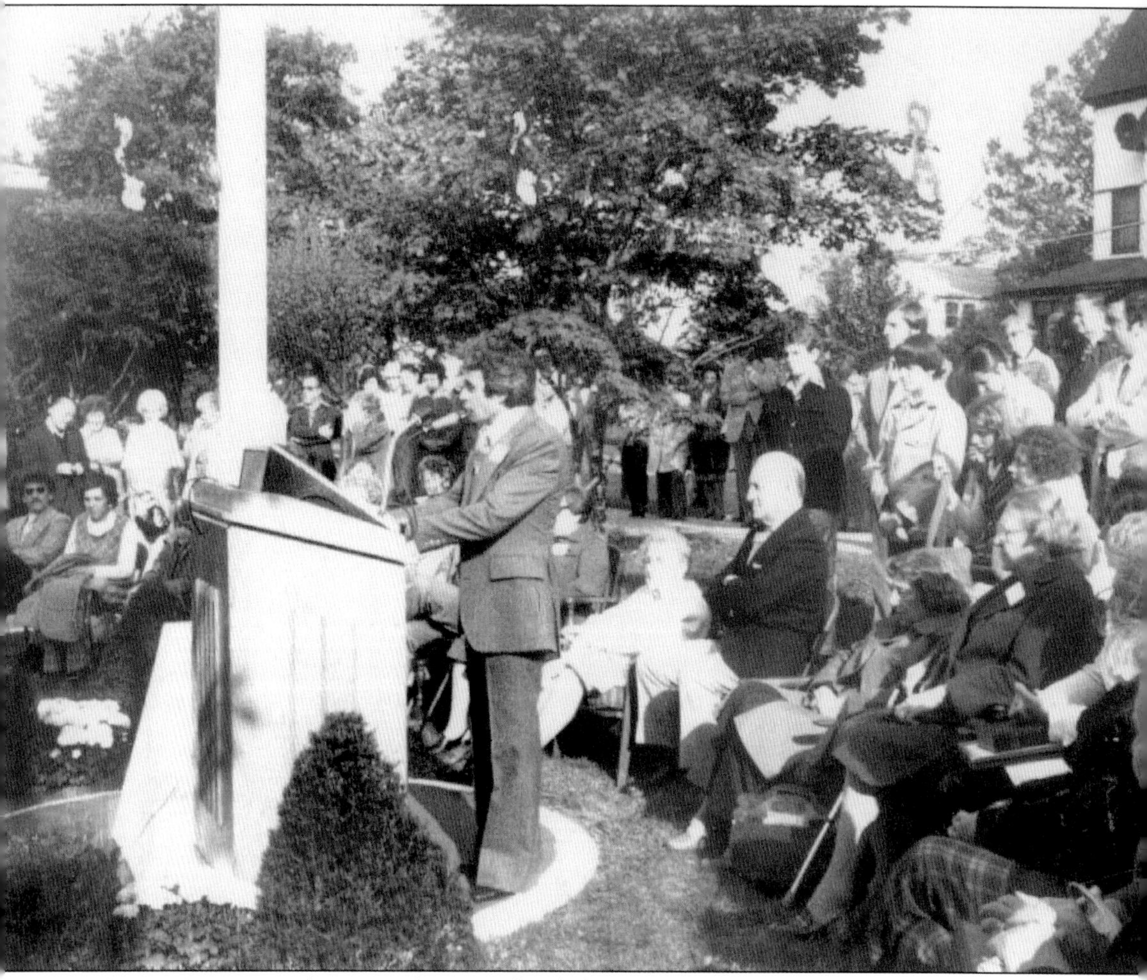

Mayor Peter Incardone presides over the dedication of the Bianchi House to the borough of Wood-Ridge. Many members of the Bianchi family are in attendance.

Five

The Police and Fire Departments

The Wood-Ridge Fire Department was established in July 1897. Originally, it only had hose carts (inherited from Carlstadt Hose No. 2) and steam engines that needed to be pulled by hand or horses. The department has continually improved and added to its service. It now has state-of-the-art equipment. The Wood-Ridge Emergency Squad became a part of the fire department in the late 1930s.

At the time of incorporation in 1894, police service consisted of a marshal or a constable. The police department grew into a small law enforcement body, continuing to grow into the modern police department of today. Arthur Ketschke was the first police chief, appointed in the early 1920s. Emile Bugnon became chief in 1927 and served until 1965—the longest tenure of any chief in Bergen County. One case during Bugnon's time became an episode on the *Gang Busters* radio program. The Marshal Association was developed to act as an auxiliary to the police department. It is now known as the auxiliary police.

Wood-Ridge residents can boast of having a safe place to live and raise a family due to the efforts of both departments, which include highly dedicated volunteers and employees.

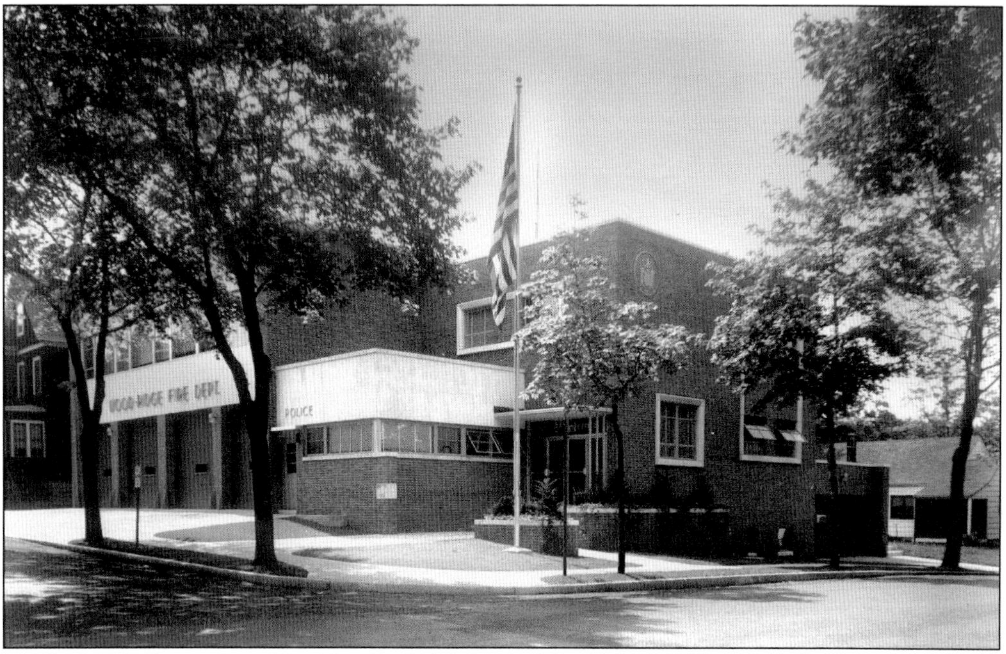

The newly built municipal building is pictured in 1952. It provided one central location for the Wood-Ridge borough offices, the police, and the fire departments.

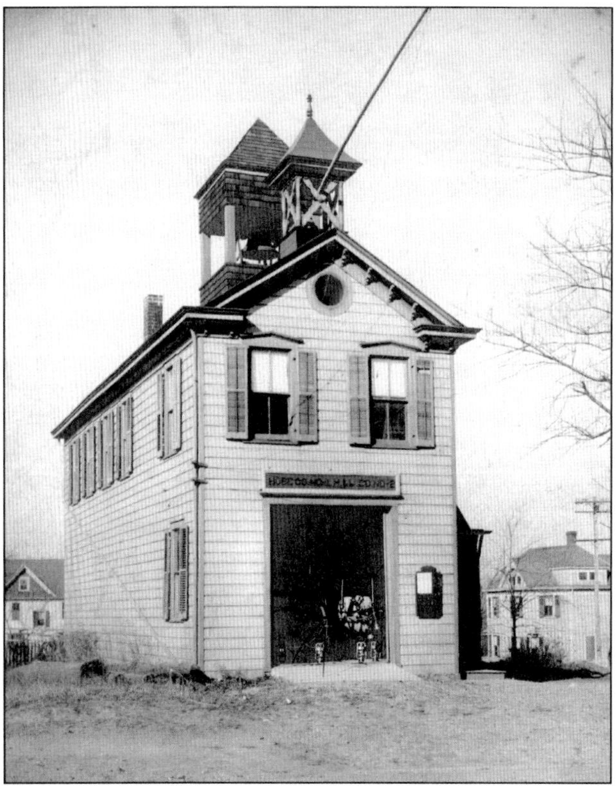
This was the original fire department headquarters c. 1910.

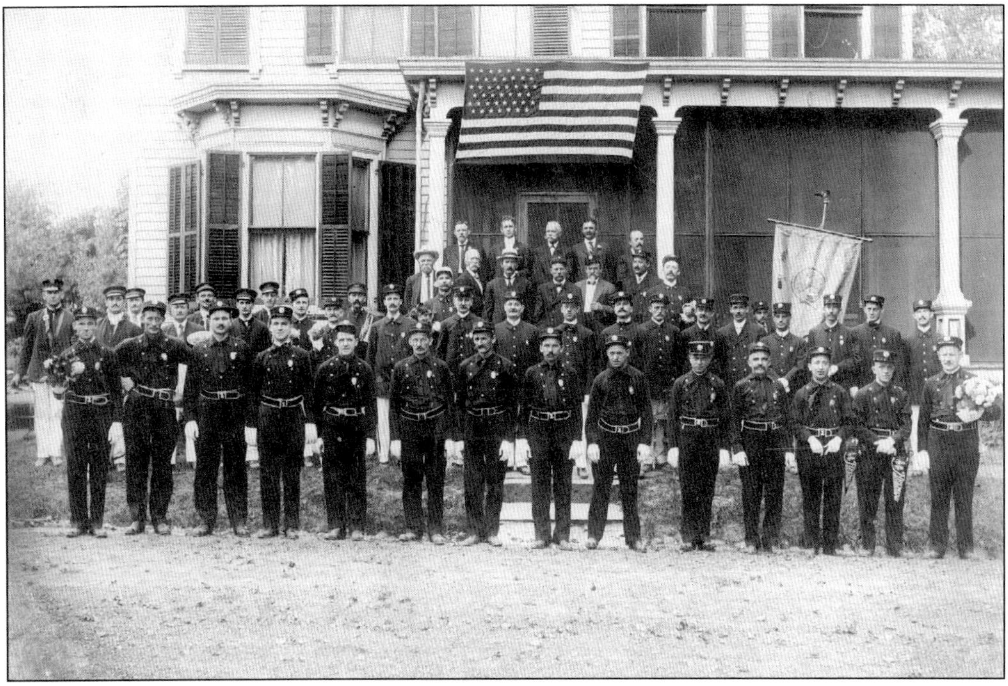

Members of the Wood-Ridge Fire Department pose *c.* 1913. From left to right are the following: (first row) W. Koegel, Charles Rumsby, Frank Castagnetta, Jack O'Brien, S. W. Osthagen, J. Kempfner, William Kour, C. Fred Schiesswohl, A. Von Glahn, William Chippendale, L. Obermeyer Jr., John Distel, William Von Glahn, and Frank Lehmann; (second row) Tom Daley, unidentified, Herman Hofener, ? Newman, unidentified, George Hecker, Andrew Meyer, William Parlato, Eugene Winberry, C. Laurent, William White, and Joseph Beck; (third row) Case Gwinn, Jake Bloom, F. Fritsch, William Jansen, George Young, and J. Doerflinger; (fourth row) unidentified, Leopold Brandenburg, Mayor Charles Ruegger, Homer Moore, and William Purdy. The musicians are unidentified.

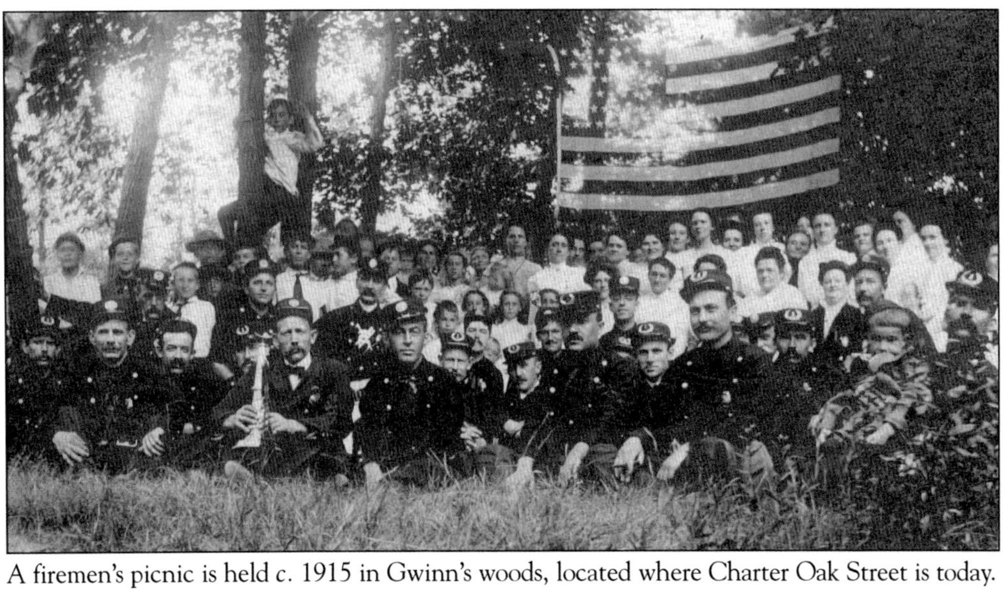

A firemen's picnic is held *c.* 1915 in Gwinn's woods, located where Charter Oak Street is today.

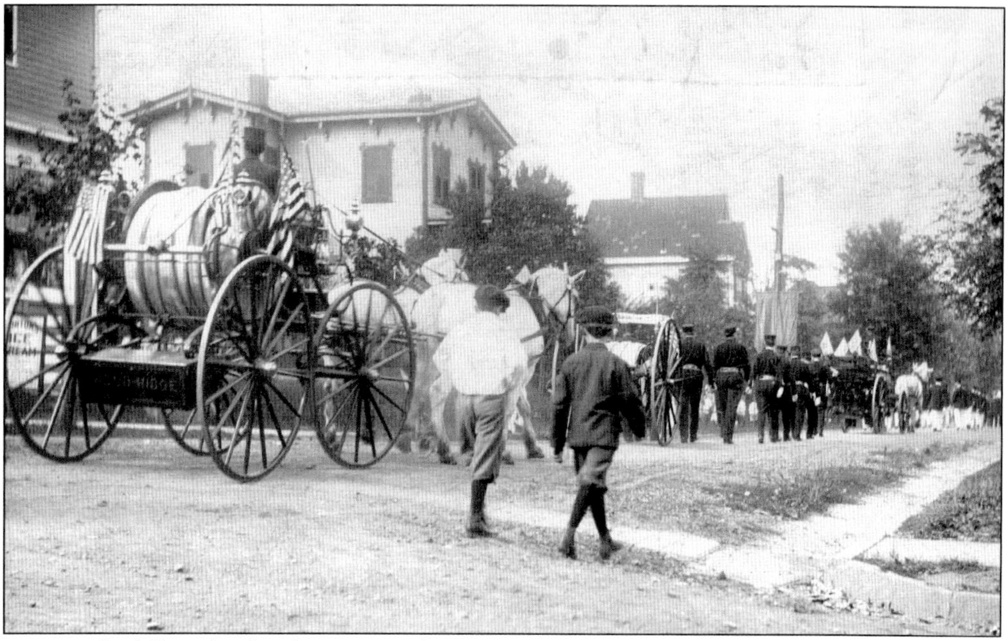

Two youths follow the fire department during a parade in 1913.

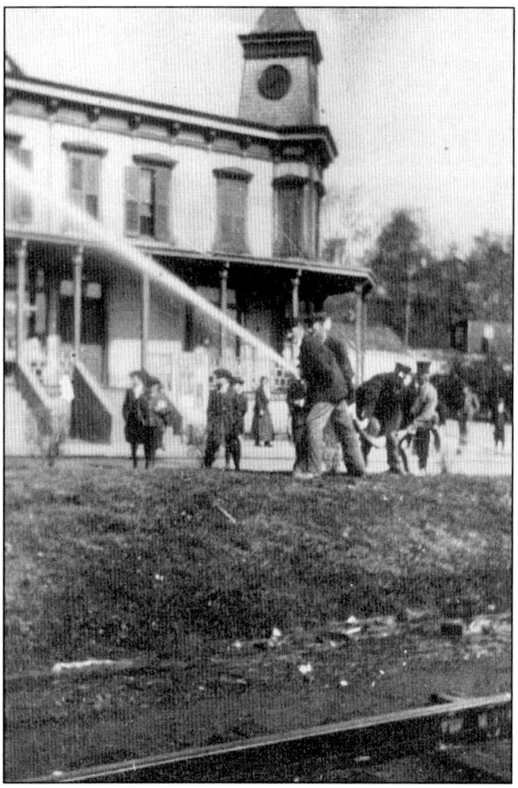

The fire department tests its equipment outside the Adelung Hotel, on Park Place East.

Firefighters test the hose on Park Place East.

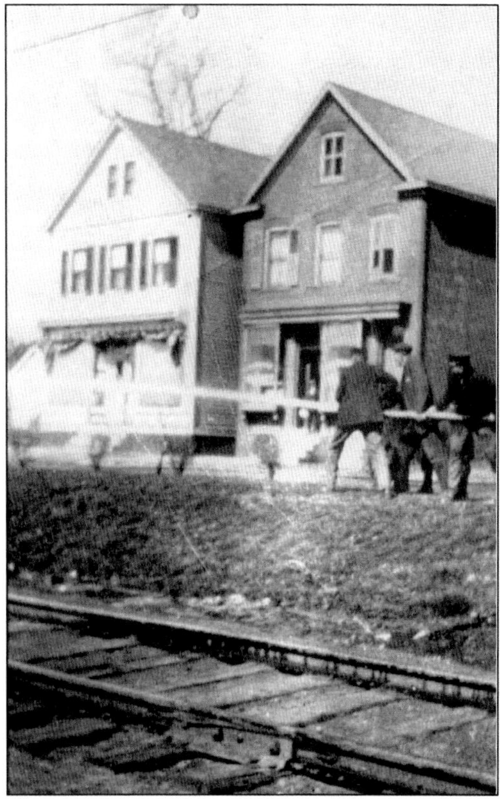

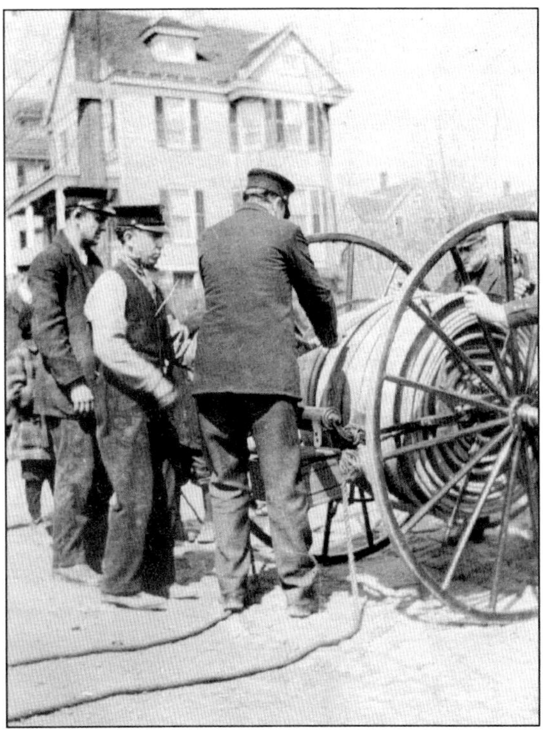

Firefighters check the hose as they put it back on the wheel.

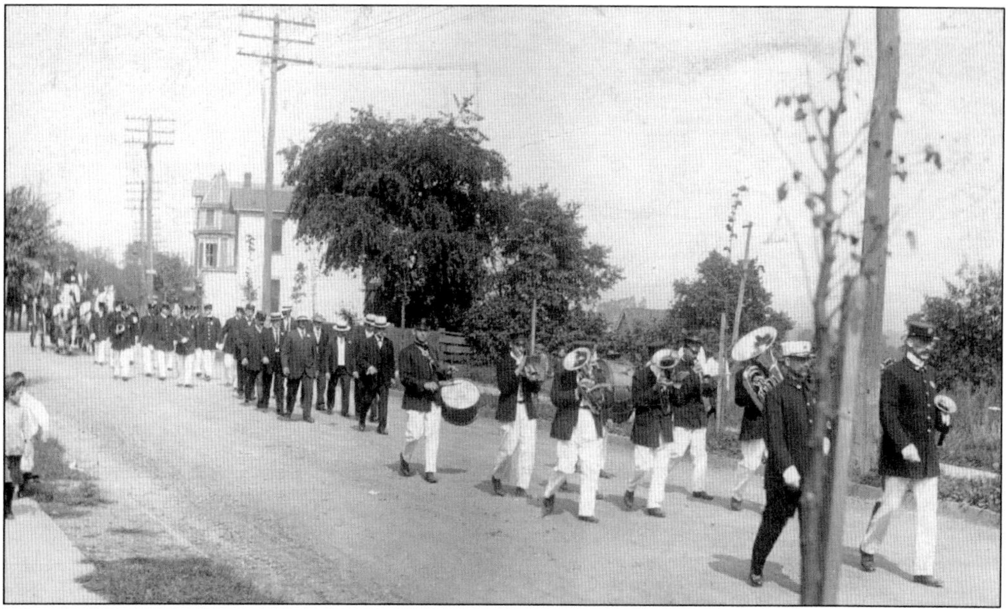

A fire department parade takes place on Hackensack Street in front of Mount Pleasant School c. 1915.

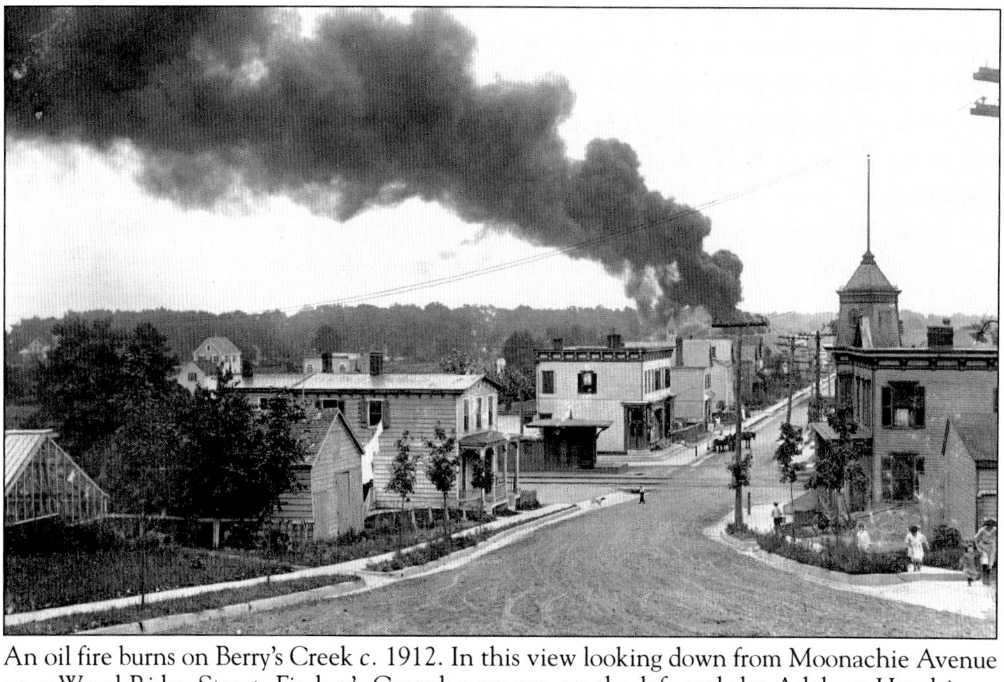

An oil fire burns on Berry's Creek c. 1912. In this view looking down from Moonachie Avenue near Wood-Ridge Street, Fischer's Greenhouses are on the left and the Adelung Hotel is on the right.

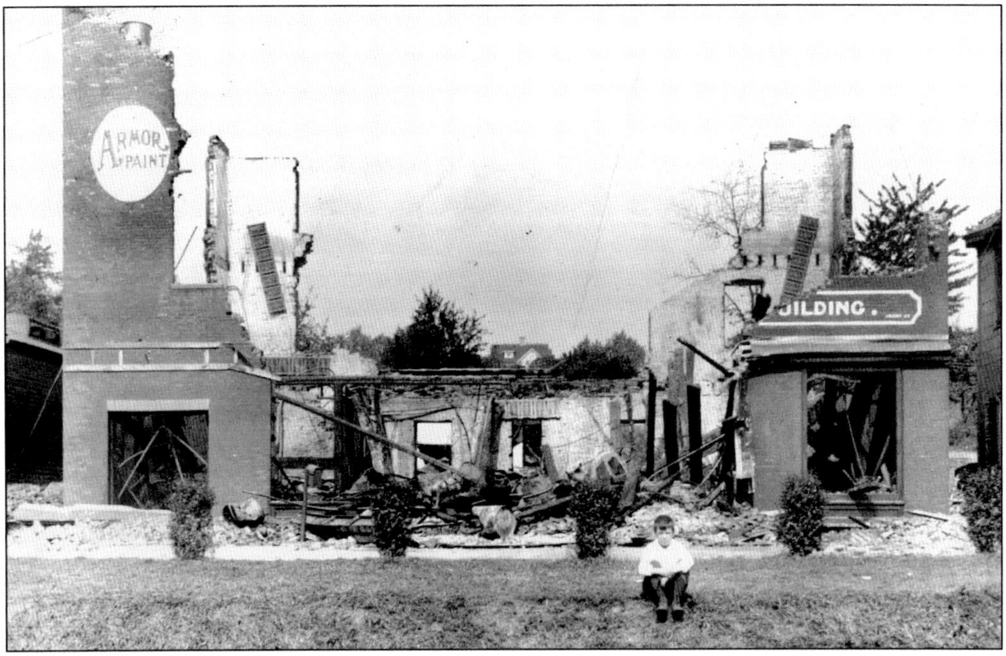

Armor Paint Factory, located near Railroad and Anderson Avenues, sustained damage in the *c.* 1912 fire. A boy sits in front of the remains.

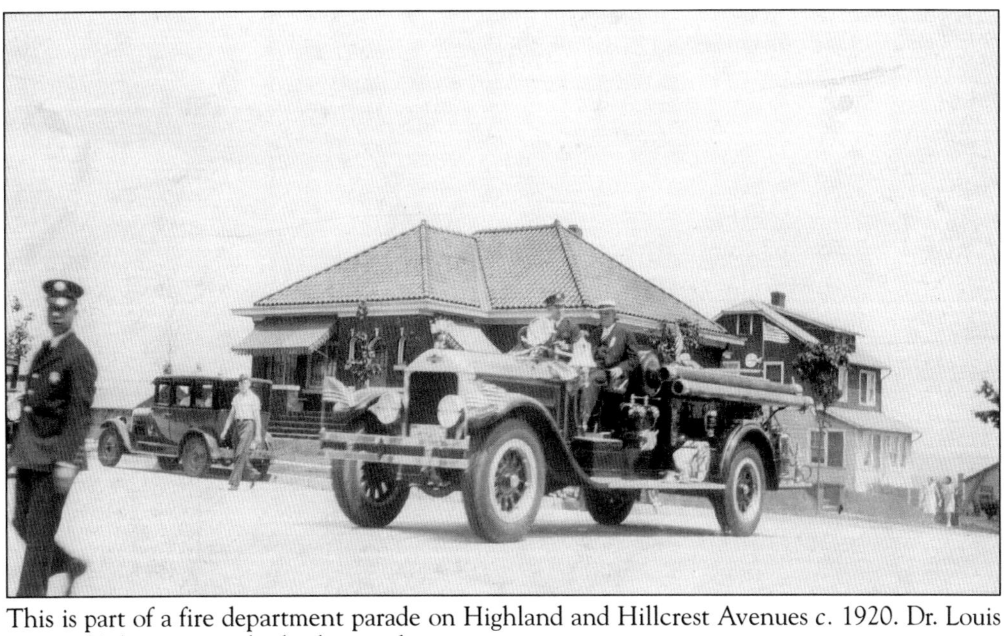
This is part of a fire department parade on Highland and Hillcrest Avenues *c.* 1920. Dr. Louis Cartnick's house is in the background.

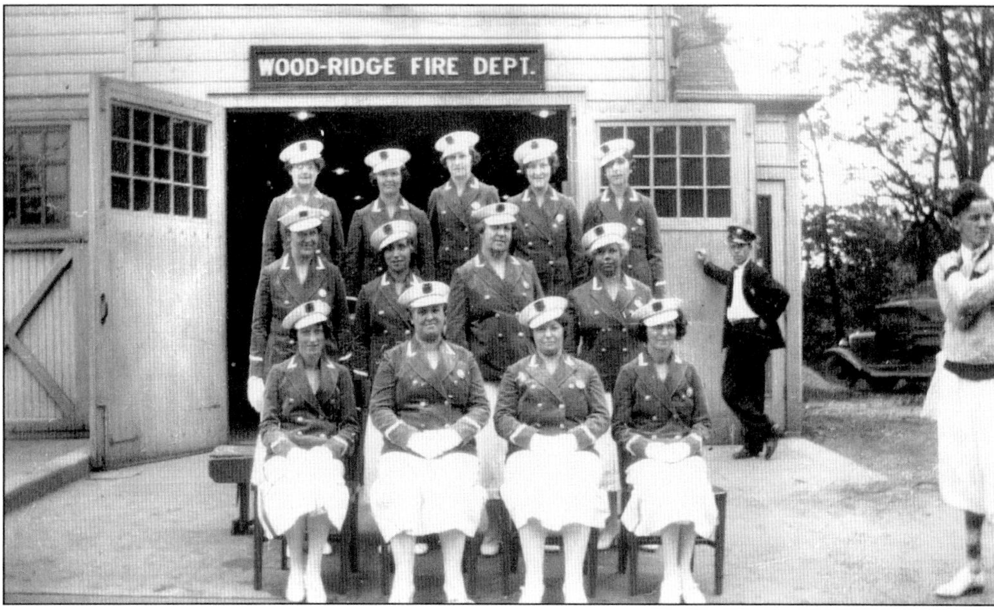

Pictured here is the Wood-Ridge Fire Department Ladies Auxiliary on July 14, 1935.

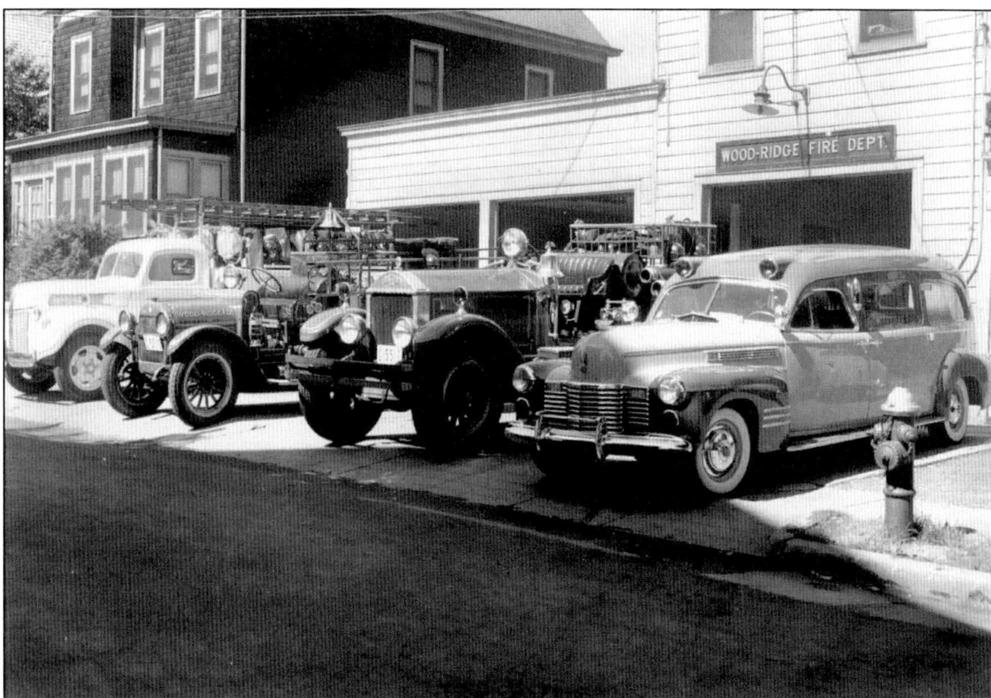

The fire department equipment is shown in this *c.* 1940 photograph. The old fire and police department building remains in this same location on Humboldt Street today.

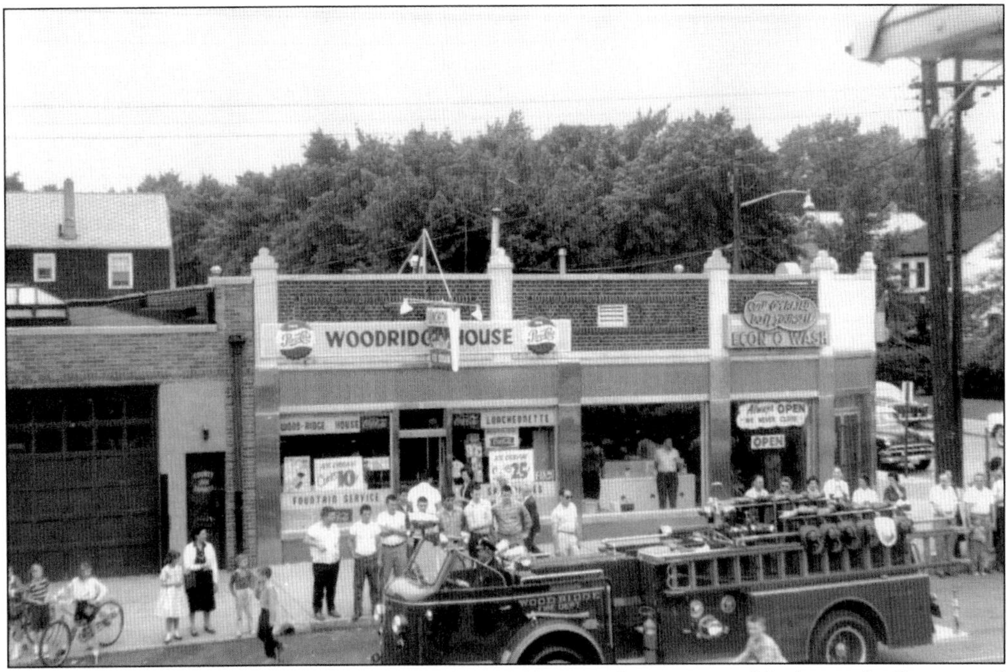

A celebration for Decoration Day in May 1960 is under way on Hackensack Street and Windsor Road.

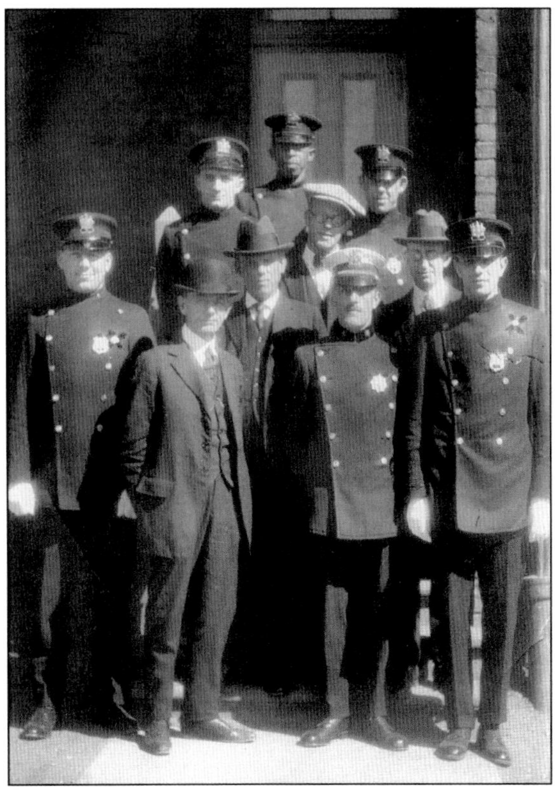

Pictured is the Wood-Ridge Police Department c. 1926. From left to right are the following: (first row) Mayor Walter Innes, Police Chief Arthur Ketschke, and patrolman Ed Bishop; (second row) patrolman Emile Bugnon (later, chief), Councilman William Purdy, and Harry Coston; (third row) Councilman John Ford (later, mayor after Innes died in office); (fourth row) patrolmen Charles Aimone and Bill Smith; (fifth row) school marshal Holmes Robinson.

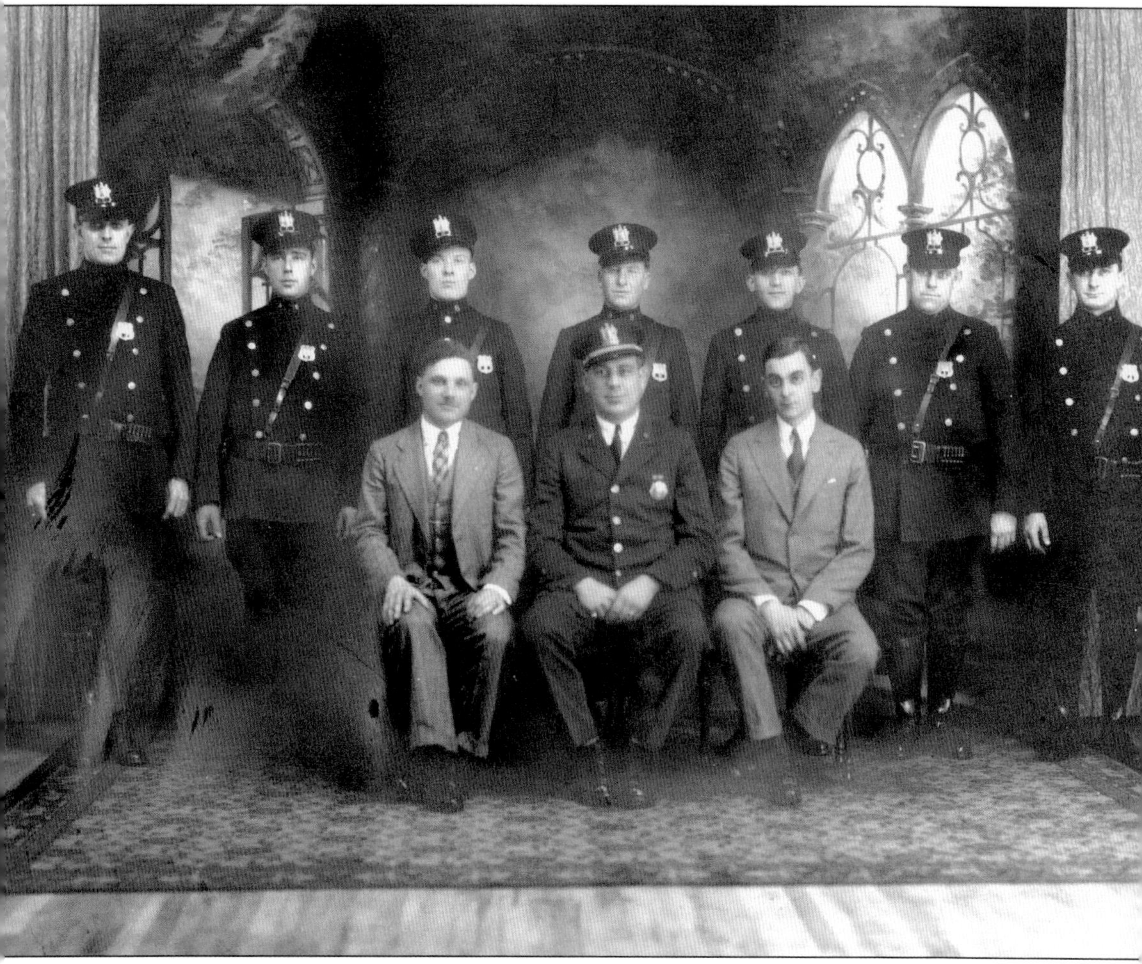

The Wood-Ridge Police Department is pictured *c.* 1933. From left to right are the following: (first row) Mayor William Staubach, Police Chief Emile Bugnon, and Police Commissioner Dan Royer; (second row) patrolmen Ed Bishop, Winnie Davis, Ed Barlow, Charles Prince, Robert Kuhl, Joseph Schmidt, and Charles Aimone.

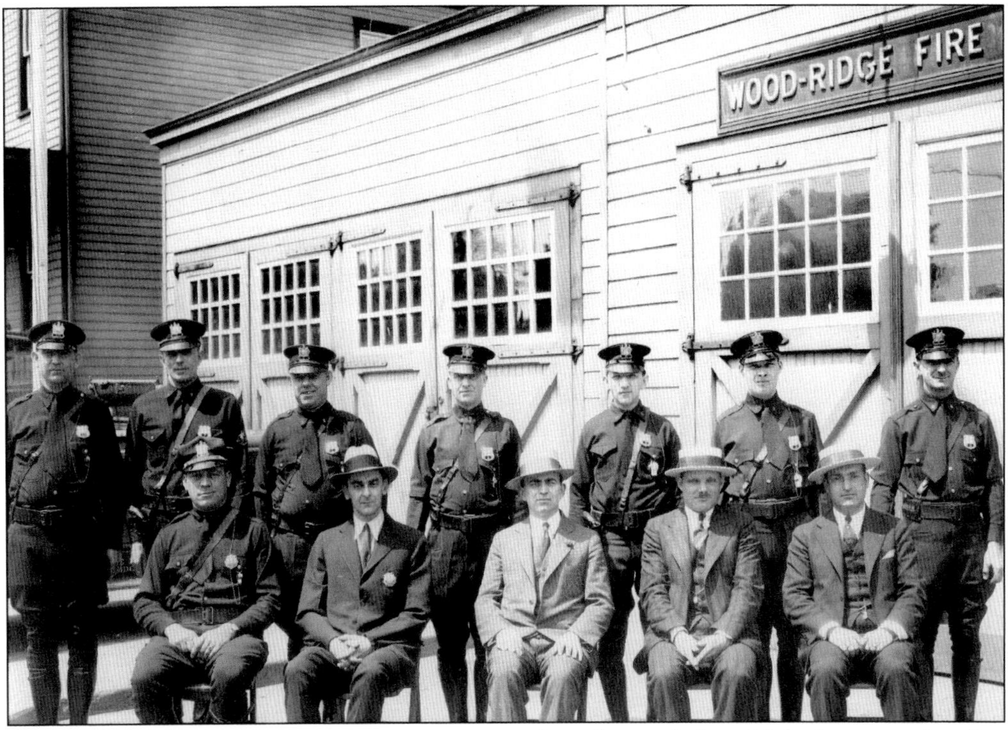

The Wood-Ridge Police Department is pictured in front of the old firehouse and police department. From left to right are the following: (first row) Chief Emile Bugnon, D. Royer, A. Alessi, Mayor William Staubach, and Albert Gorab; (second row) J. Van Note, Ed Bishop, W. Smith, C. Prince, R. Kuhl, E. Barlow, and C. Aimone.

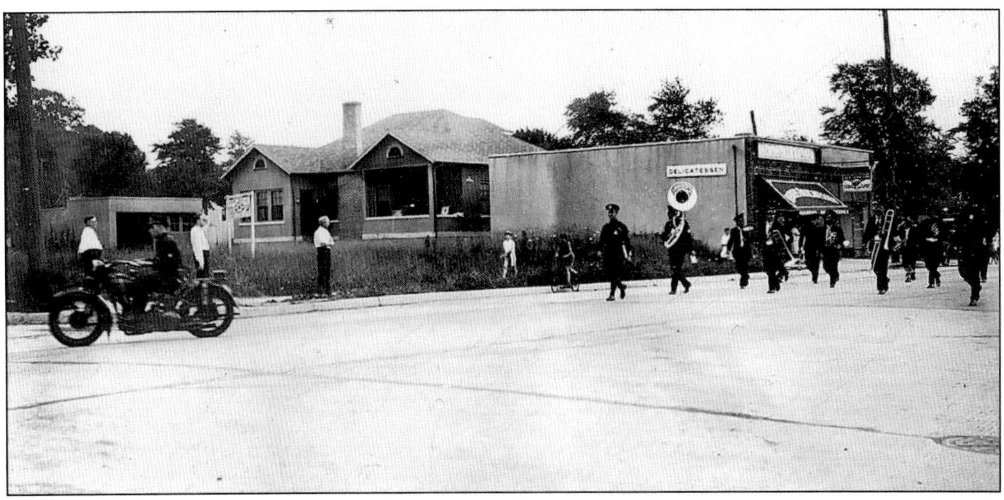

The police department leads the parade on Valley Boulevard near Wood-Ridge Avenue.

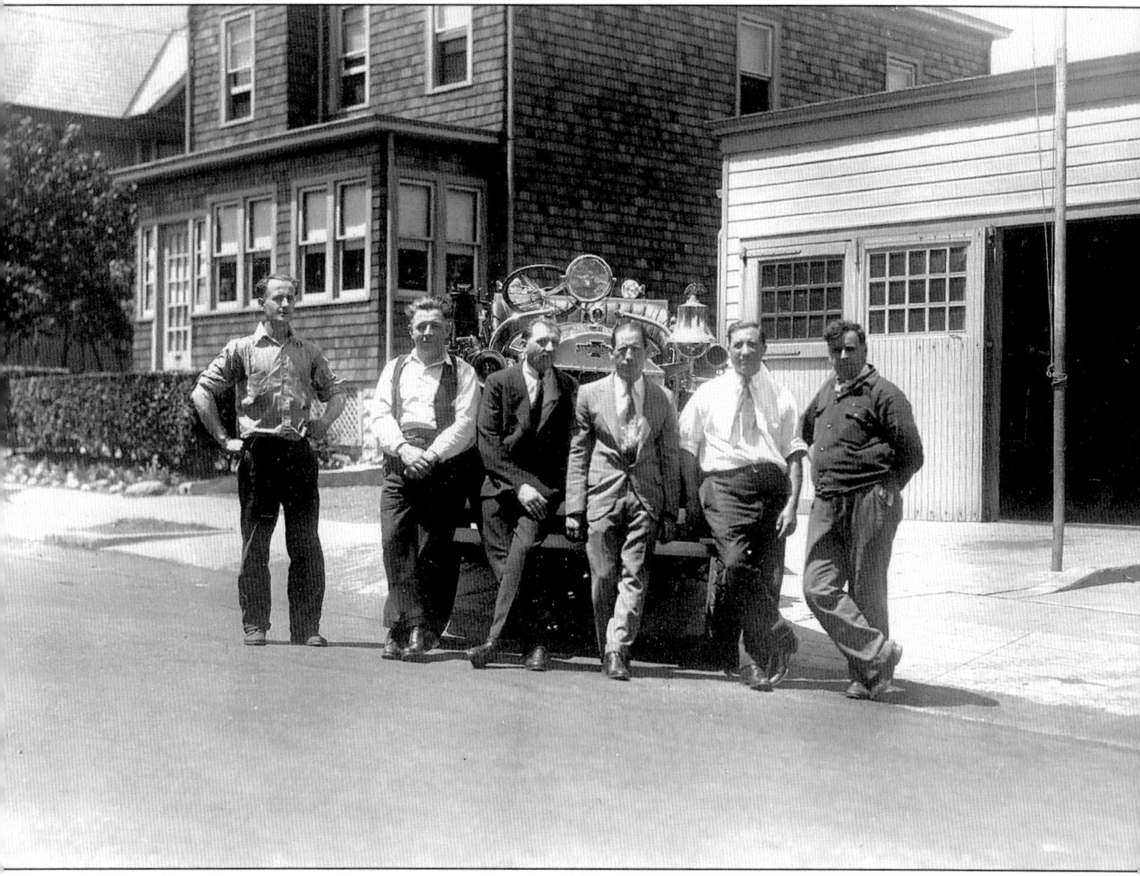

The first big piece of equipment for the Wood-Ridge Fire Department was an American LaFrance engine. Standing in front of the engine and the old firehouse on Humboldt Street, from left to right, are Emil Dross, William Meade, Bob Kuhl, Charles Suehnholz, Raphael Roccuzzo, and William Kour.

Six

HOUSING DEVELOPMENTS

Frederick Kohbertz is considered to be one of the earliest developers of Wood-Ridge. He purchased parcels of land and then sold them to builders.

In 1911, the Lint, Butscher, and Ross building firm developed the area of Wood-Ridge Avenue, Columbia Boulevard, and the south side of Highland Avenue from Hackensack Street to Twelfth Street. Other cross streets were planned, but only Hillcrest Avenue was completed. Hillcrest Avenue was a broad road with island parks in the center. The islands were removed in the 1950s.

In the 1920s and 1930s, Sunshine City was developed. After that, the town stayed basically the same for the next decade.

Following World War II, construction booms hit nearly every town in the nation. In the late 1940s and 1950s, the last major development occurred in Wood-Ridge.

It was called Wood-Ridge Heights. It encompassed the area of Twelfth Street and below, including Fourteenth Street, Jay Street, Laurel Drive, Arnot Place, Burnett Place, and Jocelyn, Helm, Wood-Ridge, Industrial (now Donna Drive, named in memory of Wood-Ridge resident Donna Ricker) and Main Avenues.

With nearly every piece of private property built upon, it seemed any further housing development in Wood-Ridge was unlikely.

However, in 2001, the Curtiss-Wright Corporation informed the borough that it would be selling its entire 100-plus-acre property.

In the fall of 2001, New York real estate developer Rubin Schron purchased the property. In mid-2002, Somerset Development was named redeveloper.

During 2002–2003, dozens of meetings took place between the borough, Schron, and the mayor's advisory committee to make recommendations and exchange ideas. Schron had a concept plan of creating a traditional neighborhood.

Committee members were introduced to the concept and made several trips to visit the closest of the traditional neighborhoods, called Kentland's, in Gaithersburg, Maryland.

The council and committees were pleased with what they saw. The next step was to bring the town in so the rest of the residents could provide input.

The Somerset Development Group hired world-renowned planner Andres Duany of Duany Plater-Zybeck in Miami, Florida.

In August 2003, the group held a charrette, an intensive planning session at which citizens, designers, and others collaborated on a vision for development.

The planners considered all ideas offered at the charrette and came up with a transit village concept: mixed-use housing and businesses, at least eight acres of open space, and improvements to the remaining property. Duany also had designs for the entire Curtiss-Wright property, planning to incorporate the existing building for development at some time in the future.

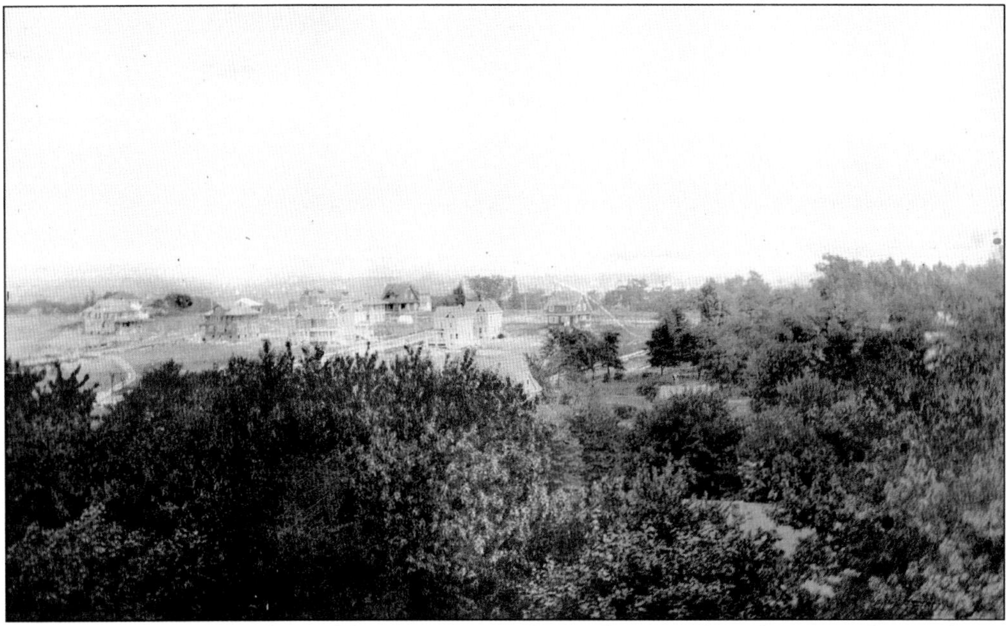

This view, taken from the Kohbertz Mansion, shows the Lint, Butscher, Ross homes being constructed near Wood-Ridge and Highland Avenues between 1910 and 1920.

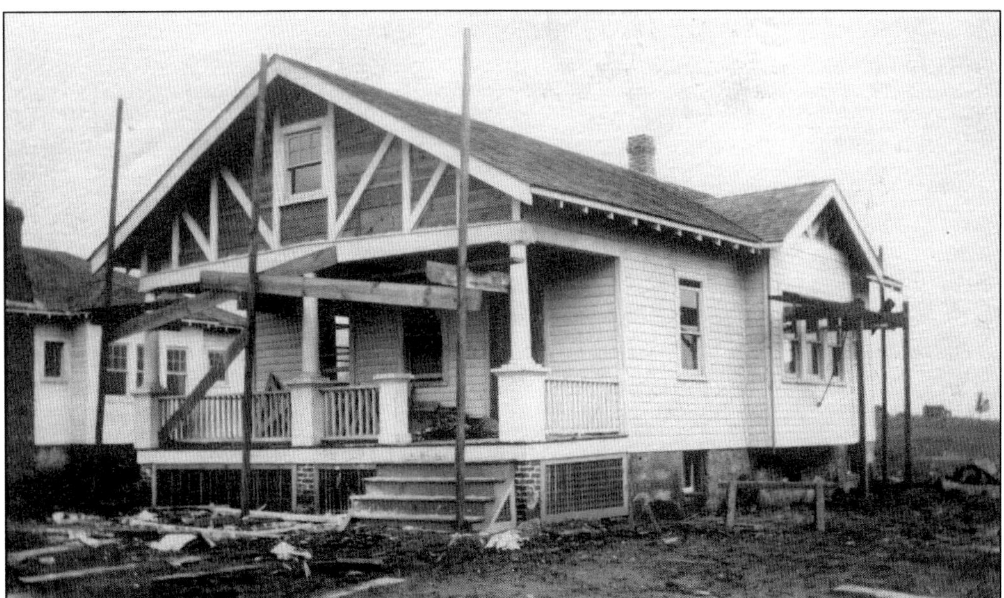

A Lint, Butscher, and Ross house is being constructed *c.* 1915.

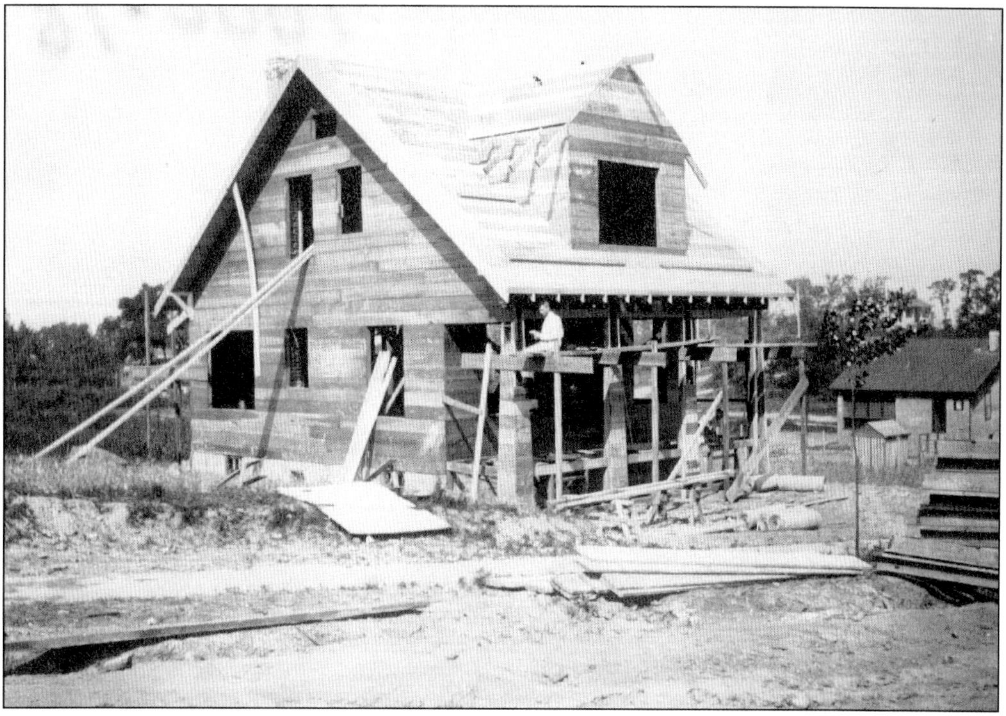

On June 18, 1914, construction is under way on the Hampel residence, located on Columbia Boulevard near Tenth Street.

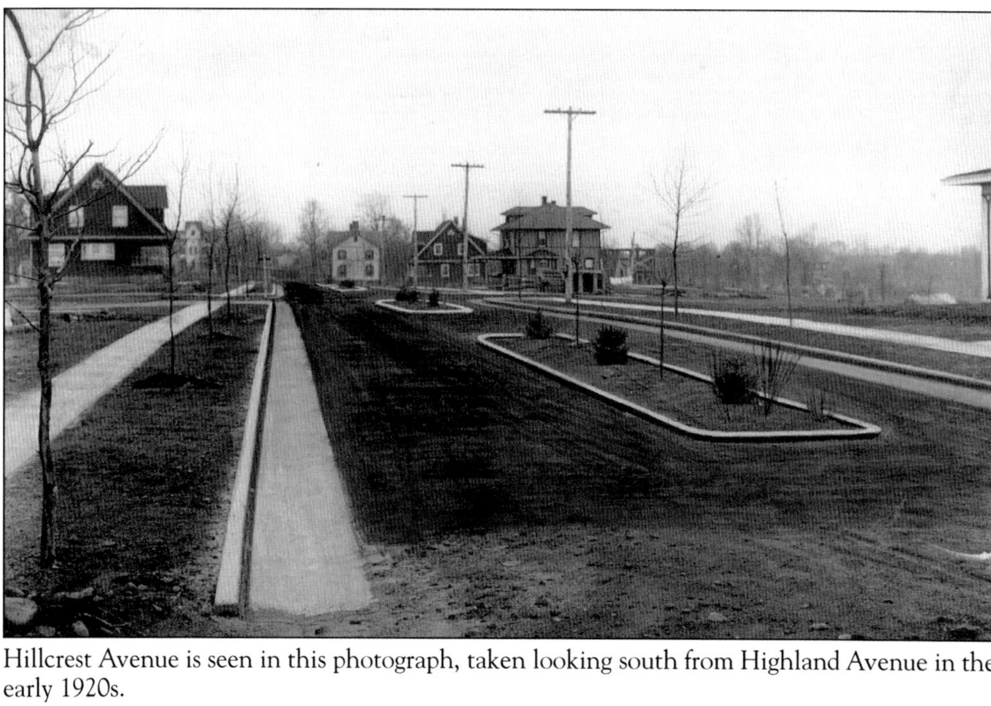

Hillcrest Avenue is seen in this photograph, taken looking south from Highland Avenue in the early 1920s.

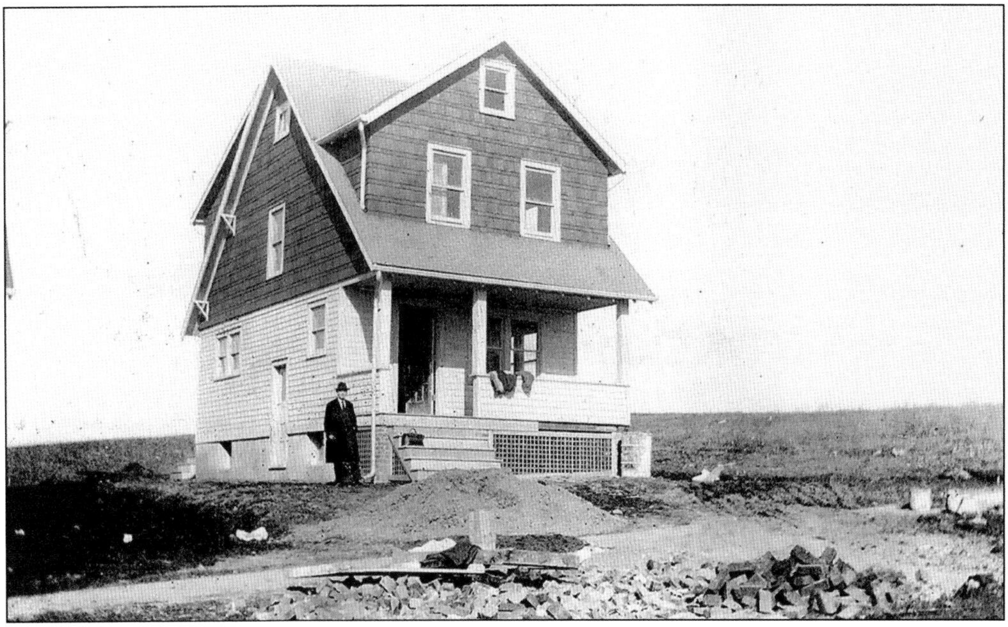

Shown is one of the Lint, Butscher, and Ross homes built between 1910 and 1920.

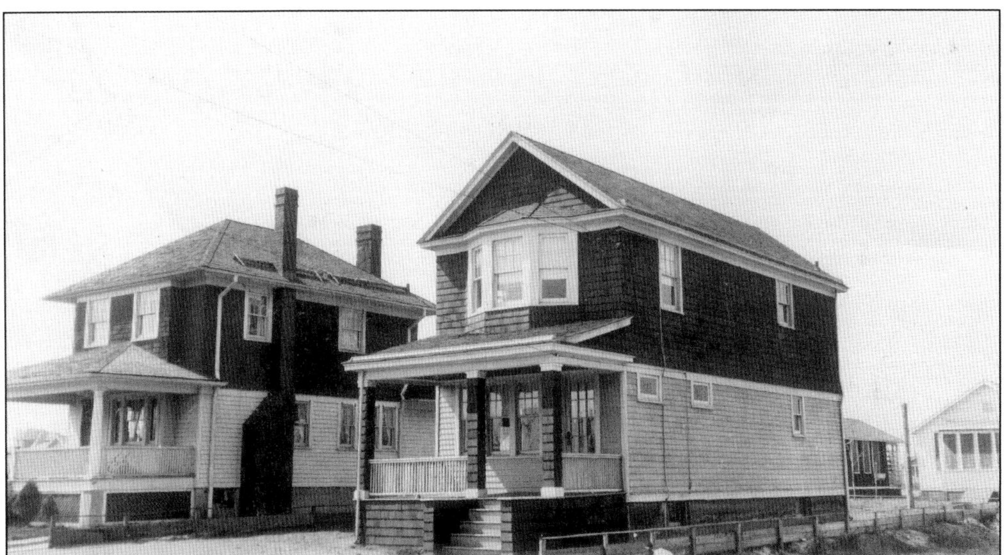

Pictured are two typical designs of the Lint, Butscher, and Ross homes.

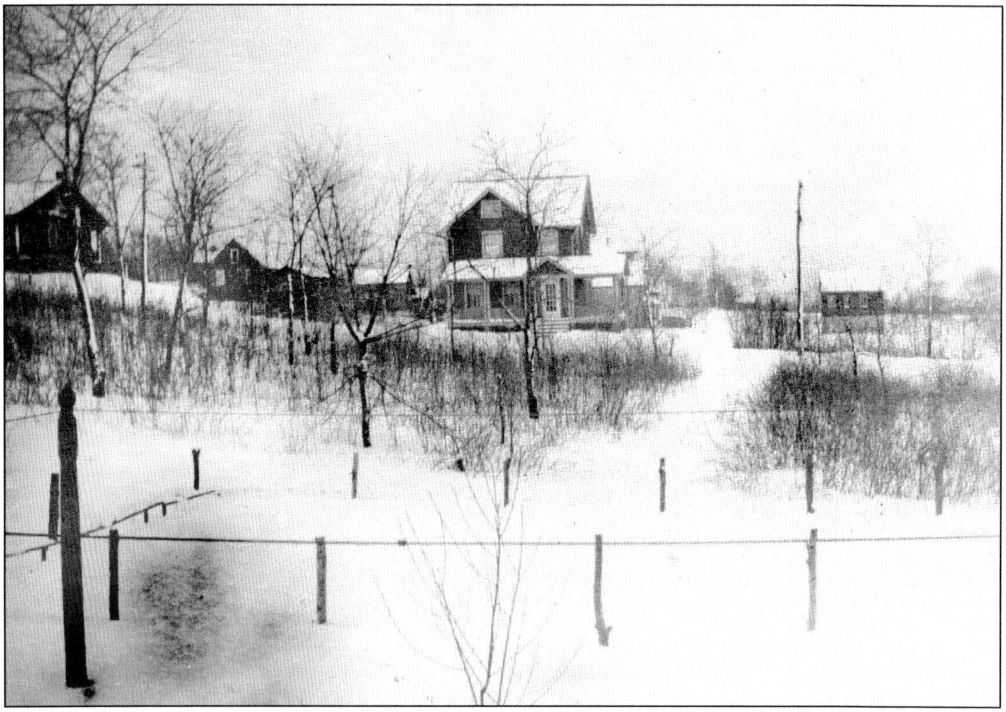

This photograph of Columbia Boulevard between Seventh and Tenth Streets was taken looking toward Wood-Ridge Avenue in 1916.

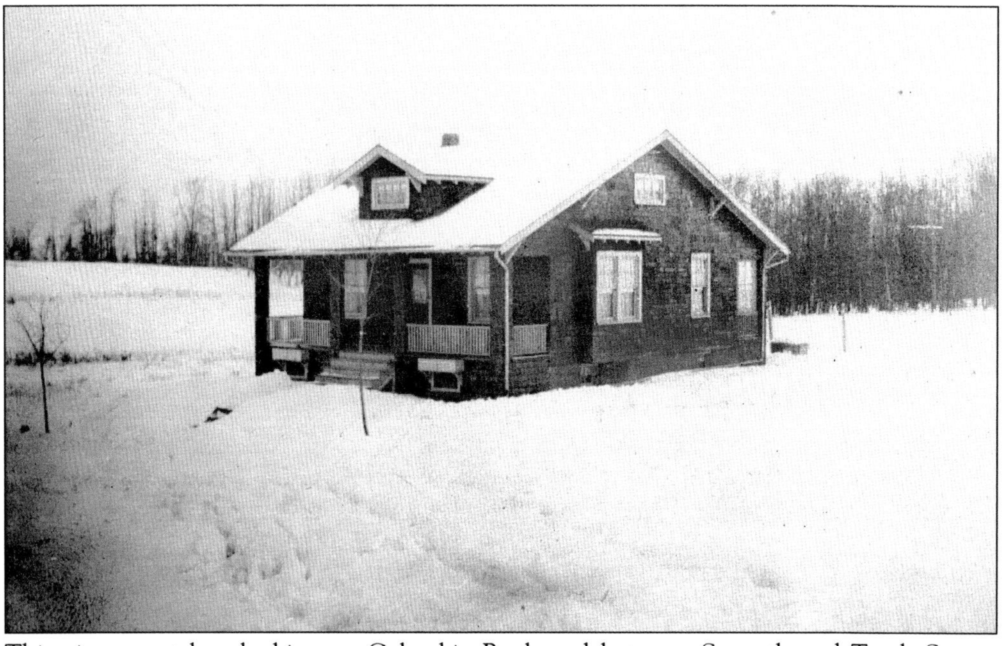

This view was taken looking up Columbia Boulevard between Seventh and Tenth Streets in 1916.

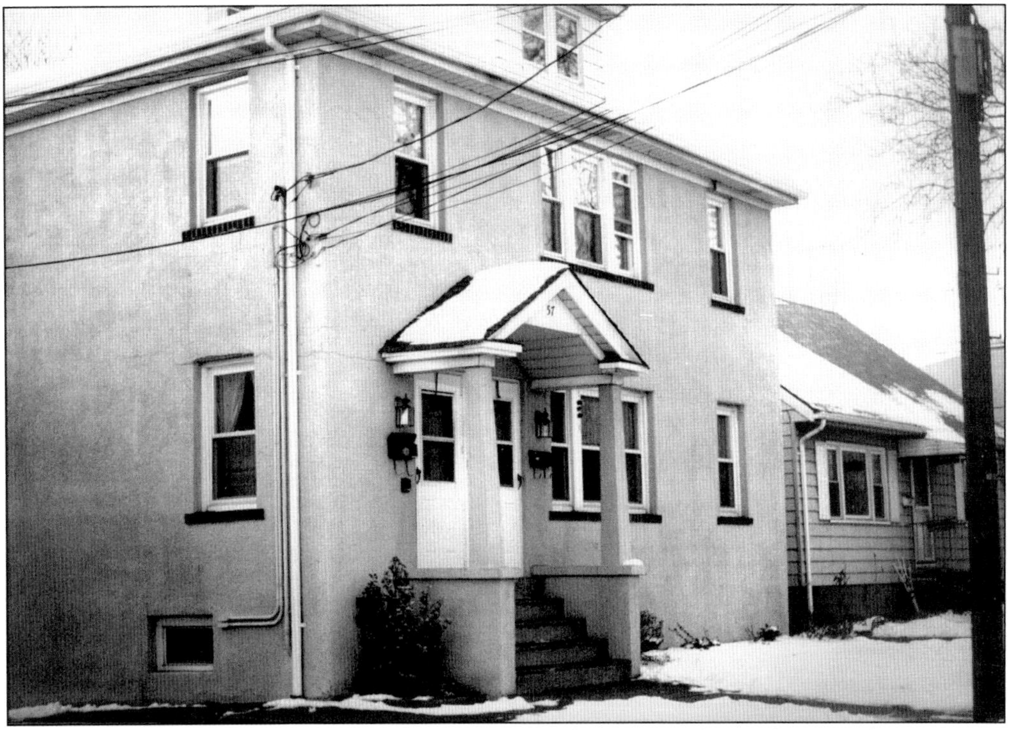

Shown is an example of a Nicholas Spadola house. This home is located on Tenth Street.

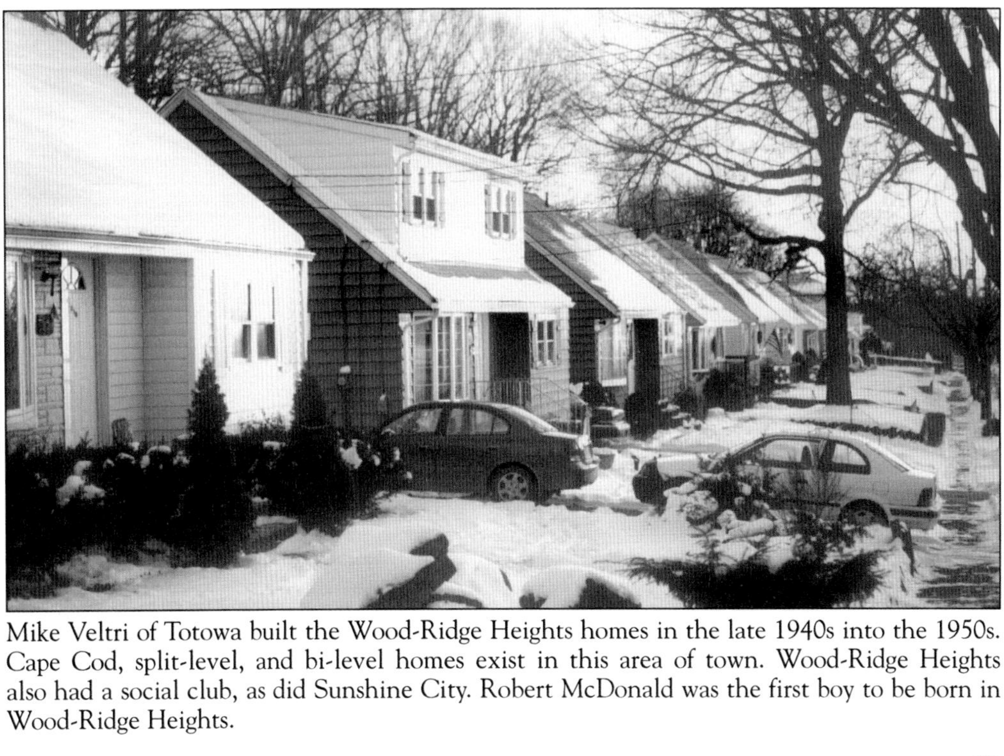

Mike Veltri of Totowa built the Wood-Ridge Heights homes in the late 1940s into the 1950s. Cape Cod, split-level, and bi-level homes exist in this area of town. Wood-Ridge Heights also had a social club, as did Sunshine City. Robert McDonald was the first boy to be born in Wood-Ridge Heights.

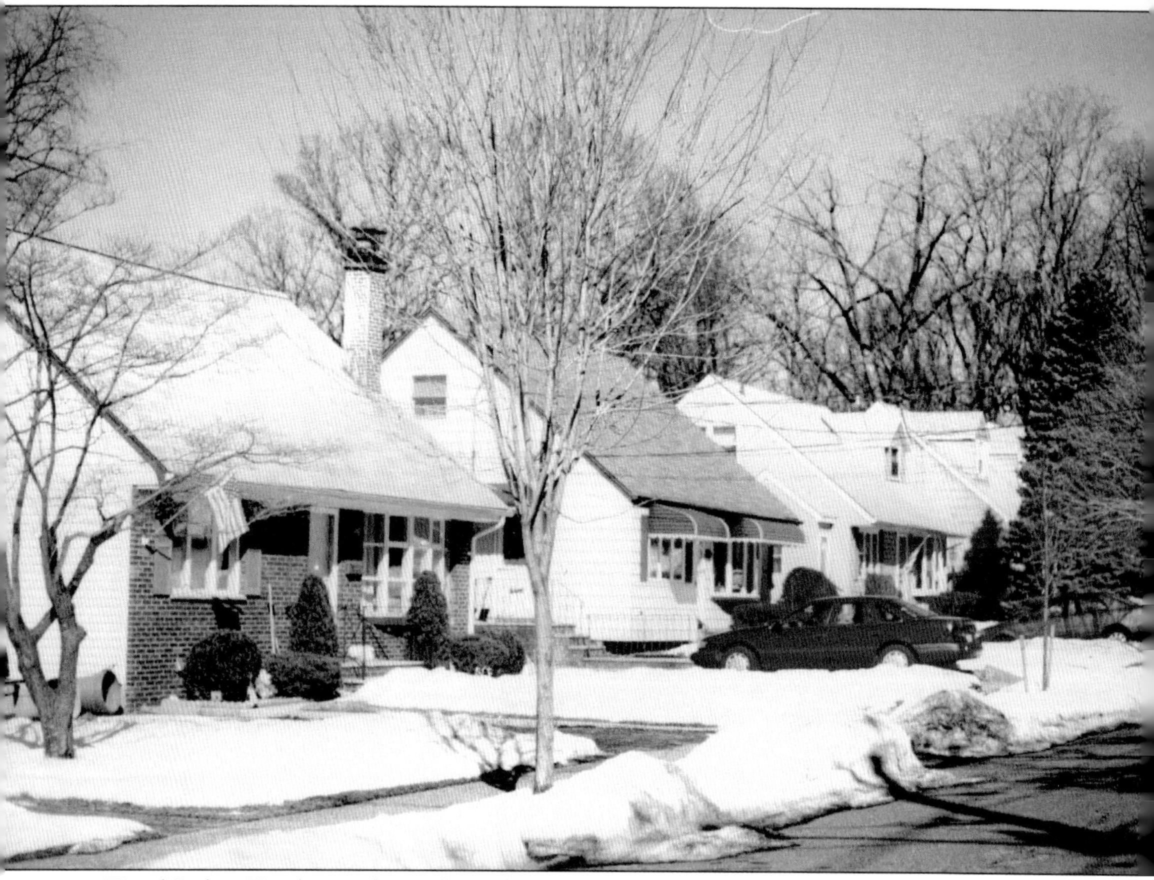

Wood-Ridge Heights is located in the area that was called "back the hill" by longtime residents. Many of the original owners and their families still live there. This postwar housing development brought in numerous families with children. This is one of the main reasons for the construction of Catherine Doyle School. As with all of Wood-Ridge, the Wood-Ridge Heights area was a good place to raise a family. There were always children to play with and many places to explore, such as wooded areas and Burma Road, which surrounded Curtiss-Wright. A favorite pastime of the children was to watch the helicopters land at the army camp located in Wallington, right across the Bergen Short Cut Railroad line.

Seven

SUNSHINE CITY

One of the most ambitious undertakings in housing development was the result of the vision of a young real estate broker named Charles Reis. At the age of 21, Reis entered the homebuilding business when he began construction of more than 10,000 homes in River Edge, Tenafly, Englewood, Oradell, Clifton, Englewood Cliffs, and Paramus.

During the late 1920s, Reis envisioned a development of small and moderate sized, well-built homes convenient to New York City and surrounding cities. His plan attracted much attention among those in the local building area. He purchased the land west of Hackensack Street between Marlboro and Sussex Roads and parts of Lincoln Avenue southwest of Valley Boulevard. The development ended at the wooded area near the western boundary of town. There, he built approximately 1,000 homes.

In September 1927, the founding of Sunshine City, as this development was named, formally began with a celebration. At that time a model of the one-family home was introduced to the public. It was estimated that the population would increase by some 5,000 people.

One of the highlights of Sunshine City was the spectacular view of the New York skyline, which residents in the elevated areas of town would see. The original flyers and newspapers advertised it as overlooking Times Square.

The development of Sunshine City brought great change to Wood-Ridge. Families moved here from the cities, and the need for more services quickly became apparent.

Government services increased, and civic groups were formed. Before Sunshine City was built, Wood-Ridge retained a country feel, with many farms still being operated. With Sunshine City, Wood-Ridge became part of modern suburbia. Other housing developments followed, as more people looked to live in a family-friendly community such as Wood-Ridge.

The new residents formed an organization called the Wood-Ridge Manor Community Club. Its members were concerned with many aspects of community living. They encouraged attendance at school board meetings and eventually supported plans to build a local high school. (Previously, Wood-Ridge students attended out of town high schools.)

They saw the need for police to ensure the safe crossing of schoolchildren on Valley Boulevard and Hackensack Street and the problems that arose as more people began owning automobiles.

The club printed a monthly newsletter to inform residents of happenings in town, including church events, youth activities, public health and safety issues, Scouting news, and civic activities. During the Great Depression, the newsletter reported on relief efforts. Throughout

World War II, it provided updates on local people in the armed services.

The Manor Club also featured a garden club that hosted an annual flower show. One of the goals of the organization was to encourage the owners of the new homes to beautify their property by landscaping.

One of the later newsletters of the 1950s concerns the expansion of Teterboro Airport and the dangers of planes taking off and landing near residential areas. As early as 1928, when Sunshine City was first built and the organization formed, it was suggested that a delegation spur the mayor and council to do something about low-flying planes in the area. These concerns remain the same today.

The club remained in existence through the 1950s. Sunshine City and its residents changed the landscape of Wood-Ridge, as well as the role citizens played.

This is an early advertisement for Sunshine City, developed by Charles Reis.

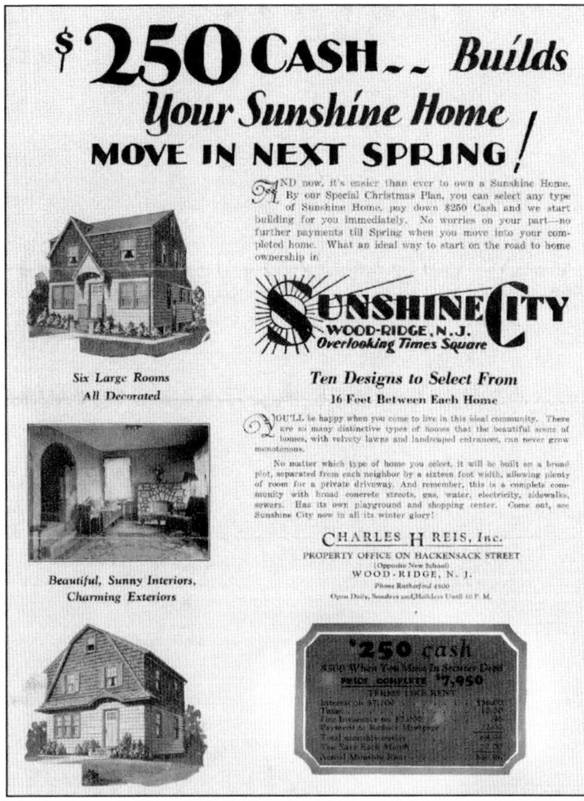

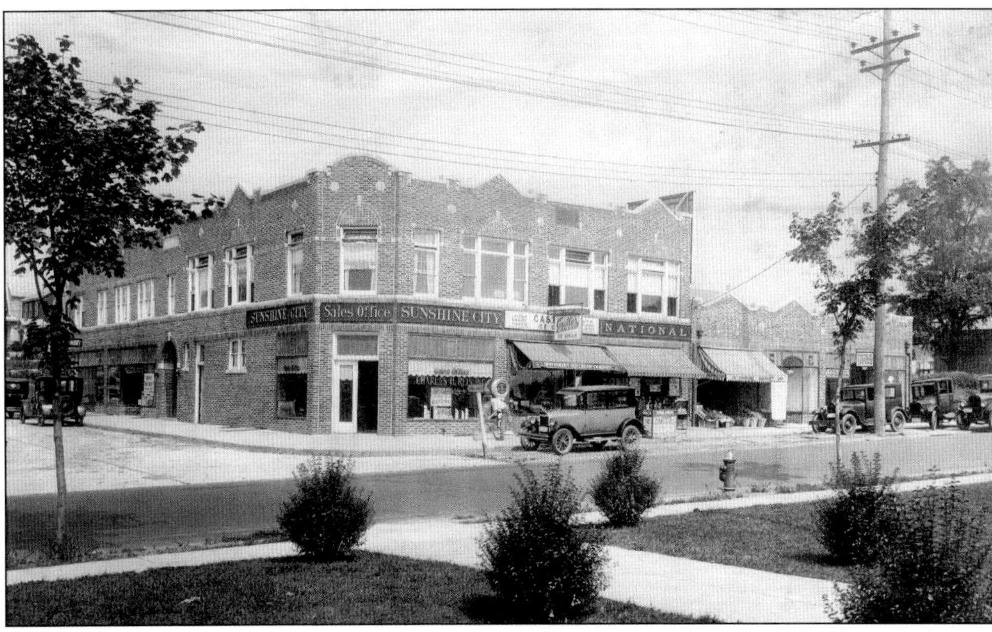

This photograph shows a later sales office for Sunshine City. The original office was located across the street where a multistoried apartment building now stands. The original sales office building was then moved behind the Brinkerhoff-Brandenburg House, where it became the Baptist church and, later, the civic center.

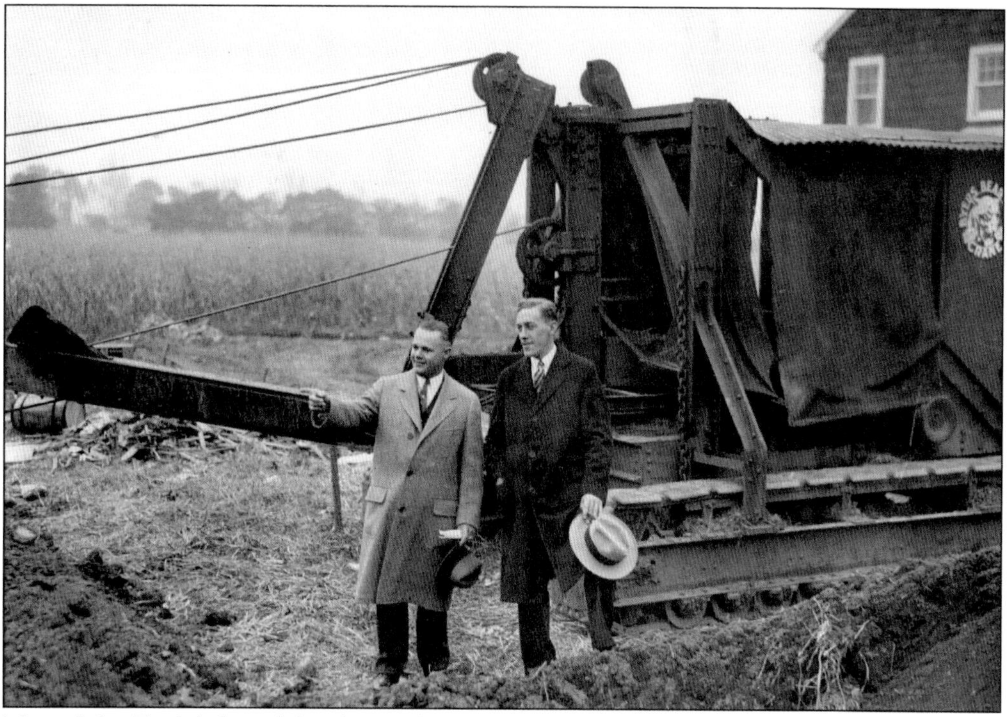

Mayor John Ford, left, and developer Charles Reis look over the Brandenburg farm during the construction of Sunshine City *c.* 1928.

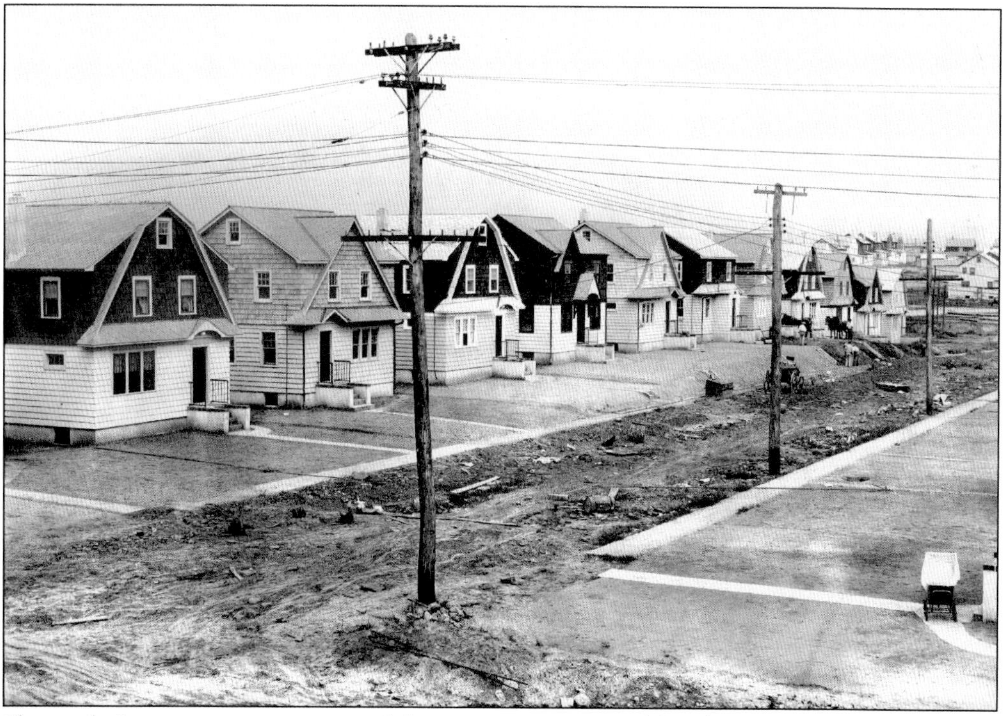

Shown during construction is one of the numerous streets of Sunshine City. William Mueller was the first baby boy to be born in Sunshine City. He continues to reside there.

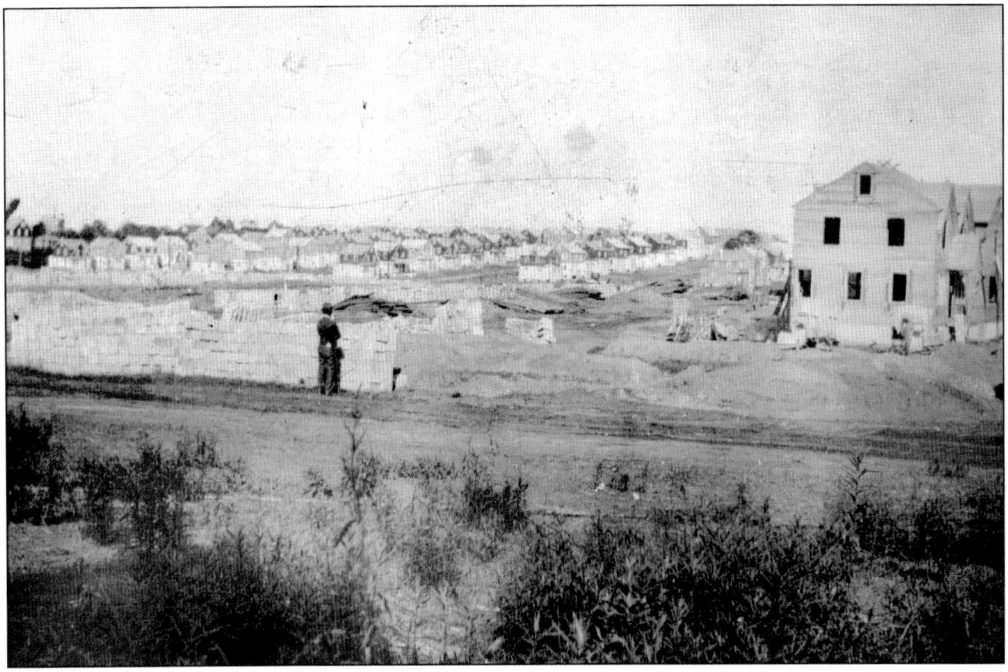

This photograph shows Sunshine City while under construction *c.* 1927.

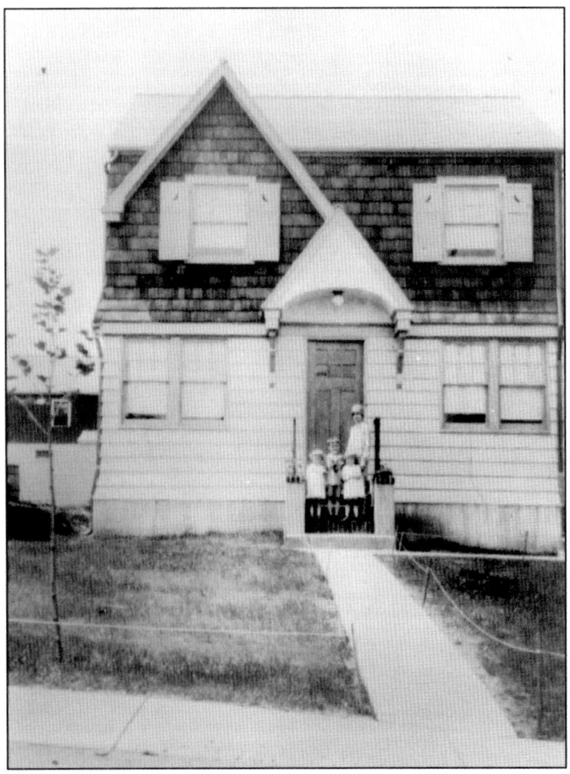

The original owners of 422 Innes Road were the Salmons. From left to right are Joseph, Martha, and Mary Salmon, with an aunt. This photograph was taken on July 8, 1928.

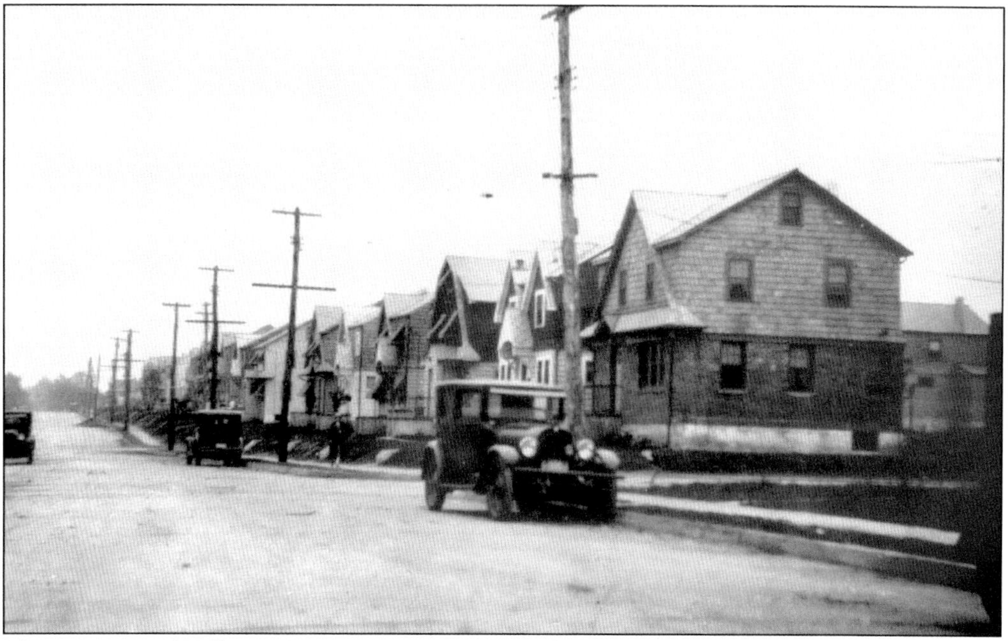

This is a view of Hillcrest Avenue near Sussex Road *c.* 1930.

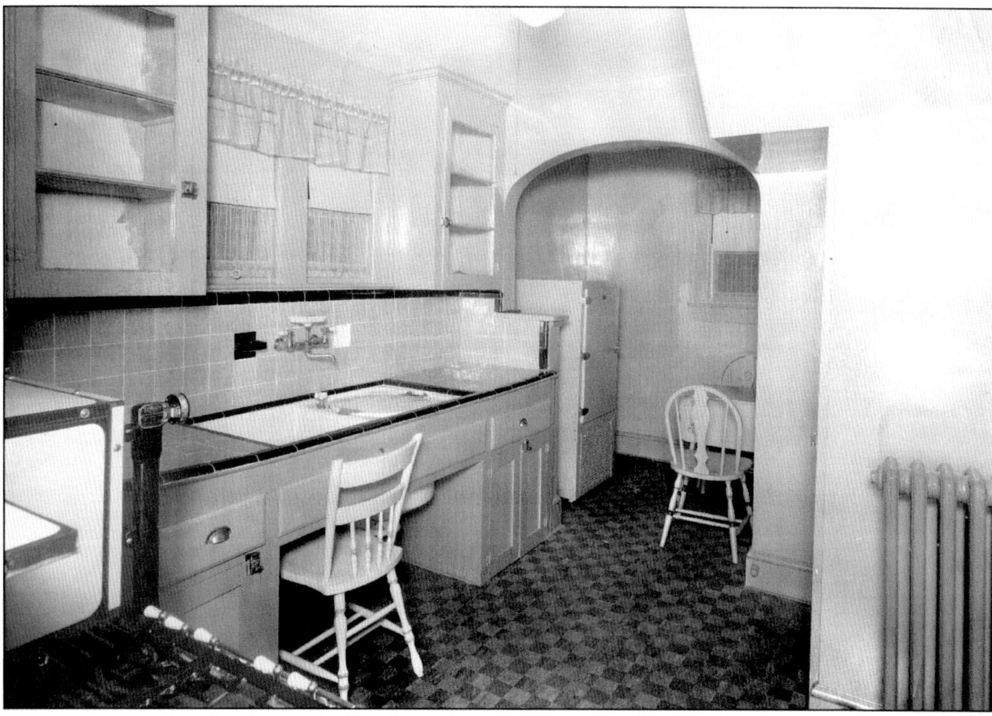

Here is the modern kitchen of a Sunshine City house. Note the Walker dishwasher in the right side of the sink. Some of the features these homes boasted were American Radiator steam heat with low radiators, American Standard plumbing fixtures, copper plumbing, General Electric wiring, tiled kitchen with breakfast nook, and in some models, the Walker electric dishwasher, which was very modern for the time.

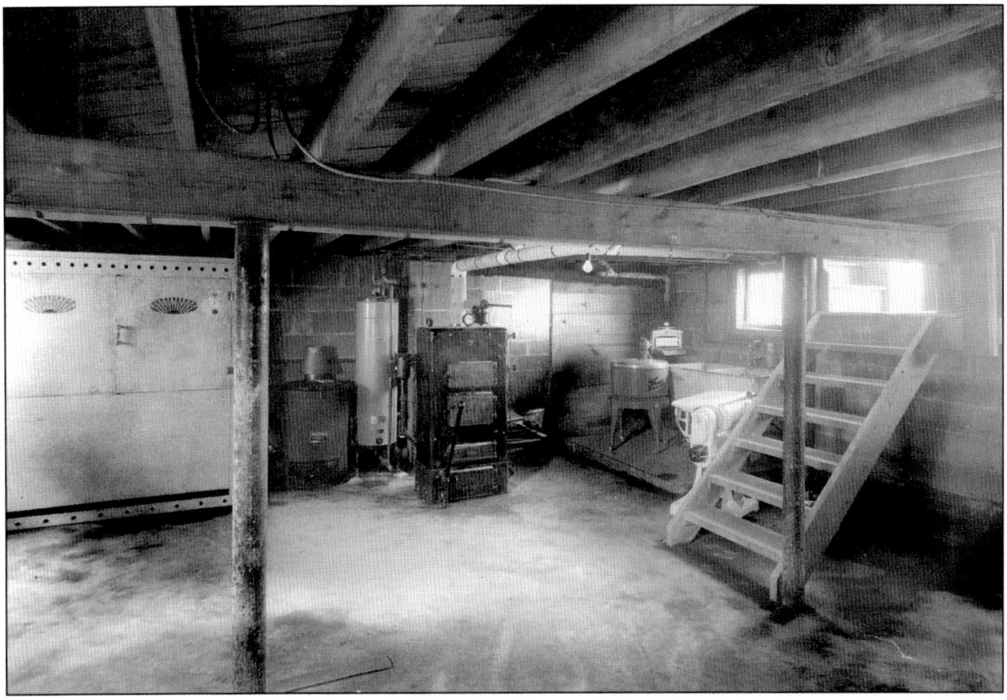

Shown are the modern conveniences that could be found in the basement of a Sunshine City house *c.* 1930. Many homes were open for inspection on Sunday afternoons.

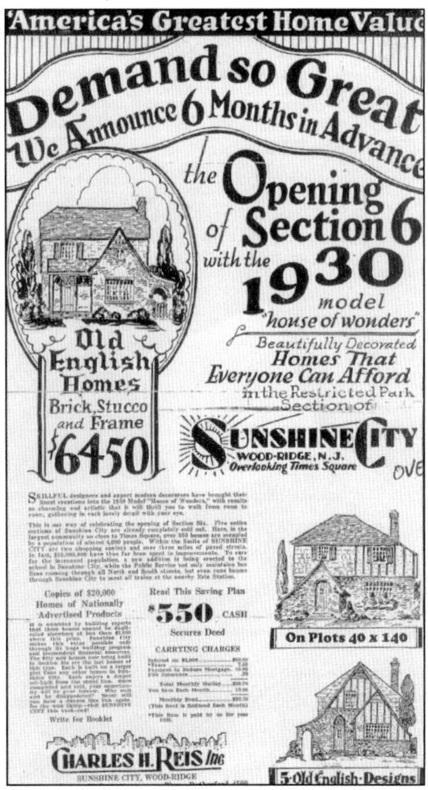

This *c.* 1929 advertisement is for the Manor section of Sunshine City, the last section to be built. It is a neighborhood of Old English–style houses of brick, stucco, and frame. The houses, although small, were considered charming, with lovely details at a low cost that everyone could afford, according to the advertisements. The houses were built partly in a hilly area, and many of the old ash and maple trees were left intact. The roads west of Tenth Street became dead ends and abutted parts of the last remaining woods in Wood-Ridge, thus adding a country feeling for the residents.

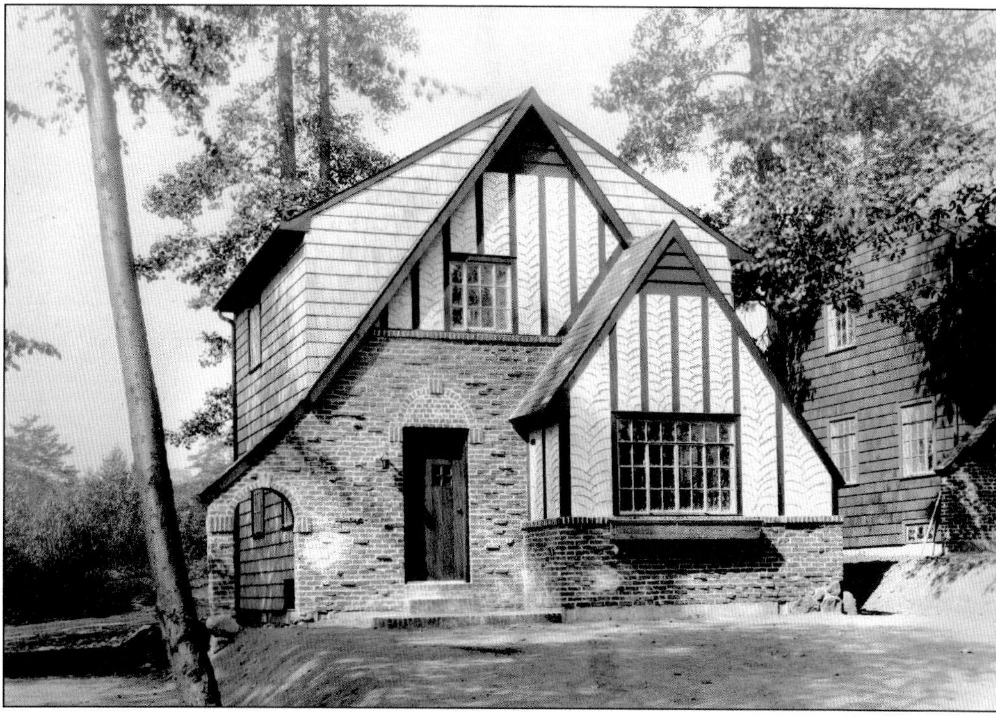

This is a typical Tudor-style Sunshine City home. The photograph dates from *c.* 1929.

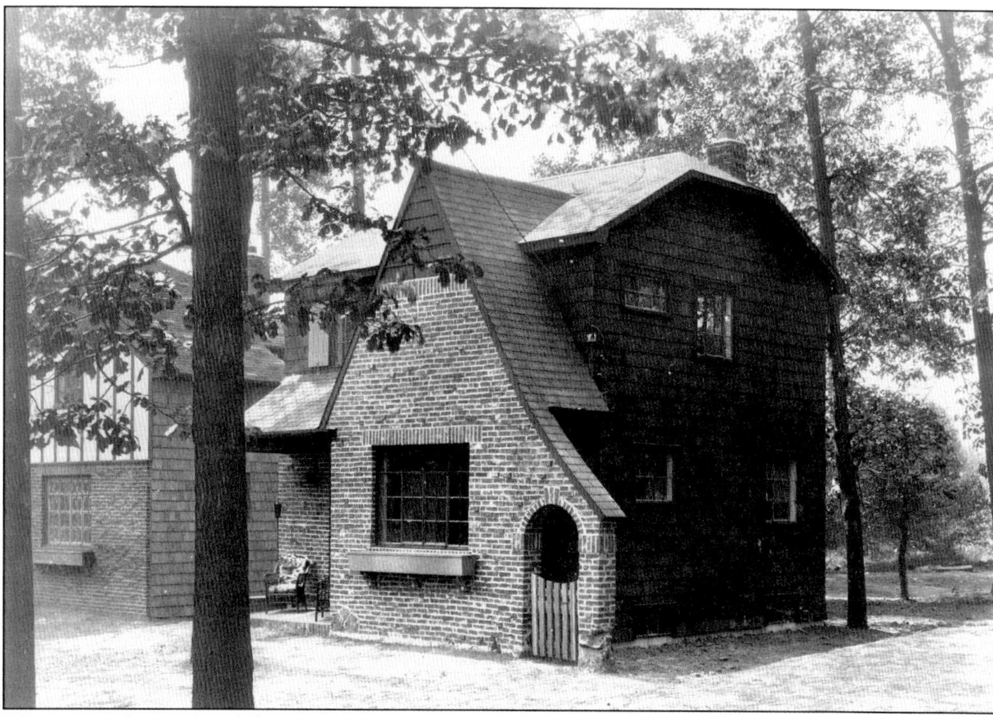

This is another style of the Tudor version of the Sunshine City home *c.* 1929. Not many houses were built in the development with this roofline. This home is located on Marlboro Road.

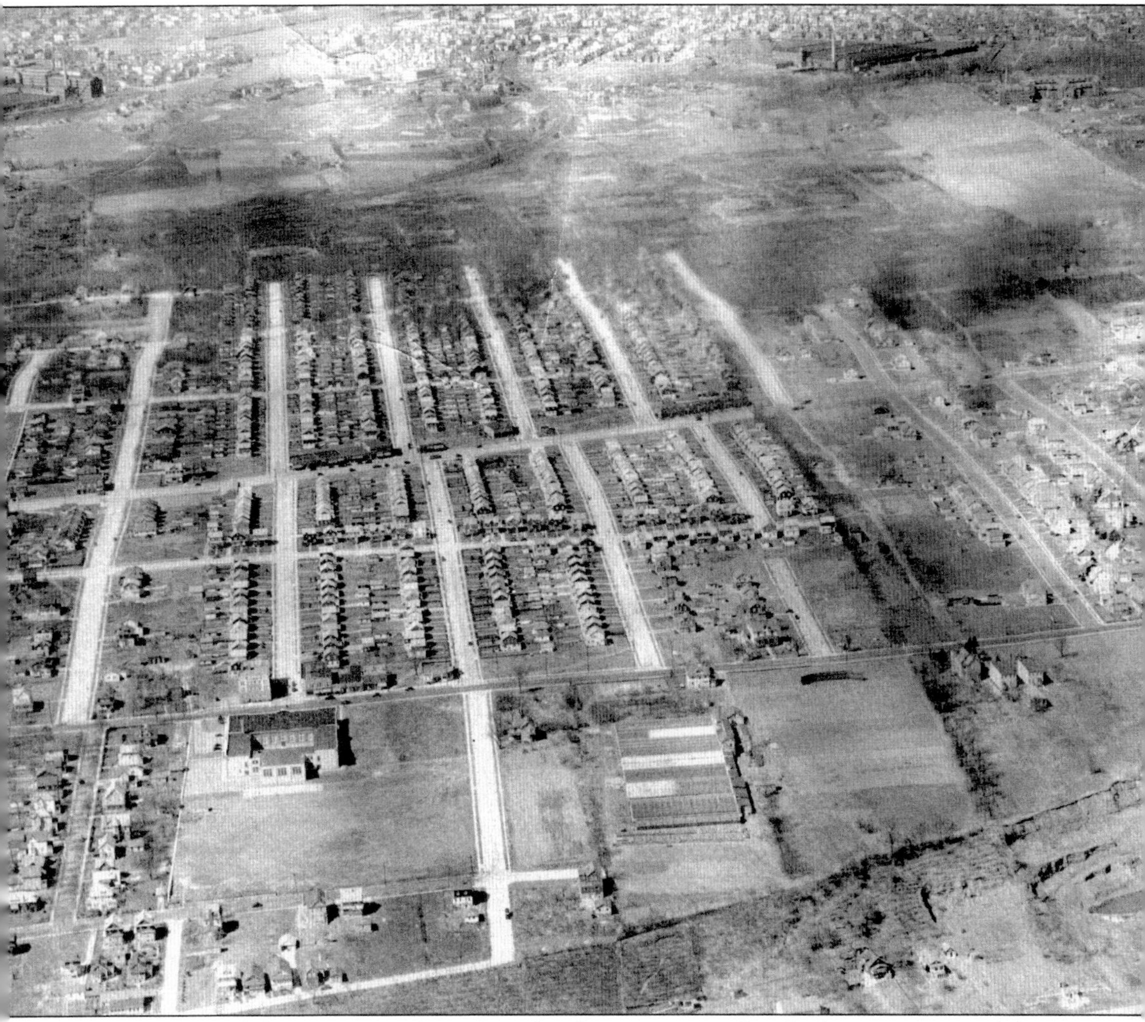

This aerial view of the entire Sunshine City development was taken looking west toward the Saddle River in 1928.

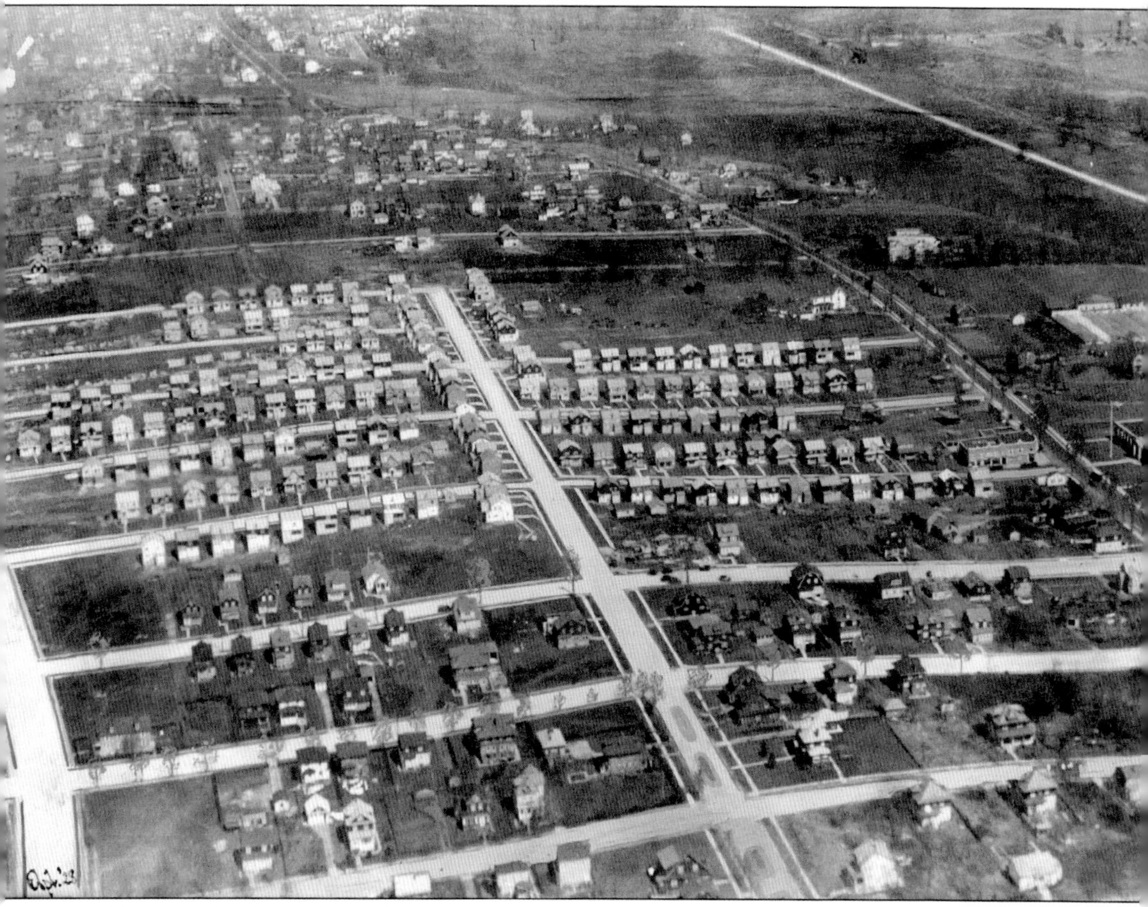

This aerial view of Sunshine City was taken *c.* 1928 looking north toward Hasbrouck Heights.

Eight

CURTISS-WRIGHT

Until the United States entered World War II, Wood-Ridge had remained a residential town with farmland and woods still covering much of the area. In the spring of 1939, the Wright Aeronautical Corporation (Curtiss-Wright) received approval to build its largest plant in the country in the northwest corner of Wood-Ridge, on land acquired from the Standard Oil Company and the remaining parts of the Brandenburg farm. Construction equipment (some of which is said to have been used on the Boulder Dam project) was operated by hordes of men to grade the land in preparation for the windowless, red-brick two-story facility. Due to the nature of the work to be done at Wright's, the plant was completed in record time. By October 1942, the first machine was in operation. In January 1943, the first Cyclone 18 engines assembled in Wood-Ridge were packed and ready for shipment to an airframe factory.

The plant was a state-of-the-art facility equipped with the latest and finest precision instruments available at the time. Workers were trained to run the automated machines in a matter of days. Laborsaving devices were installed in order to ensure that quality products were manufactured rapidly. Built specifically to mass-produce fighter-bomber engines (for the Flying Fortress, the Super Fortress, the P-36, Fighter Hawks, and P-40 War Hawks), the Wood-Ridge plant had turned out more than 140,000 of them by the end of World War II.

When the plant was completed, both men and women were hired, many without factory experience, to man the operation. Bus companies arranged additional routes and schedules to bring the workers to and from work from areas north and south of Wood-Ridge, as well as from New York City. Traffic increased due to the automobile entrance to the parking lot at the Highland Avenue gate. During the height of war production, some 20,000 people worked at the plant around the clock.

A merger of the Wright brothers and pioneer aviator Glenn Curtiss formed Curtiss-Wright in 1929. The company's legacy includes the planes that sent Charles Lindbergh and Amelia Earhart over the Atlantic and Adm. Richard Byrd over the North Pole. The engines for the *Enola Gay*, which flew over Hiroshima, were built at the Wood-Ridge plant. Lindbergh even visited the top-secret section of the Wood-Ridge plant in 1953.

Once workers were inside the building, day turned into night and night into day. The plant ran 24 hours a day, 7 days a week. It had a full cafeteria for its employees, who were served full-course meals on all shifts. The company provided a staffed hospital and ambulance, as well as a full-time paid fire department, aided by male volunteers who worked in the plant. The work done at Wright's was highly classified, and the facility was kept under tight security. The presence of the military in the area became a common occurrence, as the plant was guarded at all times.

In June 1945, when the war in Europe was over, a B-29 called *Thumper* flew over the Wood-Ridge plant as a tribute to the workers at Curtiss-Wright. All of the employees were asked to go outside to wave to the pilots.

Curtiss-Wright began to lose its lead in aviation after the war. The famous bomber engines were insufficient for commercial passenger planes. Because the government wanted the company to concentrate on bomber engines, it did not award Curtiss-Wright funding for jet engine research. The company continued to operate in Wood-Ridge through the postwar years and then officially notified the borough in the early 1980s that it was terminating its operation here. The property was sold in 2001, and plans are under way for redevelopment. Once again, the landscape will change as it did in 1942.

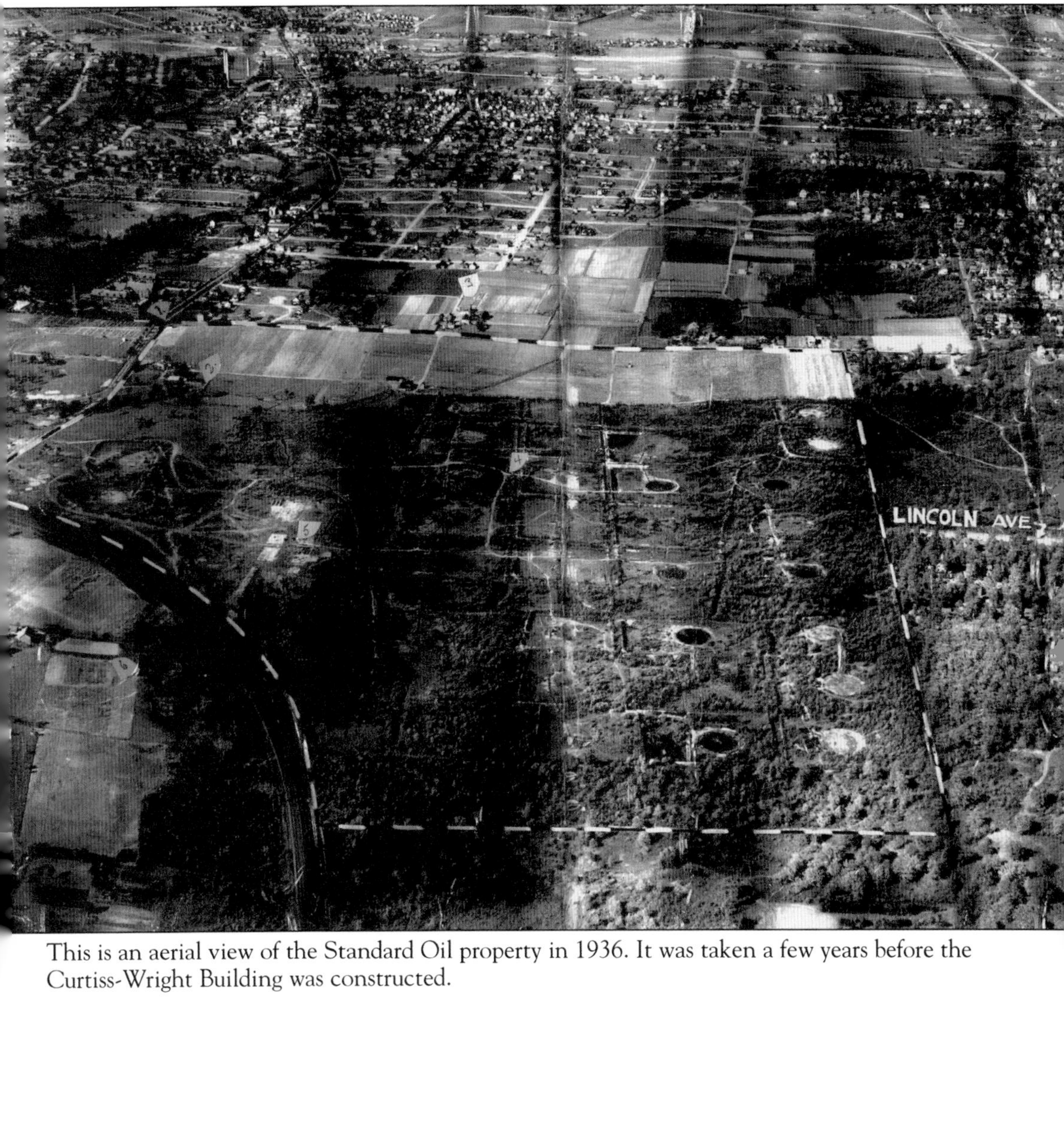

This is an aerial view of the Standard Oil property in 1936. It was taken a few years before the Curtiss-Wright Building was constructed.

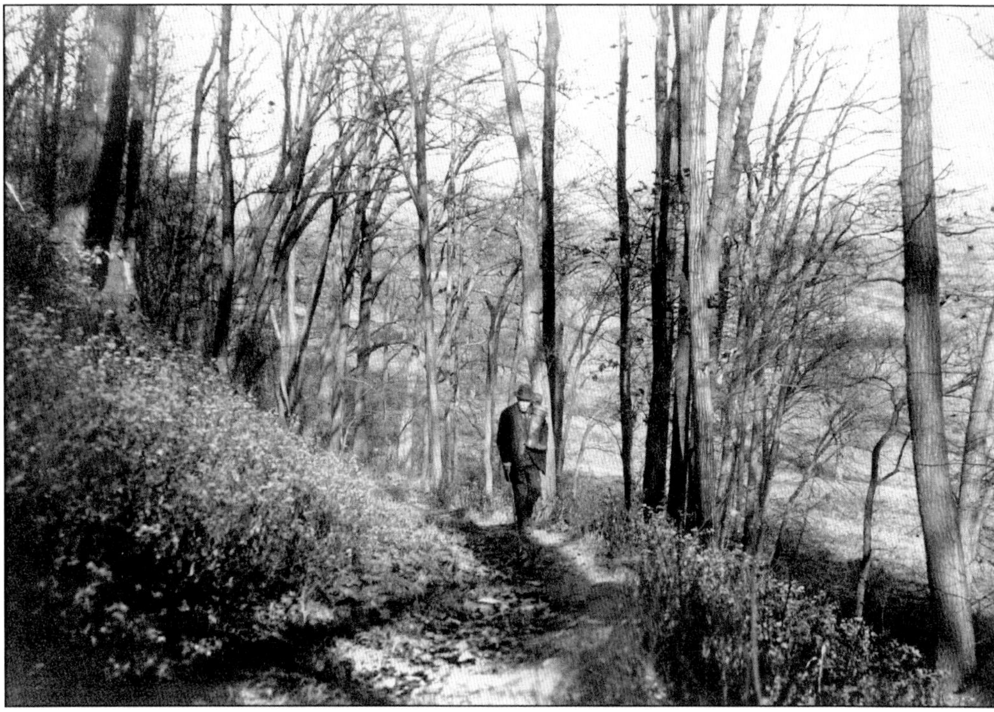

A Standard Oil watchman walks the pipeline in Wood-Ridge *c.* 1915.

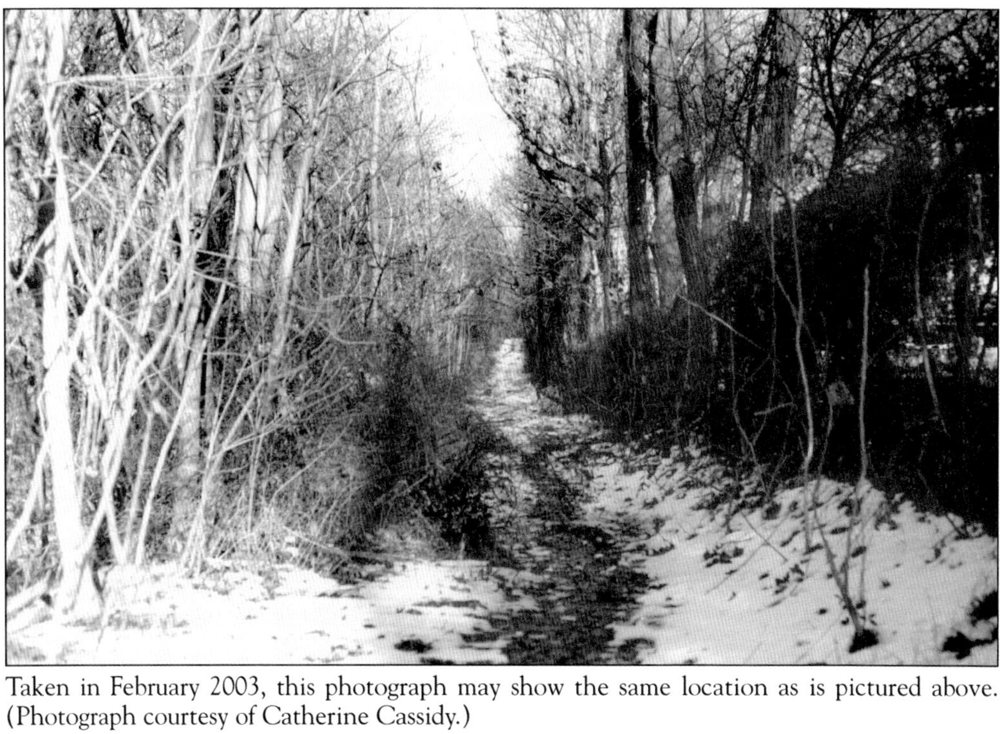

Taken in February 2003, this photograph may show the same location as is pictured above. (Photograph courtesy of Catherine Cassidy.)

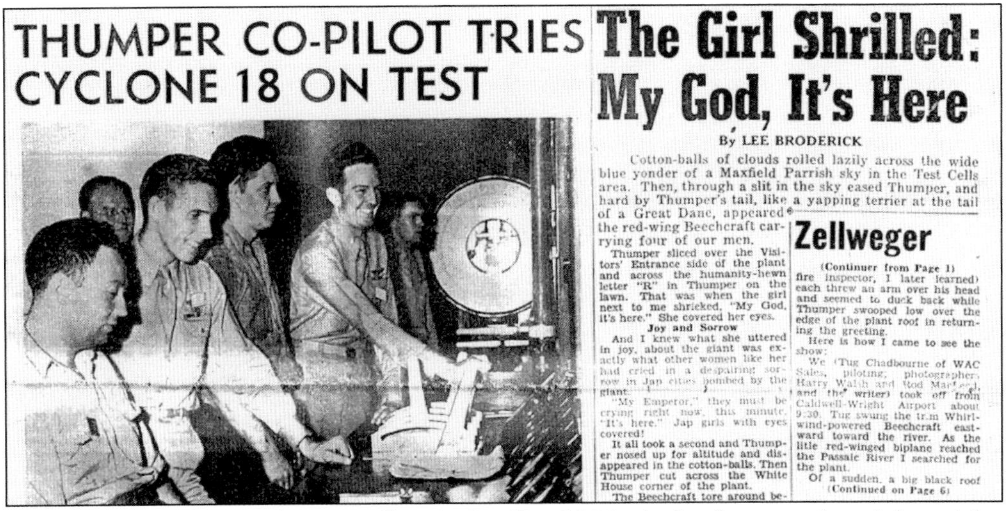

THUMPER CO-PILOT TRIES CYCLONE 18 ON TEST

The Girl Shrilled: My God, It's Here

By LEE BRODERICK

Cotton-balls of clouds rolled lazily across the wide blue yonder of a Maxfield Parrish sky in the Test Cells area. Then, through a slit in the sky eased Thumper, and hard by Thumper's tail, like a yapping terrier at the tail of a Great Dane, appeared the red-wing Beechcraft carrying four of our men.

Thumper sliced over the Visitors' Entrance side of the plant and across the humanity-hewn letter "R" in Thumper on the lawn. That was when the girl next to me shrieked, "My God, it's here." She covered her eyes.

Joy and Sorrow

And I knew what she uttered in joy, about the giant was exactly what other women like her had cried in a despairing sorrow in Jap cities bombed by the giant.

"My Emperor," they must be crying right now, this minute. "It's here." Jap girls with eyes covered!

It all took a second and Thumper nosed up for altitude and disappeared in the cotton-balls. Then Thumper cut across the White House corner of the plant.

The Beechcraft tore around be-

Zellweger

(Continuer from Page 1)

fire inspector, I later learned) each threw an arm over his head and seemed to duck back while Thumper swooped low over the edge of the plant roof in returning the greeting.

Here is how I came to see the show:

We (Tug Chadbourne of WAC Sales, piloting; photographers Harry Walsh and Rod MacLeod, and the writer) took off from Caldwell-Wright Airport about 9:30. Tug swung the trim Whirlwind-powered Beechcraft eastward toward the river. As the litle red-winged biplane reached the Passaic River I searched for the plant.

Of a sudden, a big black roof

(Continued on Page 6)

Trying out an engine in the test cell is 1st Lt. Harold Morris. Looking on, from left to right, are Herman Abraham, S.Sgt. Neal Shively, and gunner Al Kruger. The photograph was taken in June 1945.

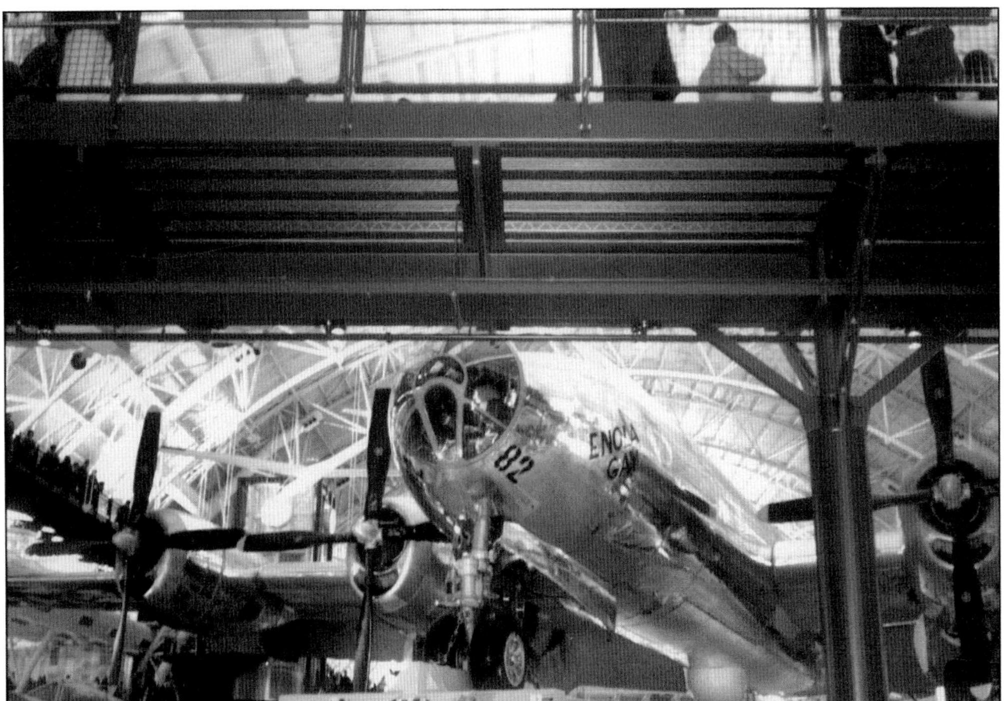

Shown here is the refurbished *Enola Gay*, with its engines made at the Curtiss-Wright Wood-Ridge facility. The photograph was taken at the Steven F. Udvar Hazy Center in Chantilly, Virginia, the newest Smithsonian facility. (Photograph courtesy of Ron and Nancy Williams.)

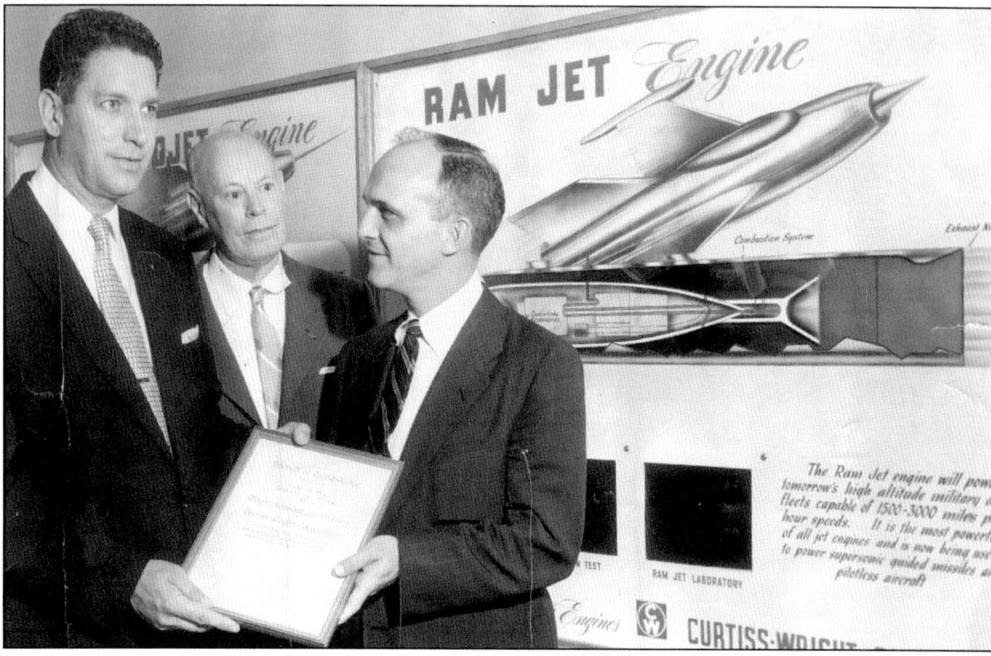

Mayor Clarence Mathe, left, presents a testimonial to officials of Curtiss-Wright. The testimonial reads "friendship, and appreciation for a pleasant and co-operative association of many years." (Photograph courtesy of the borough of Wood-Ridge.)

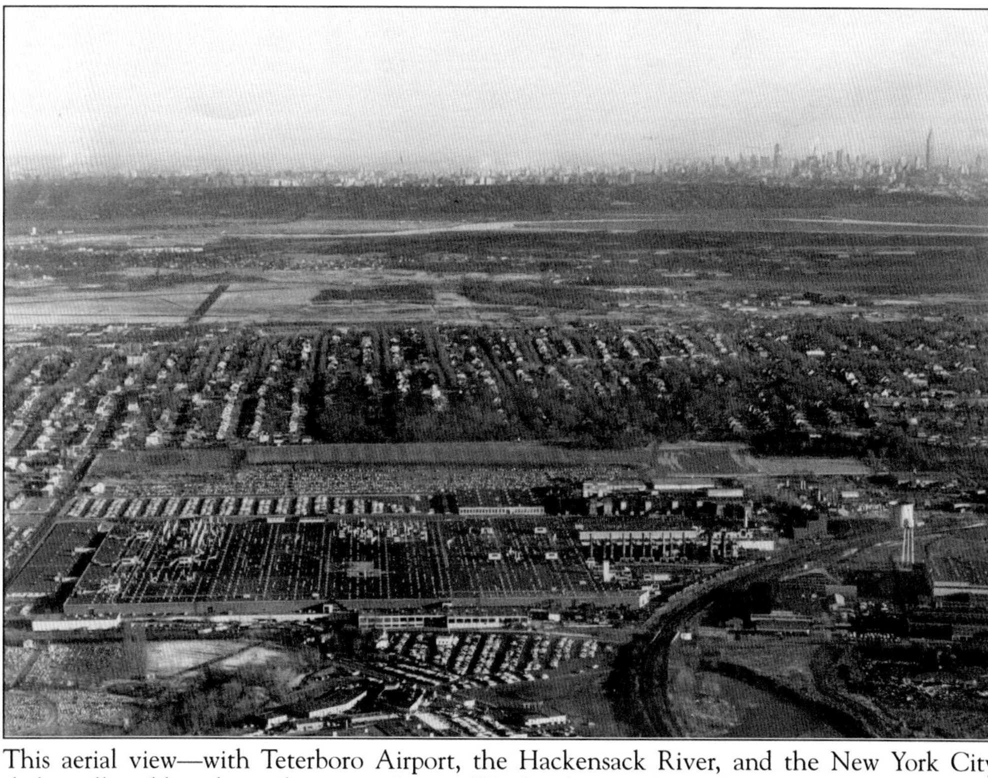

This aerial view—with Teterboro Airport, the Hackensack River, and the New York City skyline all visible—shows the entire Curtiss-Wright plant in the 1950s.

Nine

Wood-Ridge Today

Every generation witnesses change. In the early years, the people of Wood-Ridge saw horse-drawn carriages and wagons give way to automobiles, and farmlands turn into neighborhoods. Law enforcement consisting of one constable or marshal evolved into an efficient police department, and the fire department moved from using original apparatus to acquiring modern new equipment. Schools evolved from the first one-room schoolhouse to the full educational systems, both public and parochial, that Wood-Ridge boasts today. Civic organizations and borough commissions continue to enhance the lives of everyone. Changes will continue into the future. Anyone coming back for a visit after being away from Wood-Ridge for many years will be surprised at the new look in town but will remember with nostalgia the charm that this small community continues to offer.

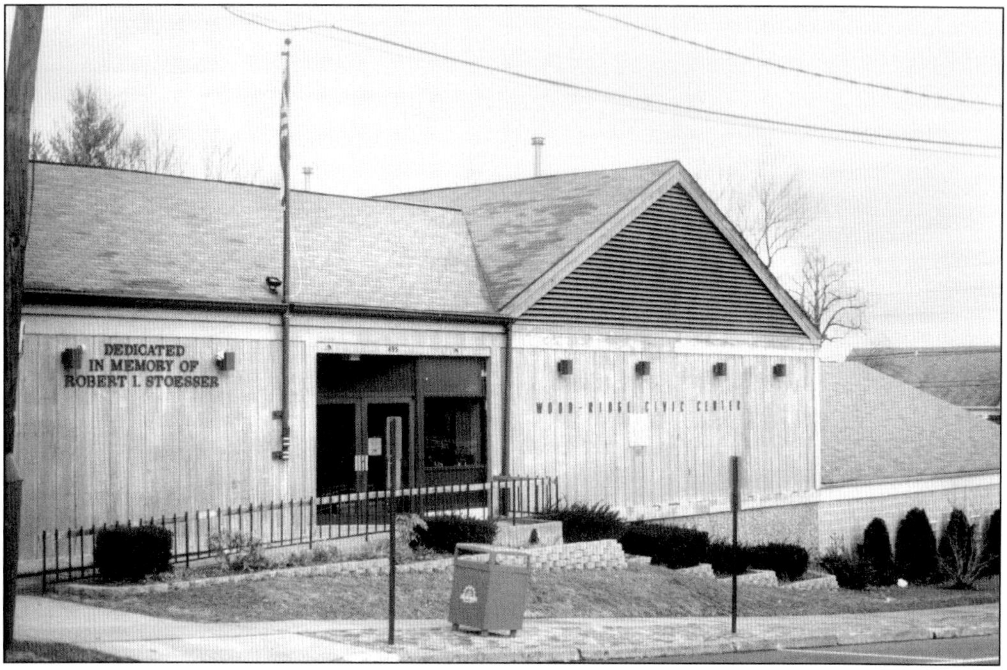

The Wood-Ridge Civic Center was dedicated in memory of Robert Stoesser, known as "Mr. Wood-Ridge." The First Baptist Church once stood here. It later served as the civic center until 1974, when the present building was constructed. A senior center was added in the 1990s.

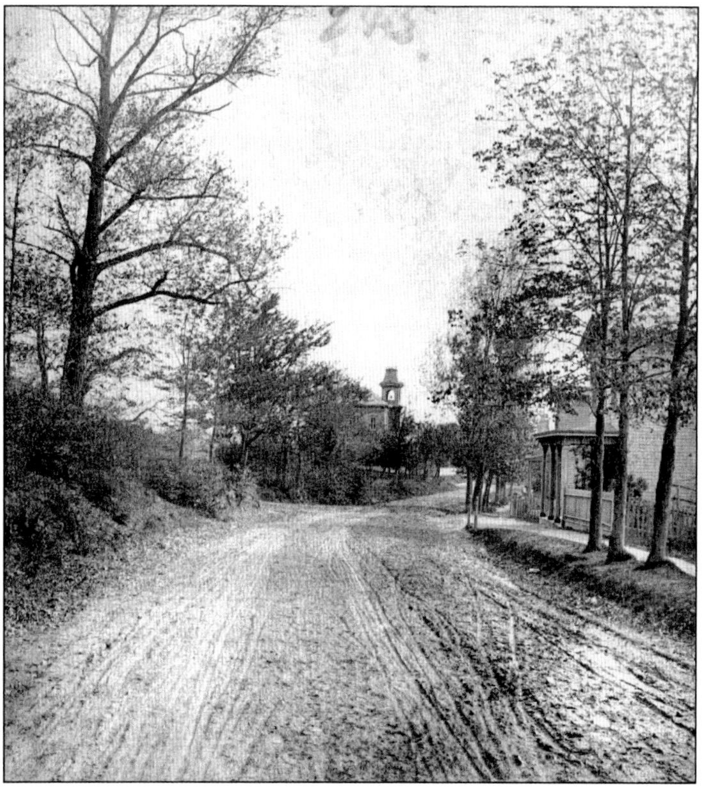

Hackensack Street is pictured in the late 19th century. Schiesswohl Bakery is on the right. This photograph was taken approximately a half block from Center Street. The bell tower of Mount Pleasant School is visible in the background.

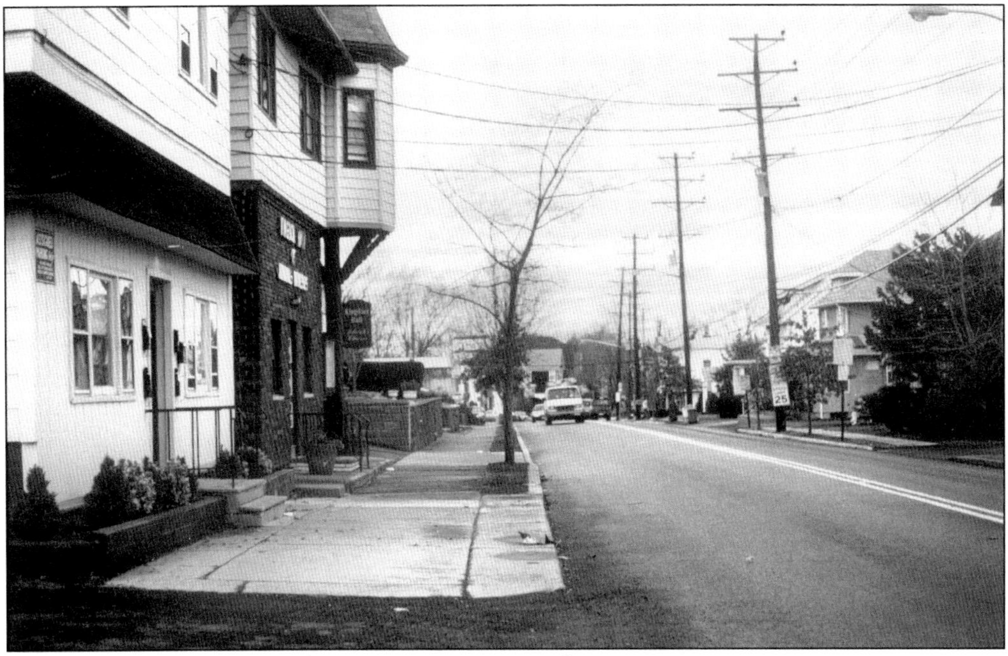

Here is a view of Hackensack Street as it appears today.

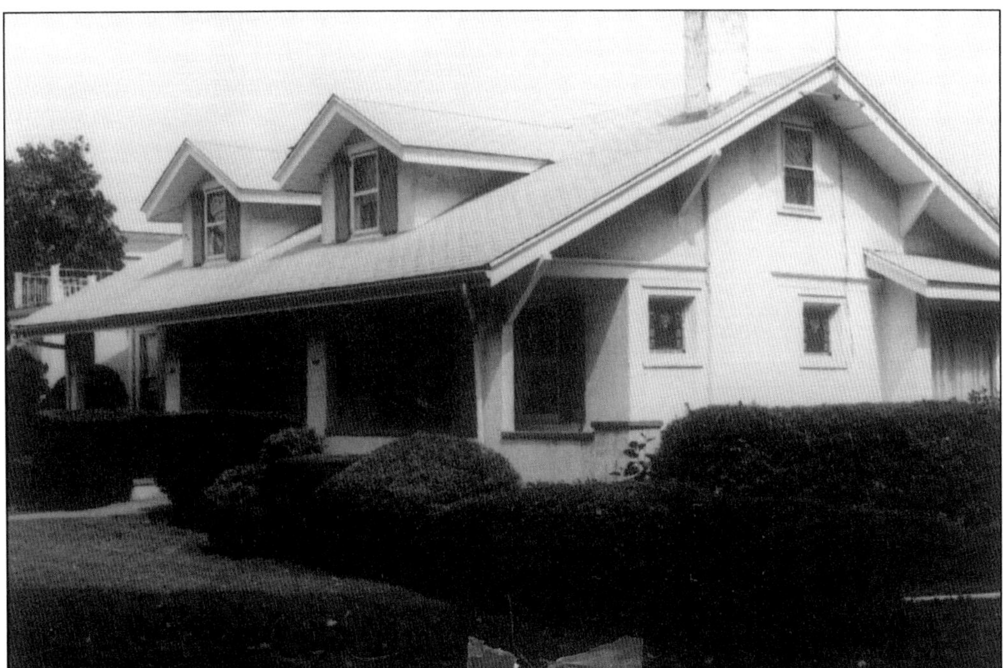

The Henry Brandenburg-Young bungalow was built in the early 1920s. The home was located next to the high school.

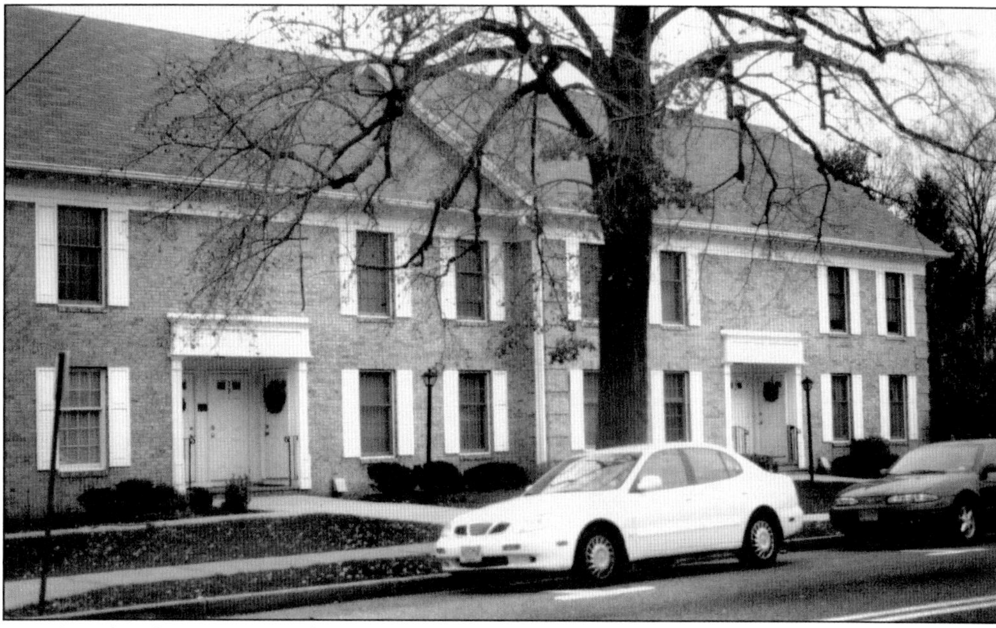

Another development was that of Ashley at Wood-Ridge. In 1986, the developers of the land where the Young family house once stood proposed a 14-unit condominium complex at the corner of Ryerson Avenue and Hackensack Street. Variances were twice approved and then negated by appellate court panels. Area residents banded together and formed Residents Against Indiscriminate Development (RAID) to fight this development. When this occurred, Ashley proposed changing the constructed building into two offices. The offices were also rejected. Finally, in 1991, the area was rezoned to multifamily housing, allowing the existing eight units to be completed.

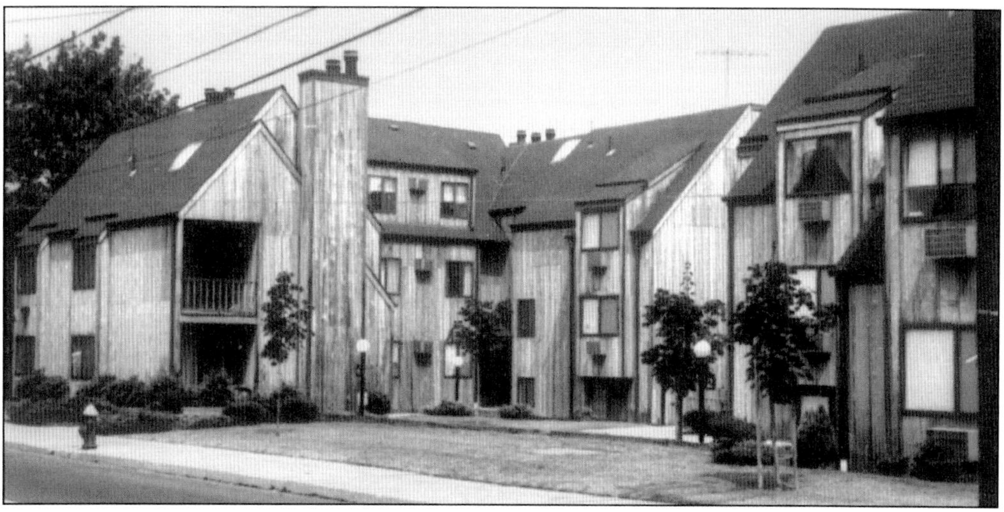

A 22-unit apartment complex called the Hilltopper Condominiums stands at the top of Hackensack Street on the Carlstadt border—the site of the old Hilltop Tavern, where the first mayor and council meeting was held on January 15, 1895. The complex was designed by architect Robert Gilchrist, designer of the Stoesser Civic Center, and was built by Rottini Construction Company. Former New York Yankee player and manager Billy Martin resided here at one time.

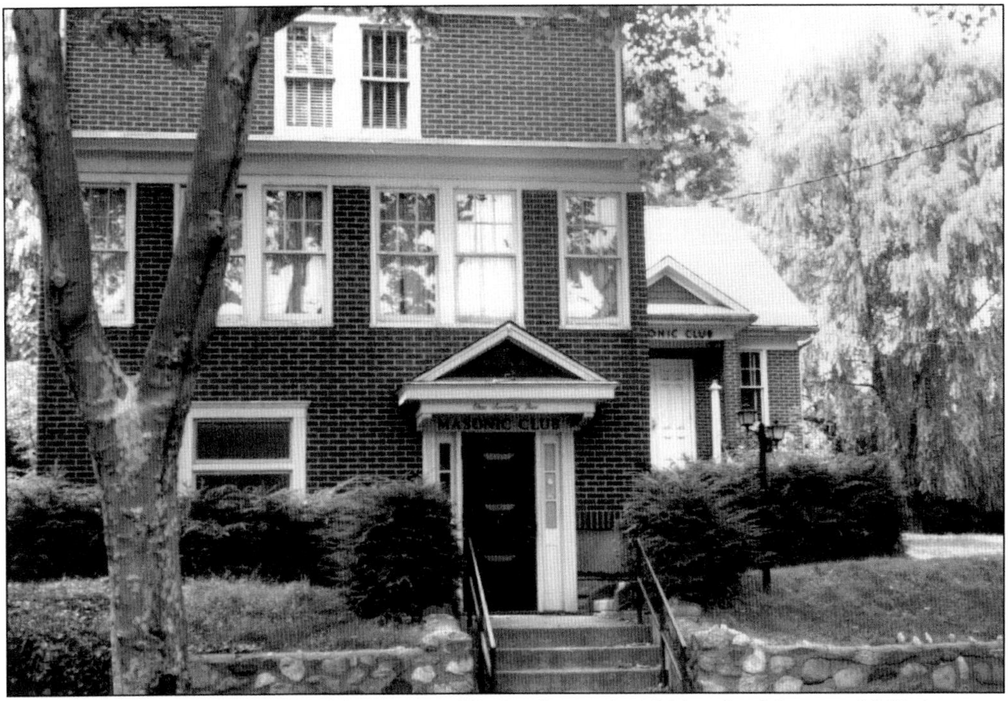

The Masonic Club is pictured here in 1975. In the early 1990s, the Masonic Hall that was located on Madison Street was torn down and replaced with two modern single-family homes. The inability of the Masons to sustain the hall led to it being demolished.

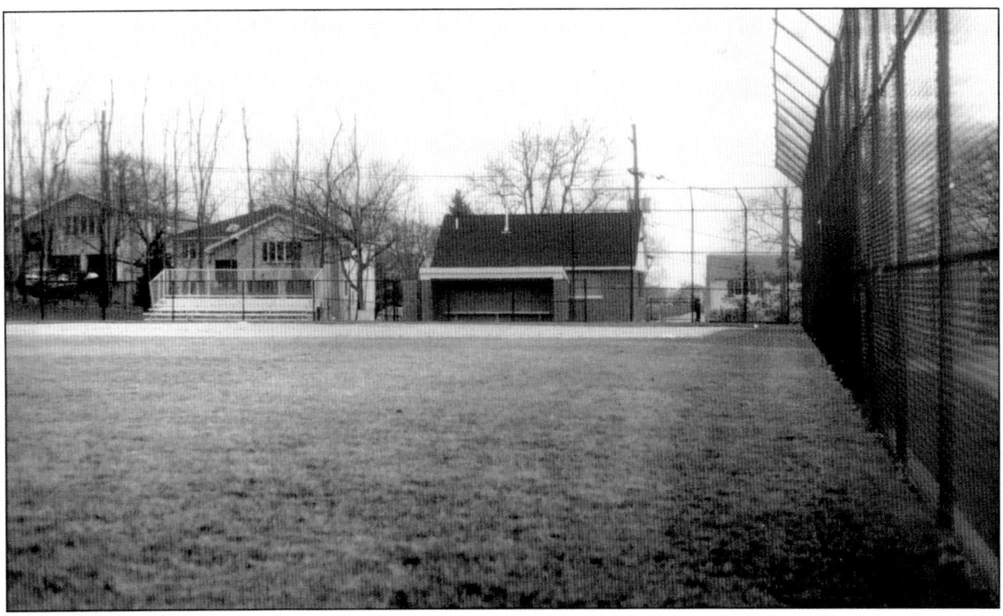

Pictured here is the newly completed field on the former Cello-Film Company site.

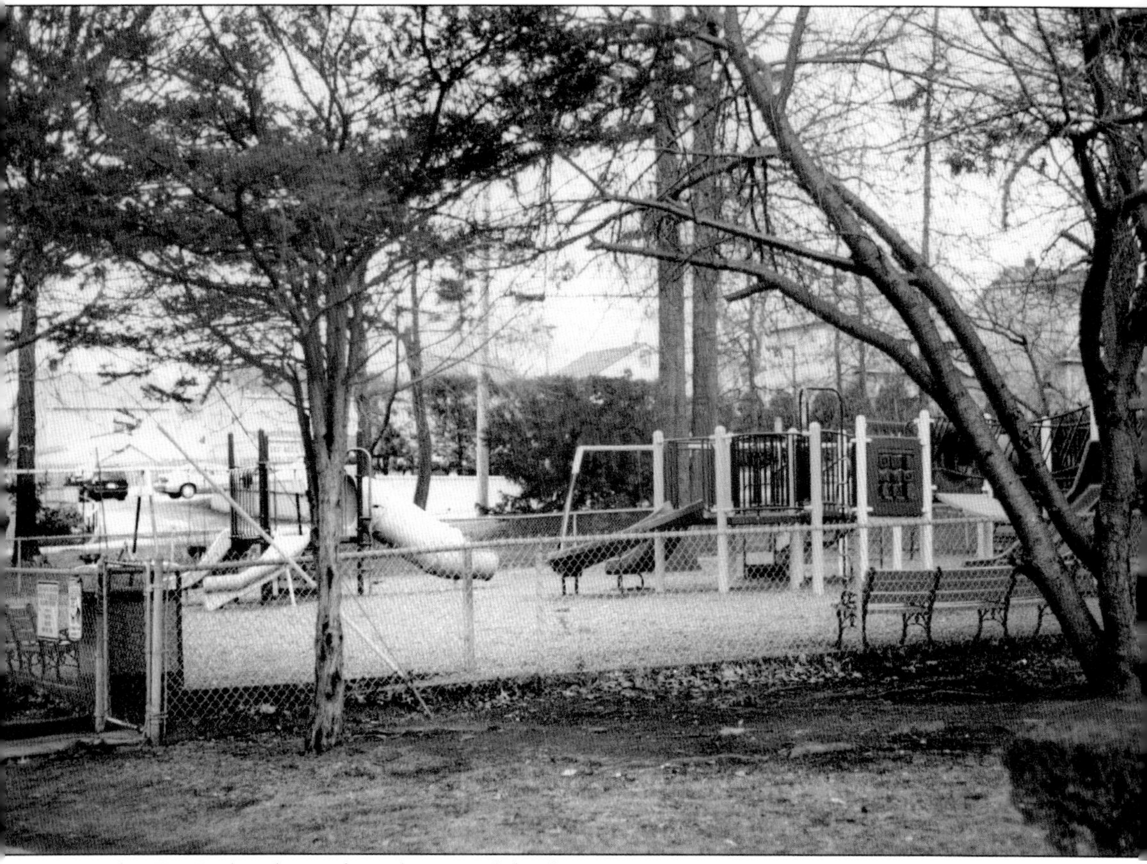

The Tot Park is located on the site of the former American Legion Hall, which was destroyed by fire in 1981.

Ten

Some Notable Wood-Ridge Residents

Researching the history of Wood-Ridge brought to light the fact that the spirit and determination of the people made the borough what it is today. Wood-Ridge has had more than its fair share of notable people. The task of selecting some of these people to name in a book was a hard one, as the more research that was done, the longer the list became. Everyone who ever resided in town has made an impact on the quality of life here. The following are only some of those with noteworthy accomplishments who proudly trace their roots back to Wood-Ridge. If space had not been limited, this list would have been endless.

Henry and Elsworth Barthen grew up in Wood-Ridge on the corner of Highland Avenue and Hackensack Street. The Wood-Ridge National Bank purchased their property to make a parking lot. Henry Barthen worked for New York Life Insurance Company in New York City. Also an artist, he developed the use of the palette knife to paint. The brothers were widely known for the beautiful roses, tulips, and dahlias that they grew.

Clement Bianchi was an Italian immigrant who worked for Sier-Bath Gear Company. Before long, he became the sole owner of the company. His last wish was to deed his home to the borough. The Bianchi House is now home to the Wood-Ridge Historical Society and the public health department.

Gustav Bickert, a World War I veteran (army sergeant), moved to Wood-Ridge in 1917 and helped organize the first library. A dental technician, he owned his own shop in Manhattan. He served Wood-Ridge as a school board member from 1928 to 1934, a Republican councilman from 1953 to 1964 (under three mayors), acting mayor after Mayor I. J. LaRosa died, and member of the Lion's Club.

Guy Calissi grew up in Wood-Ridge. A World War II veteran, he was elected mayor by 55 votes and served from 1948 to 1954. Known for fighting gambling and organized crime, he was Bergen County prosecutor from 1954 to 1970 and superior court judge in 1970. He was named Bergen County UNICO Man of the Year in 1968. He died on December 8, 1980.

Sr. Carol Ann, O.S.F., was a third-grade teacher at Assumption School. She was Wood-Ridge's version of the singing nun, having recorded more than 35 songs and 4 albums, with both United Artists and Dharma Productions.

Leonard Connors was raised in town and was a 1947 graduate of Wood-Ridge High School. He was elected to the New Jersey Senate to represent the ninth legislative district, a position he still holds.

Robert DeMarco was a Wood-Ridge resident who graduated from St. Mary's High School in Rutherford. The National Football League's St. Louis Cardinals drafted him in 1961. He was traded in 1970 to the Miami Dolphins and, later, to the Cleveland Browns, retiring from the Los Angeles Rams in 1975. He was voted to play in the Pro-Bowl three times: 1963, 1965, and 1967.

Albert Gorab was a council member from 1923 to 1930. A Syrian immigrant, poet, and published author, he started an insurance and real estate agency in Wood-Ridge in 1926. He helped negotiate sales of land involving Sunshine City and the sale of property to Curtiss-Wright. His son, Herbert Gorab, continued the business and served as councilman from 1980 to 1983 and as mayor from 1984 to 1987.

Constance Joannes graduated from Wood-Ridge High School in 1940. She was a Coty cosmetics model and television's Avon lady.

Fr. Christopher Keenan (John Keenan) was born and raised in Wood-Ridge. An Assumption School graduate, he serves at the St. Francis of Assisi mission in Manhattan. He was appointed chaplain of the New York City Fire Department in September 2001, following the death of Fr. Mychal Judge on September 11, 2001.

Frederick Kohbertz was a wine merchant in New York City. In 1870, he built a mansion on a three-acre plot bounded by Union and North Avenues, between Sixth and Seventh Streets. The 20-room mansion cost approximately $75,000 to build. Kohbertz died in 1872. His son Frederick Kohbertz bought and sold numerous parcels of land, and served three years as a councilman, beginning in 1894.

John Koster lived in Wood-Ridge from 1948 to 1971. He is the author of numerous books, including *The Atheist Syndrome* and *Road to Wounded Knee*, as well as various magazine articles.

Ludwig Metzger, a longtime resident, was appointed borough historian in 1978. Everyone who knows Metzger has heard him tell wonderful stories about Wood-Ridge.

John Molinelli was raised in Wood-Ridge. He graduated from Assumption School and Wood-Ridge High School and went on to Rutgers University and New York University Law School. Following law school, he resided in Wood-Ridge for several years and was active in the local Democratic party. In 2002, he was appointed to the position of Bergen County prosecutor.

Nicola Spadola was born in Italy and came to Wood-Ridge *c.* 1890. He operated a dairy farm until World War I. He then went into the building business and developed the west end of town, building more than 50 homes in that area.

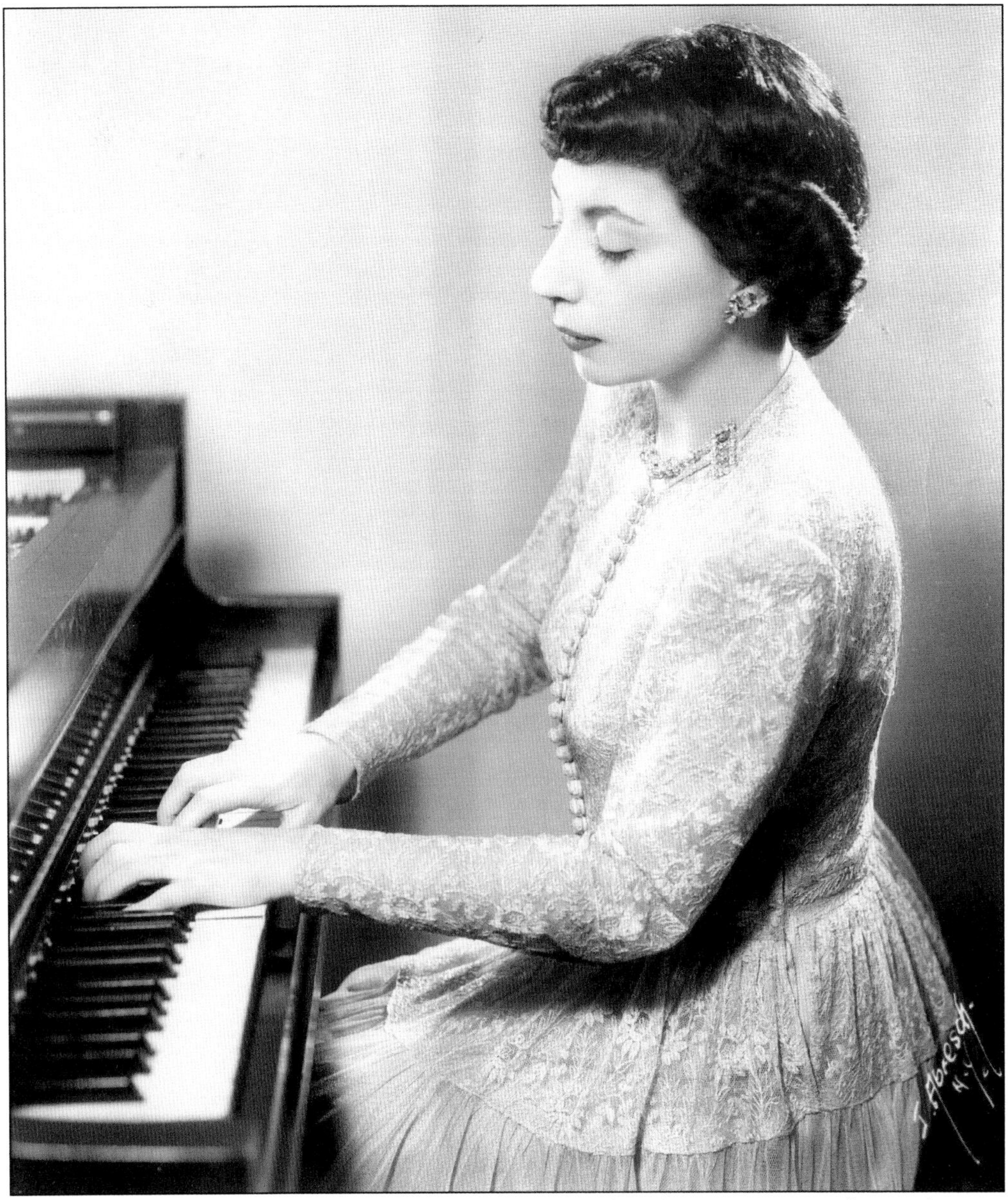

Grace Castagnetta sat at a piano at age five. She gave her first Carnegie Hall recital at age eight. She studied in Cologne, Germany, where she played for then mayor Konrad Adenauer. She also played for the king of Sweden and gave numerous performances for Presidents Franklin D. Roosevelt, Harry S. Truman, and Dwight D. Eisenhower. She became a good friend of Eleanor Roosevelt. Her career began at CBS one day when, because of technical difficulties at the station, she was asked to fill in by playing a piano recital. She was known for her great improvisational skills and was billed as "the only classically trained artist to improvise on the piano." From her days at CBS, she became acquainted with Hendrik Willem Van Loon, a noted author and illustrator, with whom she collaborated on numerous books. She was also friends with other notable people including author John Gunther and composer Richard Strauss. Although her career took her around the world, she was always proud to call Wood-Ridge her home. (Photograph courtesy of Catherine Cassidy.)

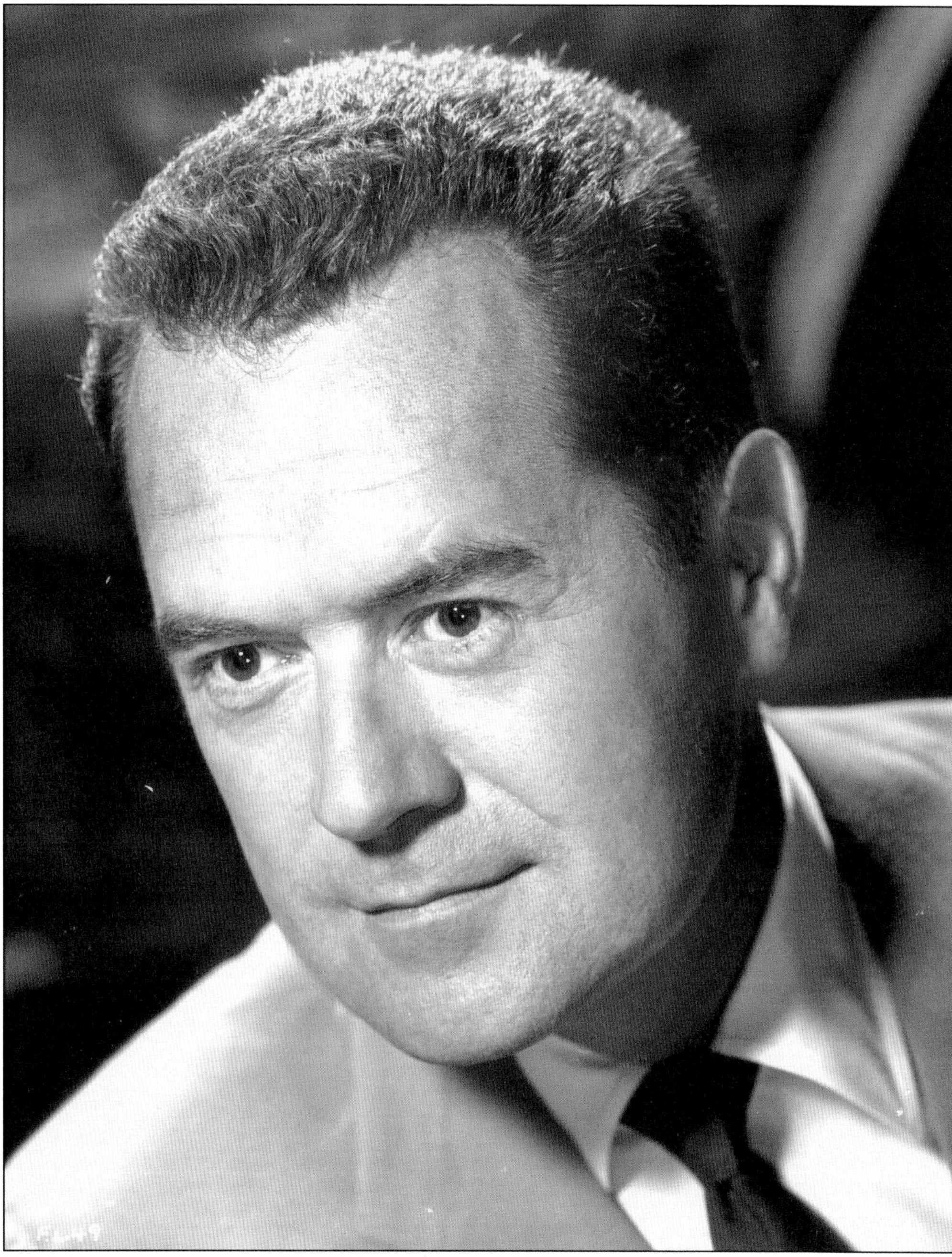

Frank Lovejoy grew up in Wood-Ridge. He made his first Broadway appearance in 1934 in *Judgement Day* and starred in the tour version of *The Best Man*. He starred in more than 18 movies and in two television series, *Man Against Crime* and *Meet McGraw*. Whenever his Wood-Ridge friends attended his live performances, they always received special consideration. (Photograph courtesy of Christopher McAlinden.)

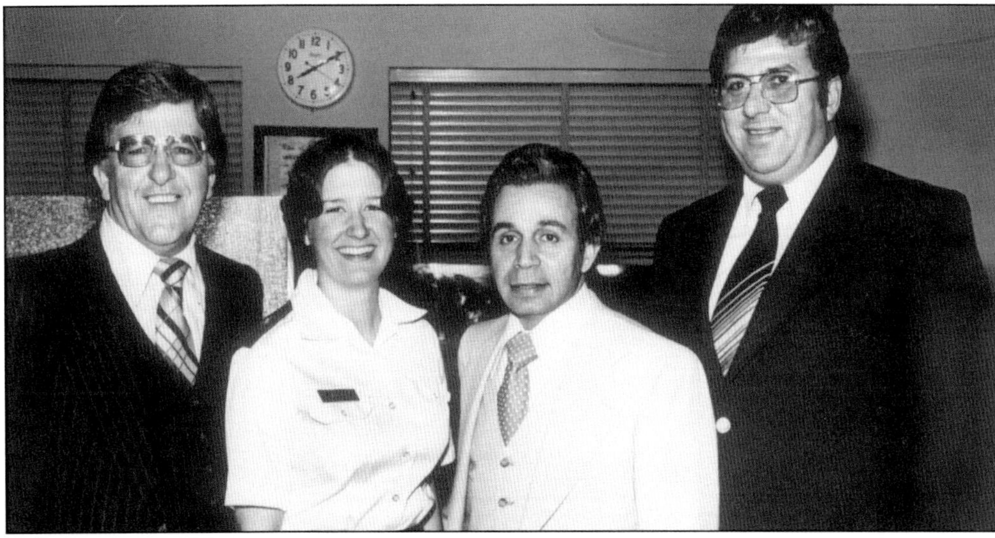

Diane Bracey attended Mount Pleasant and Assumption Schools and graduated from Wood-Ridge High School in 1976. She was a member of the first class that included women at the United States Military Academy at West Point. On July 7, 1976, she and 119 other women were sworn in as a new cadets. She was one of the 62 women who remained with the class to graduate in 1980. She served with distinction in West Germany and the United States, receiving numerous awards and commendations. She retired as a captain and worked in the private sector for General Dynamics and Dupont. Pictured with her, from left to right, are Councilman R. O'Malley, Mayor P. Incardone, and Councilman L. Cosgrove.

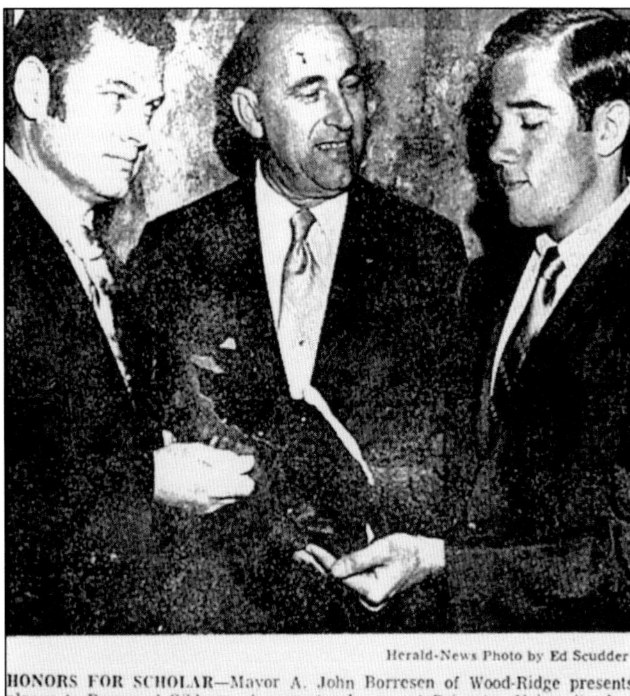

Herald-News Photo by Ed Scudder

HONORS FOR SCHOLAR—Mayor A. John Borresen of Wood-Ridge presents plaque to Raymond Gibbons who won top honors at Princeton University during his four years there and has been named a Rhodes Scholar. With them is School Trustee John Koegel. The award took place at a dinner last night in The Fiesta, Wood-Ridge, honoring Gibbons.

Raymond Gibbons graduated from Wood-Ridge High School in 1966 and from Princeton University in 1970. He went on to become a Rhodes Scholar—the first and only Wood-Ridge student to receive this honor, which is based on well-roundedness, intellectual attainment, character, leadership, and physical vigor. After Oxford University, he studied at Johns Hopkins University before graduating from Harvard Medical School. He now heads the Nuclear Cardiology Laboratory at the Mayo Clinic in Rochester, Minnesota. The Wood-Ridge Memorial Foundation honored him in 2003. (Picture courtesy of the *Herald News*.)

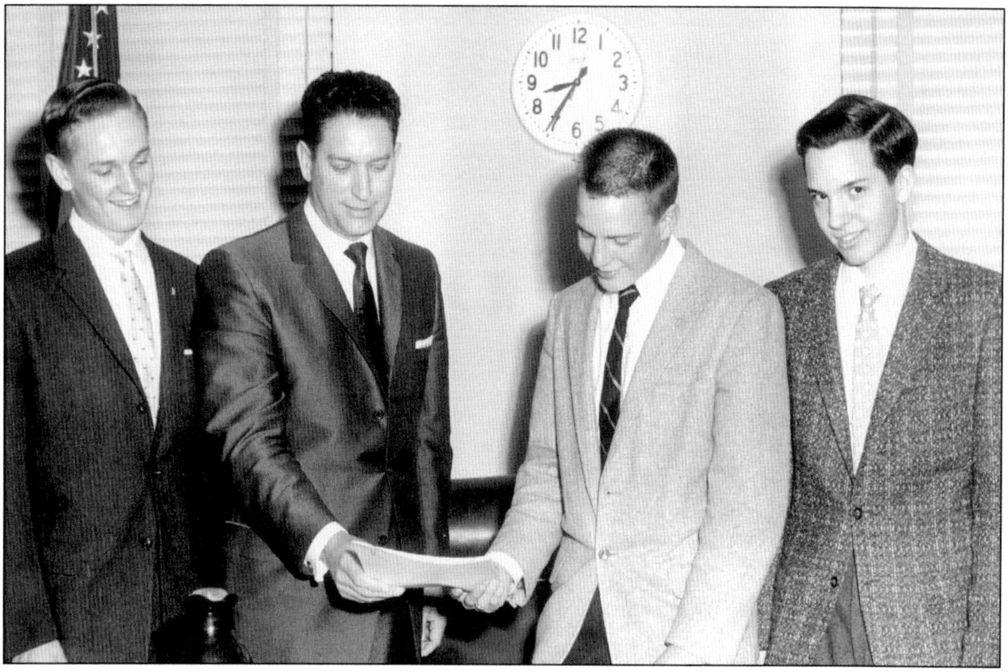

Frank Derato, right, attended Wood-Ridge schools and graduated from Stevens Institute of Technology with a degree in electrical engineering. He wrote the book *Down the Hill: Memories of Lost Wood-Ridge* in memory of his father, who was an original member of the History of Wood-Ridge Committee. He is pictured acting as councilman on Boys' Day in April 1958 with, from left to right, Frank Wells, acting as borough clerk, Mayor Clarence Mathe, and Chris Borchen, acting as mayor.

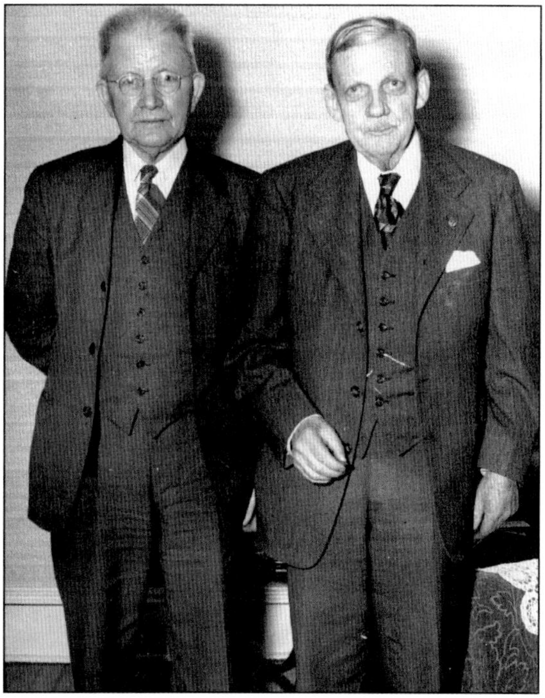

Knud Christensen, left, and Chris Madsen started their business in 1898 after meeting in England. They moved to Wood-Ridge in 1905 and pioneered the growing of potted poinsettias, becoming the first to sell them commercially in 1910. They were also founders of Tri-Boro Building and Loan, which became South Bergen Savings and Loan (now Kearny Federal Savings), and Christensen helped form the Wood-Ridge National Bank. The 14 Madsen & Christensen greenhouses spanned more than 11 acres of land. Every December, the greenhouses were opened to the public so that all could enjoy the poinsettias, which were then sent to Rockefeller Center and St. Patrick's Cathedral in New York City. Madsen & Christensen's poinsettias could always be seen at Christmastime in St. Patrick's Cathedral.

Known as "Mr. Wood-Ridge," Robert Stoesser grew up in town and graduated from Columbia University with a master's degree. He taught in the Wood-Ridge school system from 1929 to 1973. He was instrumental in starting the library in 1931 and in preserving the Brinkerhoff House by making it the current library. He served on the library board of trustees and was president from 1946 to 1954. He was borough clerk from 1948 to 1972 and councilman from 1973 to 1975. In 1991, the civic center was named in his honor.

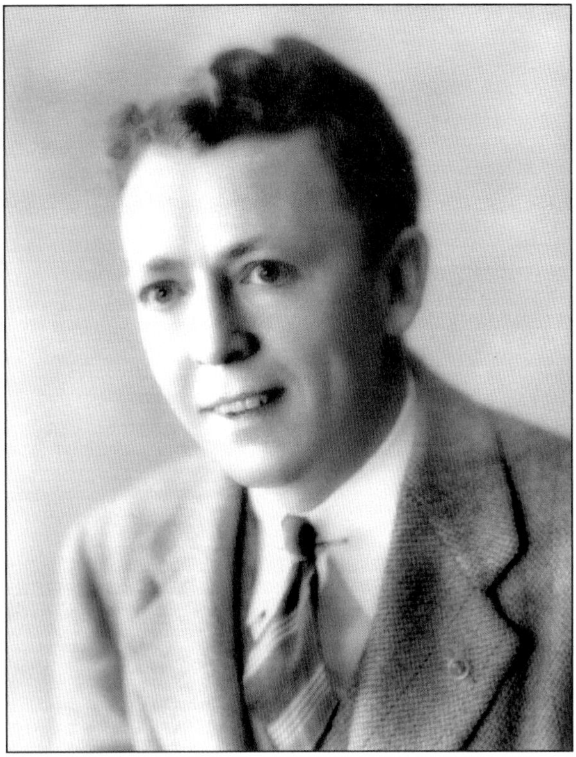

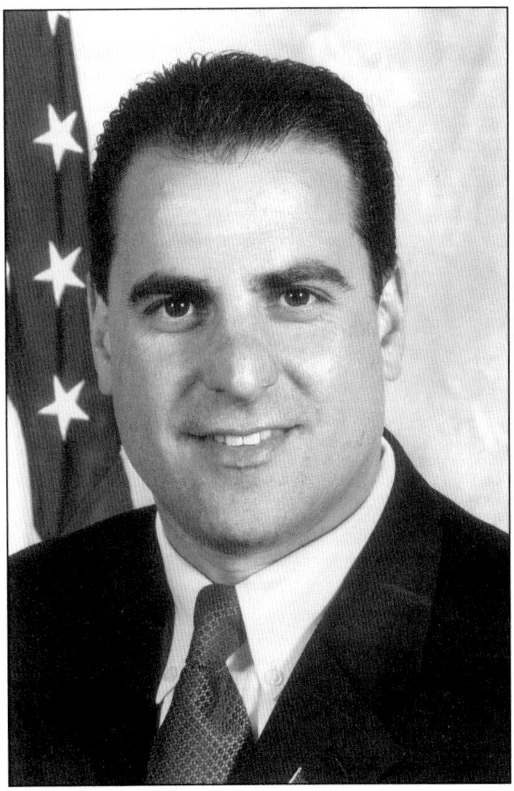

Paul Sarlo was elected to the borough council in 1994 and took office in 1995. While serving his second term as councilman, he ran for mayor and won, becoming the youngest elected mayor of Wood-Ridge. In 2001, he was chosen by District 36 Democrats to run for the state assembly. After winning that election, he was appointed state senator to fill a vacancy created by a resignation. He then ran for election as senator and won in November 2003. (Photograph courtesy of the office of Sen. Paul A. Sarlo.)

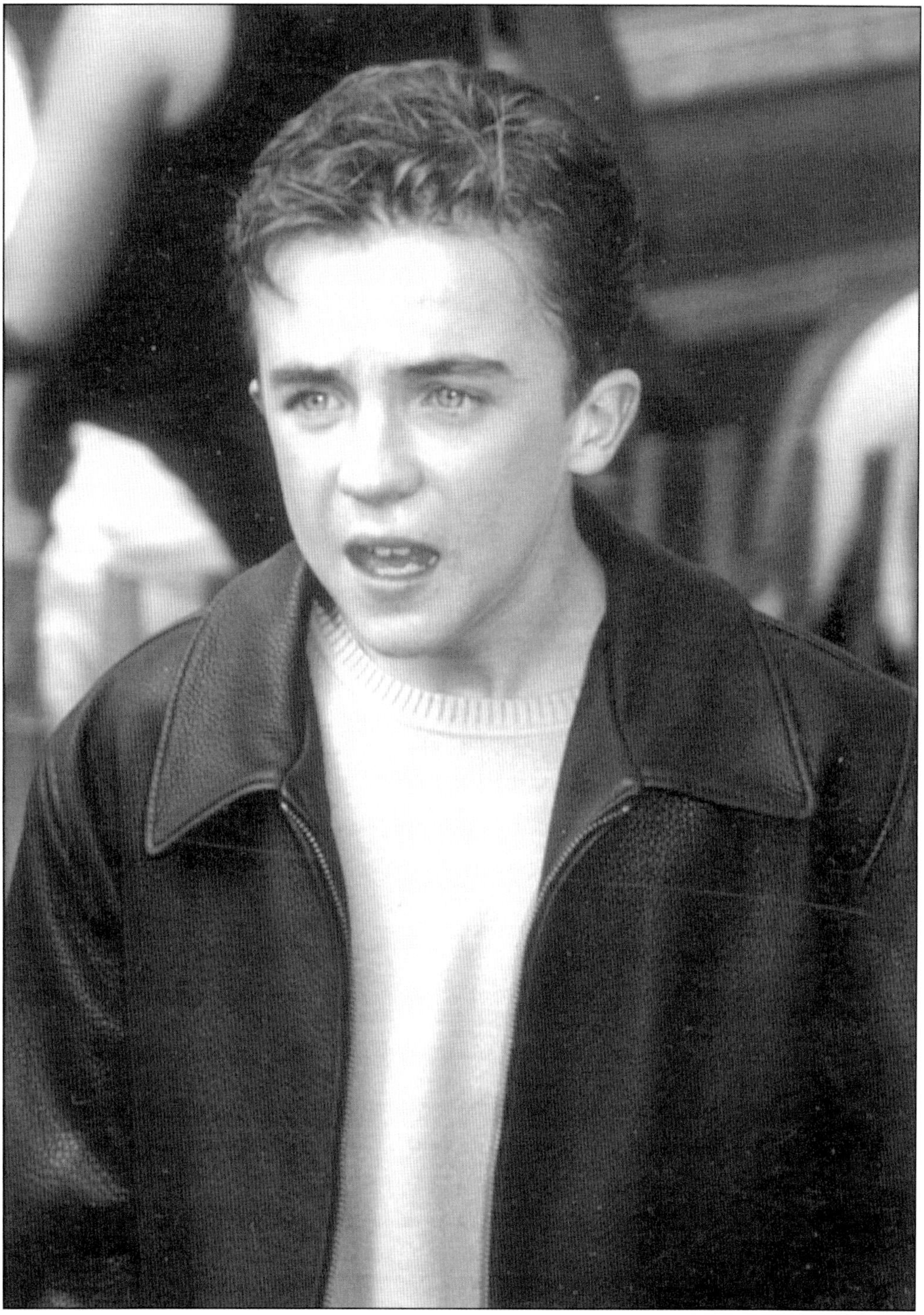

Frankie Muniz is the star of the Fox television series *Malcolm in the Middle* and the hit movies *My Dog Skip* and *Agent Cody Banks*. Born in Wood-Ridge, he lived both here and in North Carolina. California is now his home, but he comes back to Wood-Ridge to visit family. (Photograph courtesy of Martha Preli.)

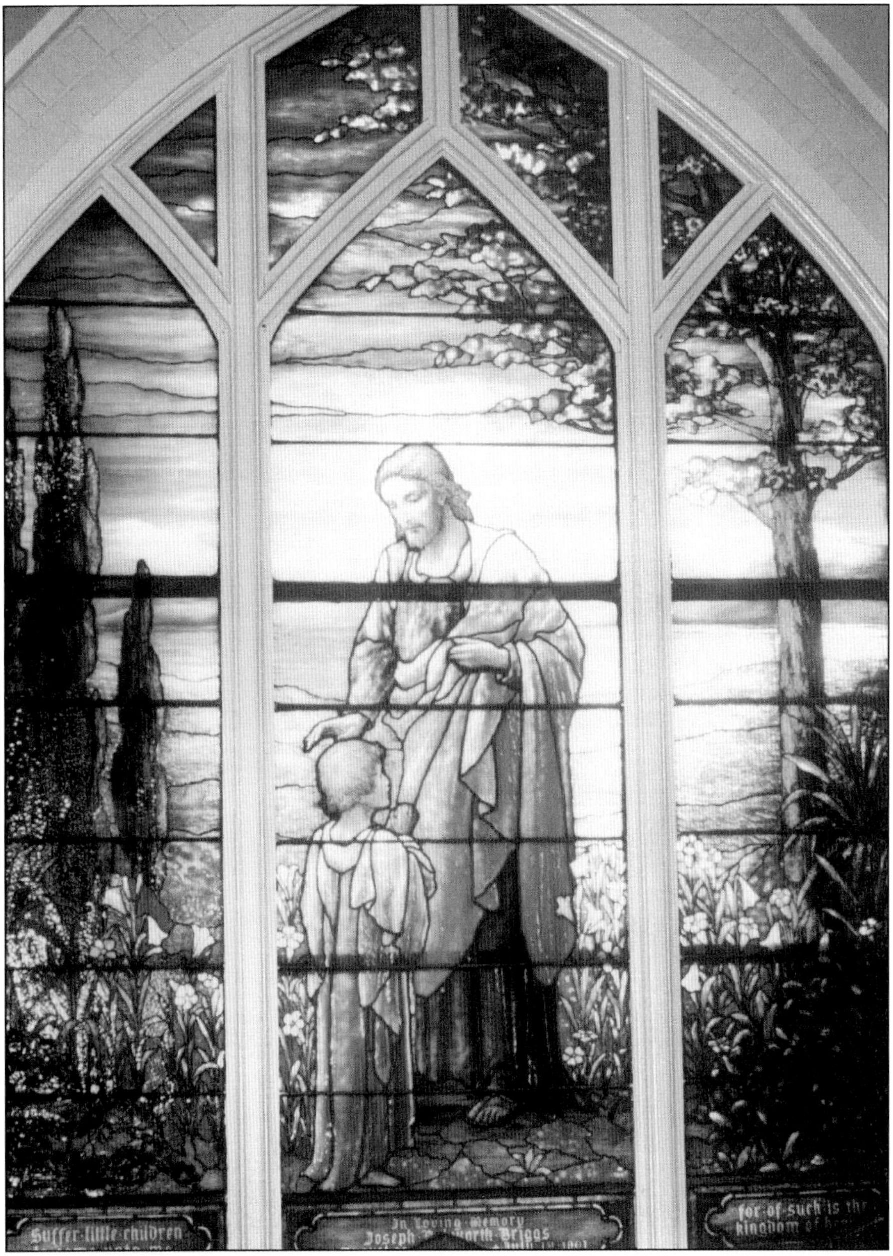

Joseph Briggs was the right-hand man to Louis Tiffany. He became president of the company and designed many of the glass windows known today. The window in St. Paul's Episcopal Church was designed by him and dedicated in his son's memory. (Photograph courtesy of Catherine Cassidy.)

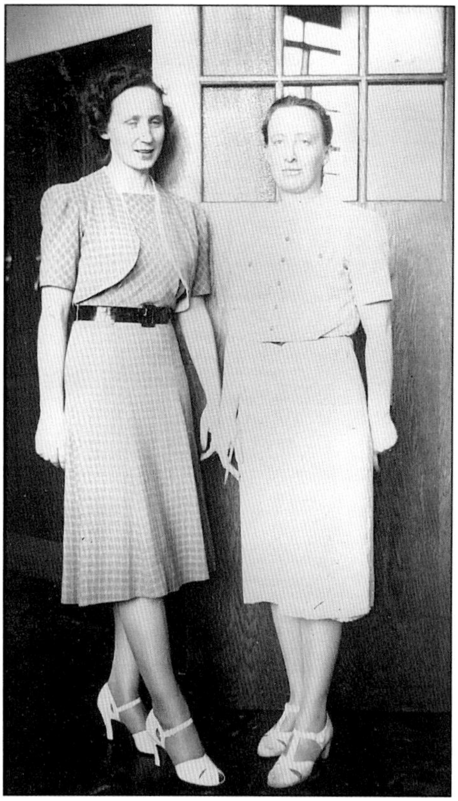

Hattie Hiecke Grimshaw, right, moved to Wood-Ridge at age 12. A longtime Wood-Ridge educator, she served as an English teacher, librarian, and the first high school guidance counselor. She was largely responsible for founding the first library in town and was instrumental in moving the library to its present-day home (the Brinkerhoff House). She volunteered for the Red Cross for 35 years and belonged to the Gallon Club of blood donors. In 1978, she moved to Florida where she lived until her death in 2002 at age 101. The Wood-Ridge Board of Education dedicated the high school library in her memory. She is pictured with Wood-Ridge High School colleague Irene Roth.

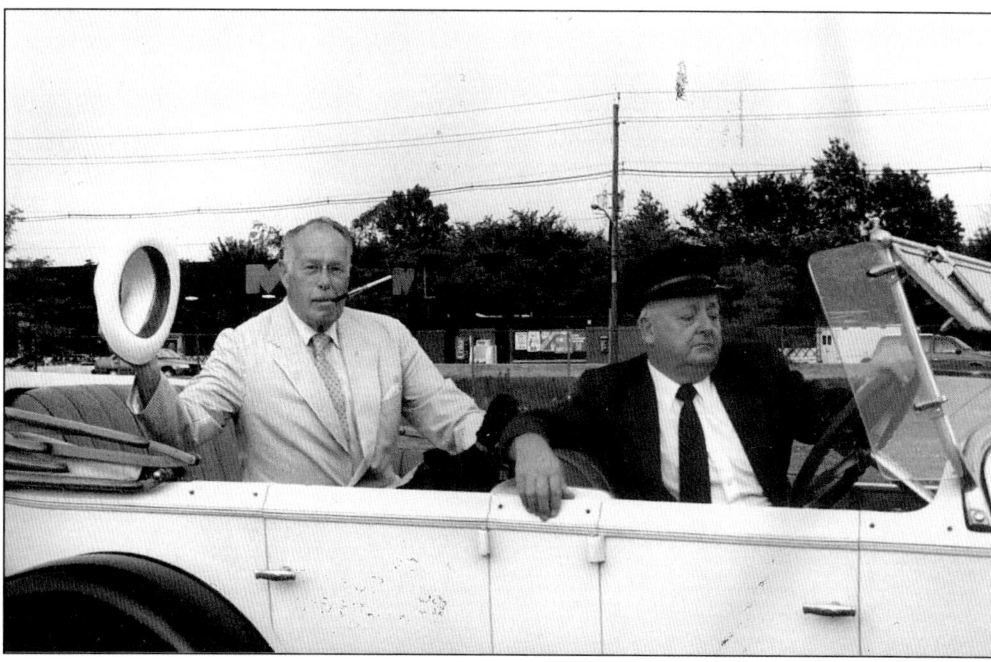

Elsworth Barthen, left, was well known for his impersonation of Franklin D. Roosevelt. Barthen appeared on television talk shows as the president. He is pictured in a Rolls Royce with its owner, Ed Meyers of Wood-Ridge.

Dr. Louis Cartnick practiced medicine in Wood-Ridge for more than 50 years. Known as "Doc," he gave free health examinations to every child at Assumption School during that time. In recognition of this service, the Louis Cartnick Memorial Fund was established to provide full tuition for a needy student each year. Shown is Cartnick's farewell letter, published in the *Wood-Ridge Independent*. (Article courtesy of Bob Hannon and the *Wood-Ridge Independent*.)

Dr. Cartnick: 53 Yrs. Worth of Thanks

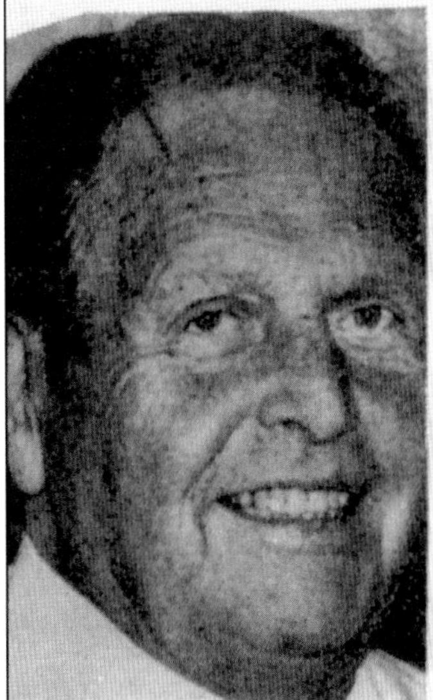

Dear Patients and Friends:

I would like to thank each of you personally for the many expressions of gratitude, prayers, and well wishes you have sent to me. I have read each of them, and am truly and deeply touched. Please know how important you have been to me throughout these many years, how much you have given me, how very much you have meant to me. We have been a gift to each other.

With some urging of family and my physicians, my wife Mildred and I, after 53 years, have decided we wish — and need — to spend a little more time together. Without saying "good-bye," we thank you for your thanks. Our prayers are with you, and our good wishes, as yours to me, are with you always.

Dr. Louis C. Cartnick
228 Hillcrest Ave., W-R

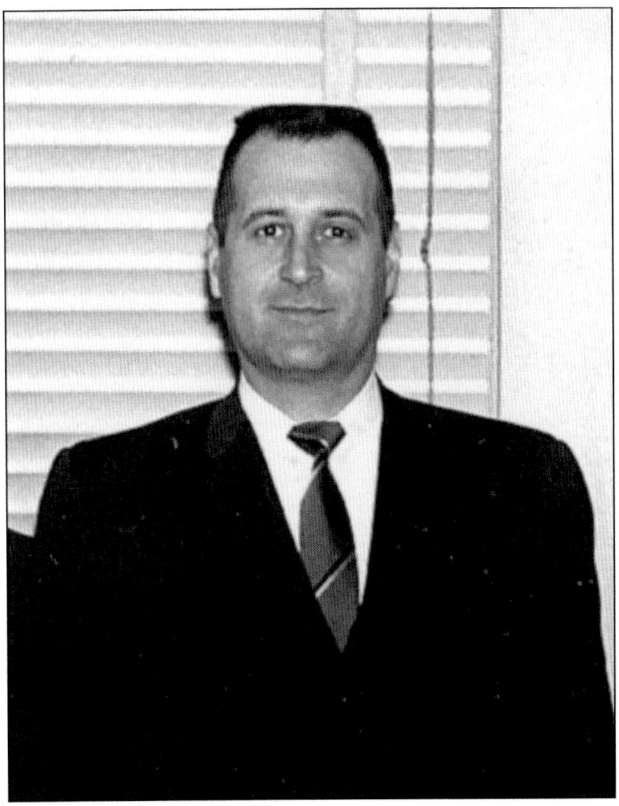

Alfred Genton graduated from Wood-Ridge High School in 1944. A local attorney, he served as assistant Bergen County prosecutor, heading the Corruption Control Bureau. In 1974, he became deputy attorney general, and in 1976, he joined the New Jersey Commission of Investigation as its counsel. He ran for New Jersey State Assembly in the 1970s, and also served as borough attorney. He died on December 5, 1989.

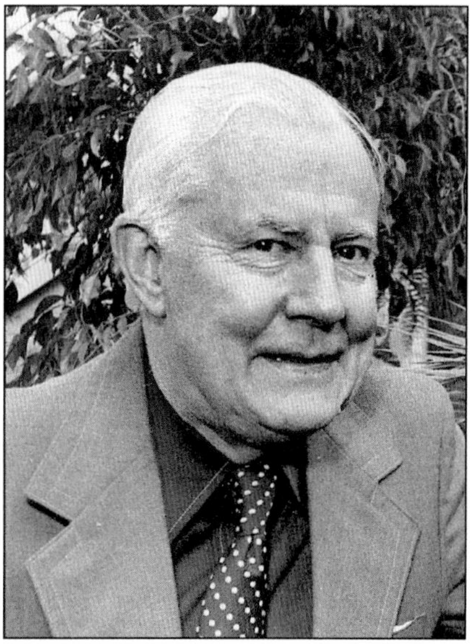

Irving "Bus" Christensen was the son of Knud Christensen. A famed horticulturist, he became president of the Madsen & Christensen Flower Company. His clientele included Rockefeller Center, McGraw-Hill–Time Life, Exxon, and Hilton. He was also a consultant to Prudential Insurance Company in Salt Lake City, Utah. Elected president of the New Jersey Board of Agriculture, he received a Distinguished Service Citation from the New Jersey Agricultural Society in 1976. He served as treasurer of the Wood-Ridge Lions Club and president of the Boy Scout Council.

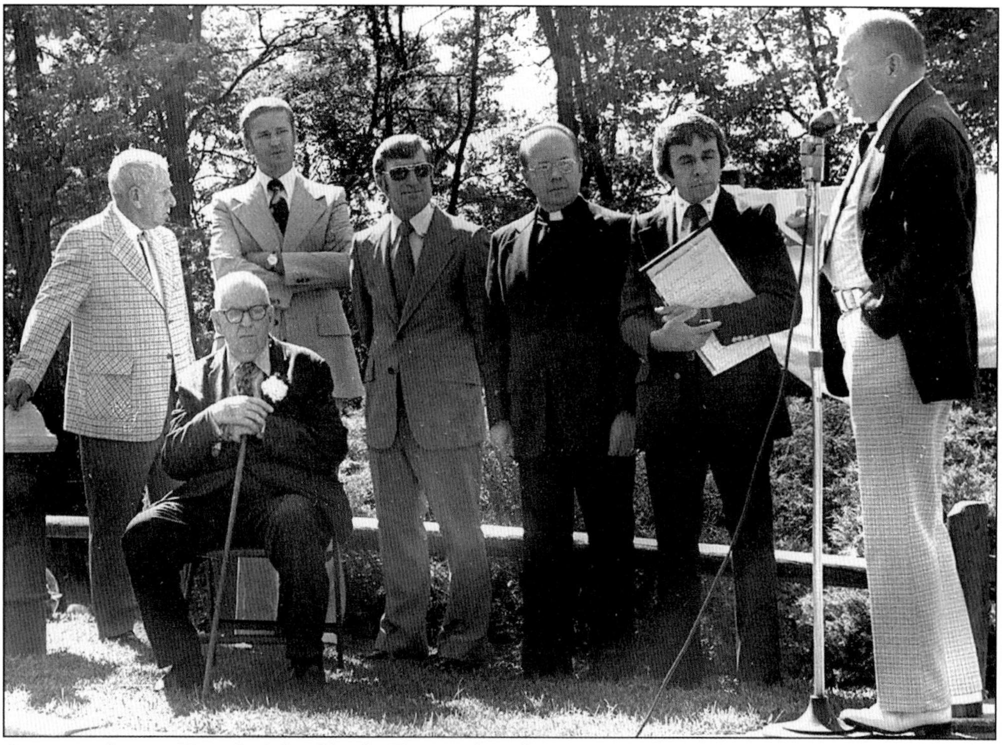

As a member and head of the Shade Tree and Park Commission, William Kour, seated, worked to save land on Thirteenth Street. He was recognized in 1976 by having Thirteenth Street Park established in his honor. Pictured with him at the dedication ceremony, from left to right, are unidentified, Councilmen Frank Wells and David Bolles, Rev. David Sutterlein of the Presbyterian church, Mayor Peter Incardone, and unidentified. Kour also helped form the Wood-Ridge Emergency Squad in 1938, served as president of the local Democratic club, and was a school board member from 1933 to 1942, a volunteer firefighter, a member of the 4-H Club, and president of the local garden club for 25-years.